MIX
Papier aus verantwortungsvollen Quellen
Paper from responsible sources
FSC® C105338

Pit Fender

Efficient Memoization Algorithms for Query Optimization

Top-Down Join Enumeration through Memoization on the Basis of Hypergraphs

Anchor Academic Publishing

Fender, Pit: Efficient Memoization Algorithms for Query Optimization: Top-Down Join
Enumeration through Memoization on the Basis of Hypergraphs, Hamburg, Anchor
Academic Publishing 2014

Buch-ISBN: 978-3-95489-336-2
PDF-eBook-ISBN: 978-3-95489-836-7
Druck/Herstellung: Anchor Academic Publishing, Hamburg, 2014

Bibliografische Information der Deutschen Nationalbibliothek:
Die Deutsche Nationalbibliothek verzeichnet diese Publikation in der Deutschen
Nationalbibliografie; detaillierte bibliografische Daten sind im Internet über
http://dnb.d-nb.de abrufbar.

Bibliographical Information of the German National Library:
The German National Library lists this publication in the German National Bibliography.
Detailed bibliographic data can be found at: http://dnb.d-nb.de

All rights reserved. This publication may not be reproduced, stored in a retrieval system
or transmitted, in any form or by any means, electronic, mechanical, photocopying,
recording or otherwise, without the prior permission of the publishers.

Das Werk einschließlich aller seiner Teile ist urheberrechtlich geschützt. Jede Verwertung
außerhalb der Grenzen des Urheberrechtsgesetzes ist ohne Zustimmung des Verlages
unzulässig und strafbar. Dies gilt insbesondere für Vervielfältigungen, Übersetzungen,
Mikroverfilmungen und die Einspeicherung und Bearbeitung in elektronischen Systemen.

Die Wiedergabe von Gebrauchsnamen, Handelsnamen, Warenbezeichnungen usw. in
diesem Werk berechtigt auch ohne besondere Kennzeichnung nicht zu der Annahme,
dass solche Namen im Sinne der Warenzeichen- und Markenschutz-Gesetzgebung als frei
zu betrachten wären und daher von jedermann benutzt werden dürften.

Die Informationen in diesem Werk wurden mit Sorgfalt erarbeitet. Dennoch können
Fehler nicht vollständig ausgeschlossen werden und die Diplomica Verlag GmbH, die
Autoren oder Übersetzer übernehmen keine juristische Verantwortung oder irgendeine
Haftung für evtl. verbliebene fehlerhafte Angaben und deren Folgen.

Alle Rechte vorbehalten

© Anchor Academic Publishing, Imprint der Diplomica Verlag GmbH
Hermannstal 119k, 22119 Hamburg
http://www.diplomica-verlag.de, Hamburg 2014
Printed in Germany

Zusammenfassung

Für ein Datenbankmanagementsystem, das Unterstützung für deklarative Anfragesprachen wie SQL bietet, ist der Anfrageoptimierer eine unerlässliche Softwarekomponente. Oft können deklarative Anfragen in verschiedene äquivalente Ausführungspläne übersetzt werden. Der Übersetzungsprozess, welcher unter allen äquivalenten Alternativen einen geeigneten Ausführungsplan auswählt, wird Anfrage-Optimierung genannt. Der Auswahlprozess beruht auf einem Kostenmodell und auf Verteilungsstatistiken über die zugrunde liegenden Daten. Für die geschätzten Ausführungskosten des Ausführungsplans ist die Reihenfolge der Join-Operationen ausschlaggebend. Dabei kann der Laufzeitunterschied zwischen verschiedenen Ausführungsplänen mit unterschiedlichen Ausführungsreihenfolgen ihrer Join-Operationen mehrere Größenordnungen betragen. Eine vollständige Suche unter allen äquivalenten Operatorbäumen ist oft zu berechnungsintensiv. Daher muss die Komplexität der Suche eingeschränkt werden, indem die Größe des Suchraumes reduziert wird. Dazu wird eine weitverbreitete Heuristik angewendet: Es werden nur die Operatorbäume erzeugt und in ihren Kosten miteinander verglichen, welche frei von Kreuzprodukten sind.

Für die Suche nach dem optimalen und damit billigsten Ausführungsplan gibt es zwei mögliche Herangehensweisen: Top-Down Join Enumeration und Bottom-Up Join Enumeration. Dabei hat Top-Down Join Enumeration einen wesentlichen Vorteil: Durch die bedarfsgesteuerte Aufzählungsreihenfolge können Branch-and-Bound-Pruning-Strategien verwendet werden. Durch Branch-and-Bound kann die Übersetzungszeit der Anfrage um mehrere Größenordnungen reduziert werden. Trotz merklicher Verkürzung der Übersetzungszeit wird in jedem Fall der optimale und somit kostengünstigste Plan erzeugt. Falls es nach dem jeweilig verwendeten Kostenmodell mehrere optimale Pläne gibt, wird einer dieser Kandidaten erzeugt.

Die vorliegende Arbeit widmet sich dem Top-Down-Join-Enumeration-Prozess. Im ersten Teil der Arbeit werden zwei gleich effiziente Partitionierungsalgorithmen für Graphen vorgestellt, die für Top-Down Join Enumeration von Relevanz sind. Jedoch gibt es bei den im ersten Teil vorgestellten Strategien zwei erhebliche Einschränkungen: (1) Die Algorithmen eignen sich nur für Anfragen mit einfachen (binären) Join-Prädikaten. (2) Anfragen, die neben inneren Join-Operationen auch auf äußere Join-Operationen zurückgreifen, können nicht verarbeitet werden.

Im zweiten Teil dieser Arbeit werden diese Einschränkungen aufgehoben. Dazu wird zunächst eine von zwei Partitionierungsstrategien für Graphen angepasst und erweitert. Anschließend wird ein generisches Framework vorgestellt, das jeden Partitionierungsalgorithmus für Graphen derart umrüstet, dass auch Anfragen mit komplexen Join-Prädikaten und äußeren Join-Operationen übersetzt werden können. Wie sich zeigen wird, ist das generische Framework effizienter als der modifizierte und erweiterte Partitionierungsalgorithmus für Graphen.

Der dritte Teil dieser Arbeit beschäftigt sich mit Branch-and-Bound-Pruning-Strategien. Als erstes werden zwei bereits bekannte Pruning-Strategien erläutert und klassifiziert. Im Weiteren wird erklärt, wie beide Strategien vereint werden können. Darauf aufbauend werden sieben Verbesserungen vorgeschlagen. Der daraus resultierende neue Branch-and-Bound-Pruning-Algorithmus verbessert (1) die Effizienz von Pruning, macht (2) Branch-And-Bound Pruning robuster und verhindert (3) Szenarien, bei denen die Übersetzungszeit durch Pruning um mehrere Größenordnungen verlangsamt wird.

Die vorliegende Arbeit evaluiert mit Hilfe verschiedener Experimente, inwieweit Laufzeitverbessungen durch die vorgestellten neuen Algorithmen erreicht werden können. Dabei werden die Anfragen der TPC-H, TPC-DS und SQLite Test Suite Benchmarks übersetzt und die Laufzeit der Optimierungsphase gemessen. Unsere Ergebnisse zeigen, dass sich die Übersetzungszeit bei Verwendung der hier vorgestellten Algorithmen für die Benchmark-Anfragen um 100% verbessert. Bei Verwendung synthetischer Workloads können sogar noch größere Laufzeitverbesserungen erreicht werden.

Abstract

For a DBMS that provides support for a declarative query language like SQL, the query optimizer is a crucial piece of software. The declarative nature of a query allows it to be translated into many equivalent evaluation plans. The process of choosing a suitable plan from all alternatives is known as query optimization. The basis of this choice are a cost model and statistics over the data. Essential for the costs of a plan is the execution order of join operations in its operator tree, since the runtime of plans with different join orders can vary by several orders of magnitude. An exhaustive search for an optimal solution over all possible operator trees is computationally infeasible. To decrease complexity, the search space must be restricted. Therefore, a well-accepted heuristic is applied: All possible bushy join trees are considered, while cross products are excluded from the search.

There are two efficient approaches to identify the best plan: bottom-up and top-down join enumeration. But only the top-down approach allows for branch-and-bound pruning, which can improve compile time by several orders of magnitude, while still preserving optimality.

Hence, this book focuses on the top-down join enumeration. In the first part, we present two efficient graph-partitioning algorithms suitable for top-down join enumeration. However, as we will see, there are two severe limitations: The proposed algorithms can handle only (1) simple (binary) join predicates and (2) inner joins. Therefore, the second part adopts one of the proposed partitioning strategies to overcome those limitations. Furthermore, we propose a more generic partitioning framework that enables every graph-partitioning algorithm to handle join predicates involving more than two relations, and outer joins as well as other non-inner joins. As we will see, our framework is more efficient than the adopted graph-partitioning algorithm. The third part of this book discusses the two branch-and-bound pruning strategies that can be found in the literature. We present seven advancements to the combined strategy that improve pruning (1) in terms of effectiveness, (2) in terms of robustness and (3), most importantly, avoid the worst-case behavior otherwise observed.

Different experiments evaluate the performance improvements of our proposed methods. We use the TPC-H, TPC-DS and SQLite test suite benchmarks to evaluate our joined contributions. As we show, the average compile time improvement in those settings is 100% when compared with the state of the art in bottom-up join enumeration. Our synthetic workloads show even higher improvement factors.

Contents

1. **Introduction**   15
   1.1. Motivation   15
   1.2. Contribution   17
       1.2.1. Graph-Aware Join Enumeration Algorithms   17
       1.2.2. Hypergraph-Aware Join Enumeration Algorithms   17
       1.2.3. Branch-and-Bound Pruning   18
       1.2.4. Conclusion and Appendix   18

2. **Graph-Aware Join Enumeration Algorithms**   19
   2.1. Preliminaries   19
       2.1.1. Graphs   19
       2.1.2. Query Graphs, Plan Classes and Costs   22
       2.1.3. Problem Specification   24
   2.2. Basic Memoization   24
       2.2.1. Generic Top-Down Join Enumeration   24
       2.2.2. Naive Partitioning   26
       2.2.3. Exemplified Execution of TDB$_{\text{ASIC}}$ 27
       2.2.4. Analysis of TDB$_{\text{ASIC}}$ 28
   2.3. Advanced Generate and Test   31
       2.3.1. TDM$_{\text{IN}}$C$_{\text{UT}}$AG$_{\text{A}}$T   31
       2.3.2. An Improved Connection Test   33
       2.3.3. Correctness of Advanced Generate and Test   34
   2.4. Conservative Graph Partitioning   39
       2.4.1. Correctness Constraints   40
       2.4.2. The Algorithm in Detail   40
       2.4.3. Exploring Connected Components   42
   2.5. Branch Partitioning   42
       2.5.1. Branch Partitioning - An Overview   42
       2.5.2. The Algorithm in Detail   44
       2.5.3. Two Optimization Techniques   46
       2.5.4. Exploring Restricted Neighbors   47
       2.5.5. Two Examples   48
       2.5.6. Complexity of Branch Partitioning   48
   2.6. Evaluation   50
       2.6.1. Experimental Setup   50
       2.6.2. Organizational Overview   50
       2.6.3. Experiments   51

3. Hypergraph-Aware Join Enumeration Algorithms   63
- 3.1. Motivation 63
- 3.2. Preliminaries 65
  - 3.2.1. Hypergraphs 65
  - 3.2.2. Graphs vs. Hypergraphs 68
  - 3.2.3. Neighborhood 69
- 3.3. Basic Memoization for Hypergraphs 70
  - 3.3.1. Generic Top-Down Join Enumeration for Hypergraphs 70
  - 3.3.2. Naive Partitioning of Hypergraphs 71
  - 3.3.3. Test for Connectedness of Hypergraphs 71
- 3.4. Conservative Partitioning for Hypergraphs 73
  - 3.4.1. Overview of MINCUTCONSERVATIVEHYP 74
  - 3.4.2. The Algorithm in Detail 76
  - 3.4.3. Avoiding Duplicates 77
  - 3.4.4. GETCONNECTEDCOMPONENTS 82
  - 3.4.5. MAINTAINCSET 83
  - 3.4.6. An Example 84
- 3.5. Generic Top-Down Join Enumeration for Hypergraphs 85
  - 3.5.1. High-Level Overview 85
  - 3.5.2. Structure of the Generic Partitioning Framework 89
  - 3.5.3. Generating the Adjacency Information 91
  - 3.5.4. Composing Compound Vertices 94
  - 3.5.5. Economizing on Connection Tests 104
  - 3.5.6. Efficient Subgraph Handling 108
  - 3.5.7. Implementation Details 120
- 3.6. Evaluation 121
  - 3.6.1. Implementation 121
  - 3.6.2. Workload 121
  - 3.6.3. Organizational Overview 123
  - 3.6.4. Evaluation of Random Acyclic Query Graphs 124
  - 3.6.5. Evaluation of Random Cyclic Query Graphs 128
  - 3.6.6. Overhead Detection 129
  - 3.6.7. Performance Evaluation with Different Benchmarks 129

4. Branch-and-Bound Pruning   137
- 4.1. Motivation 137
- 4.2. Accumulated-Cost Bounding and Predicted-Cost Bounding 138
  - 4.2.1. Building a Join Tree 138
  - 4.2.2. Accumulated-Cost Bounding 138
  - 4.2.3. Predicted-Cost Bounding 139
  - 4.2.4. Combining the Methods 140
  - 4.2.5. An Example for Accumulated-Predicted-Cost Bounding . . . 140
- 4.3. Technical Advances 141
- 4.4. Evaluation 144
  - 4.4.1. Implementation 144
  - 4.4.2. Workload 145
  - 4.4.3. Performance Evaluation with Simple Query Graphs 146

4.4.4.	Performance Evaluation with Complex Query Graphs	156
4.4.5.	Performance Evaluation with Different Benchmarks	160

5. Conclusion 169
5.1. Graph-Aware Join Enumeration Algorithms 170
5.2. Hypergraph-Aware Join Enumeration Algorithms 170
5.3. Branch and Bound Pruning 170
5.4. Graceful Degradation 171
5.5. Summary 171

A. TDMinCutLazy 173
A.1. Important Notions 173
A.2. Lazy Minimal Cut Partitioning 173
A.3. Biconnection Tree Building 174
    A.3.1. Biconnection Tree Construction 174
    A.3.2. Complexity of Biconnection Tree Construction 176
    A.3.3. Computation of Ancestors and Descendants 176
    A.3.4. An Alternative to Tree Construction 178
A.4. Complexity of Lazy Minimal Cut Partitioning 178
A.5. Improved Version 180
    A.5.1. Global Reuse of the Biconnection Tree 180
    A.5.2. Analyzing the Number of Tree Buildings 180

B. Iterator Implementations 183
B.1. Conservative Partitioning 183
B.2. Branch Partitioning 188

List of Figures

2.1.	Example graph with eleven relations.	22
2.2.	Pseudocode for TDPLANGEN	25
2.3.	Pseudocode for BUILDTREE	26
2.4.	Pseudocode for naive partitioning	26
2.5.	Pseudocode for ISCONNECTED	27
2.6.	Example graph with four relations	28
2.7.	Selectivity and Cardinalities for the Query Graph of Figure 2.6	28
2.8.	Pseudocode for MINCUTAGAT	33
2.9.	Pseudocode for ISCONNECTEDIMP	33
2.10.	Pseudocode for MINCUTCONSERVATIVE	41
2.11.	Pseudocode for GETCONNECTEDCOMPONENTS	43
2.12.	Pseudocode for PARTITION$_{MinCutBranch}$	46
2.13.	Pseudocode for MINCUTBRANCH	47
2.14.	Pseudocode for REACHABLE	48
2.15.	Chain Query	48
2.16.	Cyclic Query	48
2.17.	Cost per emitted ccp	52
2.18.	Absolute and normed runtime results for chain queries.	54
2.19.	Absolute and normed runtime results for star queries.	55
2.20.	Absolute and normed runtime results for random acyclic queries	57
2.21.	Absolute and normed runtime results for cycle queries.	58
2.22.	Absolute and normed runtime results for clique queries.	59
2.23.	Absolute and normed runtime results for cyclic queries (8 vertices)	60
2.24.	Absolute and normed runtime results for cyclic queries (16 vertices)	61
3.1.	Hypergraph $H(V, E)$ with five relations	65
3.2.	A bitvector with 2^x bits	68
3.3.	Pseudocode for TDPLANGENHYP	71
3.4.	Pseudocode for BUILDTREE	71
3.5.	Pseudocode for naive partitioning for hypergraphs	72
3.6.	Pseudocode for ISCONNECTEDHYP	73
3.7.	Pseudocode for GETSIMPLECOMPONENTS	73
3.8.	Pseudocode for MERGECOMPONENTS	74
3.9.	Hypergraph with five relation and a disconnected hypernode.	77
3.10.	Pseudocode for MINCUTCONSERVATIVEHYP	78
3.11.	Sample Hypergraph	78
3.12.	Pseudocode for MAINTAINXMAP	80
3.13.	Pseudocode for CHECKXMAP	80
3.14.	Hypergraph $H(V, E)$ with five relations	81

3.15. Pseudocode for MAINTAINXMAP$_{NoFN}$ 83
3.16. Pseudocode for CHECKXMAP$_{NoFN}$ 83
3.17. Pseudocode for GETCONNECTEDSETS 84
3.18. Pseudocode for MAINTAINCSET 84
3.19. (a) Overlapping hyperedges, (b) and (c) simple graphs 87
3.20. (a) Hypergraph, (b) simple graph and (c) final graph 88
3.21. Pseudocode for PARTITION$_X$ 91
3.22. Call graph for the top-level case of PARTITION$_X$ 92
3.23. Struct *StackEntry* 95
3.24. Struct *HyperEdge* 95
3.25. Global Variables 95
3.26. Pseudocode for INITIALIZEINFOSTACK 95
3.27. Pseudocode for COMPUTELOOKUPIDX 95
3.28. Struct *Overlap* used by COMPUTEADJACENCYINFO 96
3.29. Pseudocode for COMPUTEADJACENCYINFO 97
3.30. Pseudocode for STORECOMPLEXHYPEREDGE 98
3.31. Pseudocode for DEREFERENCE 98
3.32. Pseudocode for STOREADJACENCYINFO 98
3.33. Pseudocode for COMPOSECOMPOUNDVERTICES 99
3.34. Pseudocode for MANAGEADJACENCYINFO 100
3.35. Pseudocode for GETBCCINFO 102
3.36. Pseudocode for FINDINITIALCOMPOUNDS 103
3.37. Pseudocode for MAINTAINLABELS 103
3.38. Pseudocode for DECODE 104
3.39. Pseudocode for CONNECTIONTESTREQUIRED 105
3.40. (a) Hypergraph, (b) simple graph and (c) final graph 106
3.41. Pseudocode for MAXIMIZECOMPOUNDVERTICES 107
3.42. Call graph for the top-level case of PARTITION$_X$ 109
3.43. Pseudocode for MANAGEINFOSTACK 110
3.44. Pseudocode for COMPUTEFILTERS 110
3.45. Pseudocode for CLEANSEHYPERNEIGHBOURS 112
3.46. (a) Hypergraph, (b) simplified graph and (c) final graph 114
3.47. (a) Sub-hypergraph of Figure 3.46 (b) a disconnected graph 114
3.48. (a) Hypergraph, (b) simplified graph and (c) final graph 116
3.49. (a) Sub-hypergraph of Figure 3.48 (b) simple graph 116
3.50. Pseudocode for RECOMPOSECOMPOUNDVERTICES 118
3.51. Pseudocode for ADJUSTCOMPOUNDFILTER 119
3.52. Pseudocode for REMANAGEADJACENCYINFO 120
3.53. Acyclic/inner/complex 126
3.54. Acyclic/non-inner/simple 127
3.55. Cyclic/inner/complex with 10 relations 130
3.56. Cyclic/inner/complex with 15 relations 131
3.57. Cyclic/non-inner/simple with 10 relations 132
3.58. Cyclic/non-inner/simple with 15 relations 133

4.1. Pseudocode for BUILDTREE 138
4.2. Pseudocode for TDPG$_{ACB}$ 139

4.3.	Pseudocode for TDPG_{PCB}	140
4.4.	Pseudocode for TDPG_{ACBI}	142
4.5.	Relation and domain sizes for random join queries	145
4.6.	Performance results for chain queries.	151
4.7.	Performance results for star queries.	152
4.8.	Performance results for random acyclic queries	153
4.9.	Density plot of random acyclic queries.	154
4.10.	Performance results for cycle queries.	155
4.11.	Performance results for clique queries.	156
4.12.	Performance results for random cyclic queries with 10 vertices.	157
4.13.	Performance results for random cyclic queries with 15 vertices.	158
4.14.	Density plot of random cyclic queries.	159
4.15.	Performance of different Pruning Advancements.	160
4.16.	Acyclic/inner/complex	161
4.17.	Acyclic/non-inner/simple	162
4.18.	Cyclic/inner/complex with 10 relations	163
4.19.	Cyclic/inner/complex with 15 relations	164
4.20.	Cyclic/non-inner/simple with 10 relations	165
4.21.	Cyclic/non-inner/simple with 15 relations	166
4.22.	Density plots for TDMCBHYP_{APCBI} with TDMCBHYP as norm	167
4.23.	Density plots for TDMCBHYP_{APCBI} with DPHYP as norm	167
A.1.	Pseudocode for MINCUTLAZY	174
A.2.	Pseudocode for BUILDBCT	176
A.3.	Pseudocode for BUILDBCTSUB	177

List of Tables

2.1.	Exemplified execution of TDBASIC for the input graph of Figure 2.6 .	29
2.2.	Multiple calls to BUILDTREE during the enumeration process	29
2.3.	All connected (sub) sets S and the corresponding $P_{ccp}^{sym}(S)$	30
2.4.	Sample values for inner counter and number of calls to BUILDPLAN .	30
2.5.	Exemplified execution of MINCUTBRANCH for Figure 2.15	49
2.6.	Exemplified execution of MINCUTBRANCH for Figure 2.16	49
2.7.	Names and abbreviated names of different plan generators	51
2.8.	Minimum, maximum and average of the normalized runtimes	56
2.9.	Minimum, maximum and average of the normalized runtimes	56
3.1.	MINCUTCONSERVATIVEHYP emits a duplicate ccp	82
3.2.	Exemplified execution of MINCUTCONSERVATIVEHYP	86
3.3.	Names of different plan generation algorithms	124
3.4.	Performance results for random queries	125
3.5.	Normed runtimes for Chain, Star, Cycle and Clique queries	129
3.6.	Normed runtimes for some TPC-H Queries	134
3.7.	Runtimes for TPC-H Queries	135
3.8.	Runtimes for TPC-DS Queries	135
3.9.	Runtimes for SQLite test suite queries	135
4.1.	Exemplified execution of TDPG$_{APCB}$	141
4.2.	Abbreviated names of different algorithms	146
4.3.	Normed runtimes for chain and star queries	148
4.4.	Normed runtimes for random acyclic and random cyclic queries . . .	148
4.5.	Normed runtimes for cycle and clique queries	149
4.6.	Number of optimal join trees built and failed join tree requests	150
4.7.	Abbreviated names of different algorithms	157
4.8.	Performance results for random queries	160
4.9.	Normed runtimes for some TPC-H Queries	162
4.10.	Runtimes for TPC-H Queries	163
4.11.	Runtimes for TPC-DS Queries	165
4.12.	Runtimes for SQLite test suite queries	166
A.1.	Number of biconnection tree buildings	182

1. Introduction

1.1. Motivation

Queries against DBMSs are often formulated in declarative languages. Prominent examples are SQL, OQL, XPath and XQuery. Writing such a declarative query has two advantages: (1) The querist does not need to decide upon the actual algorithms and execution order to access and combine the data, which in turn (2) leaves the DBMS with several degrees of freedom to choose the best evaluation and execution strategy in order to answer the query. This is a shift of complexity: from formulating the query towards how to answer it in a most efficient way. We refer to the process of transforming the declarative query in an imperative execution plan as plan generation, and we call the component in the DBMS which deals with the complexity of choosing a suitable plan from all alternatives the plan generator.

Today's plan generators are cost-based. This means that they rely on a cost model and statistics over the data in order to select from all equivalent plans the one with the lowest costs. Essential for the costs of a plan is the execution order of join operations in its operator tree, since the runtime of plans with different join orders can vary by several orders of magnitude. An exhaustive search for an optimal solution over all possible operator trees is computationally infeasible. To decrease complexity, the search space must be restricted. For the optimization problem discussed in this book, the well-accepted connectivity heuristic is applied: We consider all possible bushy join trees, but exclude cross products from the search, presuming that all considered queries span a connected query graph. Thereby, a query graph is an undirected graph where join predicates span the edges between the relations referenced in the SQL query, i.e., a graph edge between R_1 and R_2 is introduced if there exists a join predicate involving attributes of R_1 and R_2.

When designing a plan generator, there are two strategies to find an optimal join order: bottom-up join enumeration via dynamic programming, and top-down join enumeration through memoization.

Both plan generation approaches rely on Bellman's Principle of Optimality[1]: They generate an optimal join tree for a set of relations S by considering optimal subjoin trees only. This means that non-optimal, i.e., more expensive, subjoin trees can be discarded, which curtails the search space enormously[2]. Moreover, since the connectivity heuristic is applied[3], the optimal (sub) join tree needs to be constructed only for those

---

[1] The presence of properties requires additional care. For reasons of simplicity properties are ignored here.

[2] The search space is reduced from $|V|!\, \mathcal{C}(|V|-1)$ number of plans to $\frac{3^{|V|}-2^{|V|+1}+1}{2}$ where $|V|$ is the number of relations referenced in the query and $\mathcal{C}$ are the Catalan Numbers with $\mathcal{C}(n) = \frac{1}{n+1}\binom{2n}{n}$ [4]. $|V|!\, \mathcal{C}(|V|-1)$ can be simplified to $\frac{(2|V|-2)!}{(|V|-1)!}$ [13, 19, 31]

[3] Which can reduce the search space further depending on the query graph down to $\frac{|V|^3-|V|}{3}$ number of plans.

subsets of relations S that can be joined without the need of applying cross products. In other words, the subset S of relations referenced in the SQL query has to induce a connected subgraph of the original query graph.

In order to determine the best join tree for a given subset S of relations, the top-down/bottom-up plan generator must enumerate all partitions (S_1, S_2) of S such that $S = S_1 \cup S_2$ and $S_1 \cap S_2 = \emptyset$ holds. Furthermore, since we exclude cross products, S_1 and S_2 must induce connected subgraphs, and there must be two relations $R_1 \in S_1$ and $R_2 \in S_2$ such that they are connected by a graph edge. Let us call such a partition (S_1, S_2) a ccp. Denote by T_i the optimal plan for S_i. Then the query optimizer has to consider the plans $T_1 \bowtie T_2$ for all ccps (S_1, S_2) in order to compute the optimal join tree for the relations contained in S.

Thus, both the bottom-up and the top-down join enumeration face the same challenge: to efficiently compute the ccps. There has been an ongoing race between top-down and bottom-up join enumeration concerning this challenge. Traditionally, all partitioning strategies have been generate-and-test based. But depending on the shape of the query graph, most of the generated partitions are not valid ccps, i.e., are filtered out by the tests for connectivity. That is why those approaches are suboptimal and can have an exponential overhead[4].

In bottom-up join enumeration, all the connected subsets for a given set are already generated. Therefore, a partitioning strategy for dynamic programming that is not generate-and-test based should be easier to design. Moerkotte and Neumann [22] presented a dynamic programming variant called DPCCP, producing all partitions in constant time $O(1)$ per valid ccp.

For top-down join enumeration via memoization, no such equally efficient solution is known yet. Finding an analogous variant to DPCCP for memoization is very appealing, not only for the outcome of the race but also because the nature of top-down processing can leverage the benefits of branch-and-bound pruning. The beauty of those pruning strategies is that they are risk-free: They can speed up processing by several orders of magnitude, while at the same time they preserve optimality of the final join tree.

DeHaan and Tompa took up the challenge and proposed with MINCUTLAZY [5] a minimal graph cut partitioning algorithm for memoization. Nevertheless, TDMcL, which is the generic top-down join enumeration algorithm instantiated with MINCUT-LAZY, cannot compete with DPCCP. The first contribution of this work are two partitioning algorithms for top-down join enumeration that close the performance gap to DPCCP.

However, the proposed algorithms DPCCP and TDMcL are not ready to be used in real-world scenarios yet because there exist severe limitations: First, as has been argued in several places, hypergraphs must be handled by any plan generator [2, 27, 35]. Second, plan generators have to deal with outer joins and antijoins [14, 27]. In general, these operators are not freely reorderable, i.e., there might exist different orderings, which produce different results. Because it has been shown that the non-inner join reordering problem can be reduced to hypergraphs, it remains the top goal of

---

[4]In case of a chain query for example, the naive generate-and-test based approach for top-down join enumeration generates $2^{|V|+2} - |V|^2 - 3*|V| - 4$ partitions but only $\frac{|V|^3-|V|}{3}$ are valid ccps [26].

any plan generator to deal with hypergraphs [2, 21, 27, 20]. Consequently, Moerkotte and Neumann [21] extended DPCCP to DPHYP to handle hypergraphs.

The second main contribution of this work is a generic partitioning framework that transforms hypergraphs to restrictive graphs and applies some further modifications. The advantage of this approach is that existing, well performing graph-partitioning algorithms can be reused in order to efficiently handle hypergraphs.

As the third and last contribution of this book, we present advancements to the known branch-and-bound pruning strategies.

As will be shown, all combined contributions of this book result in a performance advantage of 100% over DPHYP by considering the TPC-H [34], TPC-DS [33] and the SQLite test suite [29] benchmarks. For syntactic workloads we present average runtime improvements by orders of magnitude.

The detailed contributions together with the outline of this book are described in the following section.

1.2. Contribution

1.2.1. Graph-Aware Join Enumeration Algorithms

In Chapter 2, we give a general introduction to top-down join enumeration. We explain a naive approach and give a complexity analysis that motivates three new graph-partitioning strategies. For the last partitioning algorithm, we show that it has a complexity in $O(1)$ per emitted *ccp* for acyclic and standard query graphs. A performance evaluation concludes this chapter, showing that two of the three partitioning algorithms are competitive with DPCCP. The following publications contributed to this chapter:

- [9] Pit Fender and Guido Moerkotte. Reassessing top-down join enumeration. *IEEE Transactions on Knowledge and Data Engineering*, 24(10):1803–1818, 2012

- [12] Pit Fender, Guido Moerkotte, Thomas Neumann, and Viktor Leis. Effective and robust pruning for top-down join enumeration algorithms. In *Proceedings of the 28th International Conference on Data Engineering*, pages 414–425, 2012

- [8] Pit Fender and Guido Moerkotte. A new, highly efficient, and easy to implement top-down join enumeration algorithm. In *Proceedings of the 27th International Conference on Data Engineering*, pages 864–875, 2011

1.2.2. Hypergraph-Aware Join Enumeration Algorithms

We start Chapter 3 by motivating why the handling of hypergraphs is indispensable. After that, we adjust the naive top-down join enumeration algorithm of Chapter 2 and explain the necessary changes. We continue with a description of the first hypergraph-aware partitioning algorithm. Then we present our main contribution: a generic partitioning framework that enables graph-aware partitioning algorithms to cope with hypergraphs. We show how the partitioning strategies of Chapter 2 can be reused. Then we conclude with a performance evaluation that includes the runtime results of the

TPC-H, TPC-DS and the SQLite test suite benchmarks. The hypergraph-aware partitioning algorithm and the generic framework have already been published:

[11] Pit Fender and Guido Moerkotte. Top-down plan generation: From theory to practice. In *Proceedings of the 29th International Conference on Data Engineering*, pages 1105–1116, 2013

[10] Pit Fender and Guido Moerkotte. Counter strike: Generic top-down join enumeration for hypergraphs. *Proceedings of the VLDB Endowment*, 6(14):1822–1833, September 2013

1.2.3. Branch-and-Bound Pruning

The main advantage of top-down join enumeration over bottom-up join enumeration is that it allows for branch-and-bound pruning. Chapter 4 starts with an introduction to branch-and-bound pruning. Then, we follow with seven advancements that improve pruning (1) in terms of effectiveness, (2) in terms of robustness and (3) by avoiding its potential worst case behavior otherwise observed. At the end of Chapter 4, we give an in-depth performance evaluation. Furthermore, we give results for the TPC-H, TPC-DS and the SQLite test suite benchmarks. We have published advancements and results as follows:

[12] Pit Fender, Guido Moerkotte, Thomas Neumann, and Viktor Leis. Effective and robust pruning for top-down join enumeration algorithms. In *Proceedings of the 28th International Conference on Data Engineering*, pages 414–425, 2012

1.2.4. Conclusion and Appendix

We conclude this book in Chapter 5. Appendix A gives a complexity analysis of the work of DeHaan and Tompa [5]. Furthermore, we include the C++ Code of two partitioning algorithms in Appendix B.1 and B.2.

2. Graph-Aware Join Enumeration Algorithms

For a precise description of our graph-aware join enumeration algorithms, we have to give some fundamentals. We start with the preliminaries in Section 2.1. An introduction to top-down join enumeration by explaining a naive memoization algorithm follows in Section 2.2. After that, Section 2.3 presents our first graph-aware top-down join enumeration algorithm based on an advanced-generate-and-test paradigm. We improve upon that approach by presenting conservative graph partitioning in Section 2.4. Finally, Section 2.5 explains branch partitioning which has a complexity that is in $O(1)$ for standard queries per emitted *ccp*. We conclude this chapter with an extensive performance evaluation in Section 2.6.

2.1. Preliminaries

2.1.1. Graphs

We start with the notion of a *graph* as the basis for the definitions that follow.

Definition 2.1.1. *An* undirected graph $G = (V, E)$ *is defined by a set of vertices V and a set of edges E. The set of edges E is a set of unordered pairs (v, w) for which $v, w \in V$ with $v \neq w$ holds. We assume that the nodes in V are totally ordered via an (arbitrary) relation $\prec$.*

For an edge (v, w), v and w are said to be *adjacent* to each other, and the edge is said to be *incident* with v and w. The next definition specifies what we mean by an *index* of a vertex.

Definition 2.1.2. *Let $G = (V, E)$ be an undirected graph with $v_i \in V$. Further let $\prec$ be a binary relation specifying the total order of the vertices of V. We say i is the* index *of v_i with $i = |\{w \prec v_i | w \in V\}|$.*

We continue with the notion of *node-induced subgraphs*.

Definition 2.1.3. *Let $G = (V, E)$ be an undirected graph and $V' \subseteq V$ a subset of nodes. The* node-induced subgraph $G|_{V'}$ *of G is defined as $G|_{V'} = (V', E')$ with $E' = \{(v, w) \mid (v, w) \in E \land v \in V' \land w \in V'\}$. The node ordering on V' is the restriction of the node ordering of V.*

Having defined a graph, we now specify what we mean by a path between vertices v_0 and v_l in $G = (V, E)$.

Definition 2.1.4. *Let $G = (V, E)$ be an undirected graph, then a* path $u \to^* w$ *with the length l between vertices u and w is defined as a sequence of vertices $\langle v_0, v_1, v_2, ..., v_l \rangle$*

in V such that $u = v_0$ and $w = v_l$ and $(v_{i-1}, v_i) \in E$ for $i = 1, 2, ...l$. The length l of the path is the number of edges $(v_0, v_1), (v_1, v_2), ..., (v_{l-1}, v_l)$ in the path.

With the definition of a path, we are able to give the notion of a *cycle*.

Definition 2.1.5. *Let $G = (V, E)$ be an undirected graph, then a* cycle *is a path $\langle v_0, v_1, v_2, ..., v_l \rangle$ with $\forall_{0 \leq i \leq l} v_i \in V$ where $v_0 = v_l$ holds.*

We make the following observation:

Observation 2.1.6. *Let $G = (V, E)$ be an undirected graph, then a path $\langle v_0, v_1, v_2, ..., v_l \rangle$ is free of cycles if $\forall_{0 \leq i < j \leq l} v_i \neq v_j$ holds.*

Through the definition of a path, we can express the notion of a *connected (sub)graph*.

Definition 2.1.7. *Let $G = (V, E)$ be an undirected graph. If there exists a path between each pair of vertices of V, then G is called* connected.

There is an alternative way to specify whether a graph is connected.

Observation 2.1.8. *Let $G = (V, E)$ be an undirected graph. G is connected if $|V| = 1$ or if there exists a partitioning V', V'' of V and an edge $(v, w) \in E$ such that $v \subseteq V'$, $w \subseteq V''$, and both $G|_{V'}$ and $G|_{V''}$ are connected.*

For this, we need the notion of the direct and indirect neighborhood.

Definition 2.1.9. *Let $G = (V, E)$ be an undirected graph, then the* neighborhood *of a vertex $v \in V$ is defined as*

$$\mathcal{N}(v) = \{w \mid w \in V \land (v, w) \in E\}.$$

We define the *neighborhood of a set*:

Definition 2.1.10. *Let $G = (V, E)$ be an undirected graph, then the* neighborhood *of a set $S \subseteq V$ is defined as:*

$$\mathcal{N}(S) = \{w \mid v \in S \land w \in (V \setminus S) \land (v, w) \in E\}.$$

And a set's indirect neighborhood is defined by:

Definition 2.1.11. *Let $G = (V, E)$ be an undirected graph, then the* indirect neighborhood *of a set $S \subseteq V$ is defined as:*

$$\mathcal{N}_0(S) = S$$

$$\mathcal{N}_1(S) = \mathcal{N}(S)$$

$$\mathcal{N}_{i+1}(S) = \mathcal{N}(\mathcal{N}_i(S)) \setminus (\cup_{j=0...i} \mathcal{N}_j(S)).$$

In the following observation, we give another way of testing a graph G for connectivity:

Observation 2.1.12. *An undirected graph $G = (V, E)$ is connected only if for an arbitrary vertex $v \in V$, the set of all generations of neighbors of $\{v\}$ equals V:*

$$V = \cup_{0 \le i < |V|} \mathcal{N}_i(\{v\}) \ .$$

We give the notion of a *partition* of the vertex set V.

Definition 2.1.13. *Let $G = (V, E)$ be a connected undirected graph, $V_1 \subset V$ with $V_1 \ne \emptyset$ and $V_2 = V \setminus V_1$, then (V_1, V_2) is called a* partition *of V.*

Fundamental for the algorithms described in this book is the notion of a *graph cut*.

Definition 2.1.14. *Let $G = (V, E)$ be a connected undirected graph and (V_1, V_2) a partition of V. The set of all edges $E_{cut} = \{(v_1, v_2) \in E \mid v_1 \in V_1 \wedge v_2 \in V_2\}$ crossing this partition is called a* graph cut.

It follows from the definition that a graph cut necessarily disconnects G into at least two connected subgraphs. A special case of a graph cut is a minimal cut.

Definition 2.1.15. *Let $G = (V, E)$ is a connected undirected graph and (V_1, V_2) a partition of V. If both V_1 and V_2 induce connected subgraphs, then $E_{cut} = \{(v_1, v_2) \in E \mid v_1 \in V_1 \wedge v_2 \in V_2\}$ is a* minimal graph cut.

Let $G = (V, E)$ be a connected undirected graph and (V_1, V_2) a partition of V. The set of edges produced by the graph cut to gain (V_1, V_2) is specified with $E_{cut(V_1, V_2)} = \{(v_1, v_2) \in E \mid v_1 \in V_1 \wedge v_2 \in V_2\}$. Assume that $G_{|V_1}$ is not connected. Further, let V_{1_1} be a proper non-empty subset of V_1. We can find a minimal cut producing an edge set $E_{cut(V_{1_1}, V \setminus V_{1_1})} = \{(v_1, v_2) \in E \mid v_1 \in V_{1_1} \wedge v_2 \in V \setminus V_{1_1}\}$ that partitions V into $(V_{1_1}, V \setminus V_{1_1})$, and it holds that $E_{cut(V_{1_1}, V \setminus V_{1_1})} \subset E_{cut(V_1, V_2)}$ and $V_{1_1} \subset V_1$. But if both V_1 and V_2 induce a connected graph, then the graph cut $E_{cut(V_1, V_2)}$ cannot contain another graph cut that is a proper subset. The following observation explains why it is called minimal cut.

Observation 2.1.16. *A minimal cut contains no other graph cuts as a proper subset.*

There is a special type of vertex, called an *articulation vertex* of a connected graph G. Removing such a vertex from V disconnects the graph into at least two connected subgraphs. We give its definition.

Definition 2.1.17. *Let $G = (V, E)$ be an undirected connected graph. A vertex $a \in V$ is called* articulation vertex *if there exist two vertices $v \in V$ and $w \in V$, such that every path $v \xrightarrow{*} w$ in V must contain a.*

The articulation vertices of a connected graph $G = (V, E)$ are important when determining the *biconnected components* of a graph.

Definition 2.1.18. *Let $G = (V, E)$ be a connected undirected graph. A* biconnected component *is a connected subgraph $G_i^{BCC} = (V_i, E_i)$ of G with $V_i = \{v \mid (v = u \vee v = w) \wedge (v, w) \in E_i\}$, where the set of edges $E_i \subseteq E$ is maximal such that any two distinct edges $(u, w) \in E_i$ and $(x, y) \in E_i$ lie on a cycle $\langle v_0, v_1, v_2, ..., v_l \rangle$, where $u = v_0 \wedge u = v_l \wedge w = v_1 \wedge x = v_{j-1} \wedge y = v_j \wedge 0 < j < l$ and $\forall_{0 \le i < j < l} v_i \ne v_j$ holds. If for an edge $(u, w) \in E_i$ no such cycle exists, the vertices $u, w \in V_i$ induce a biconnected component $G_i^{BCC} = (\{u, w\}, \{(u, w)\})$.*

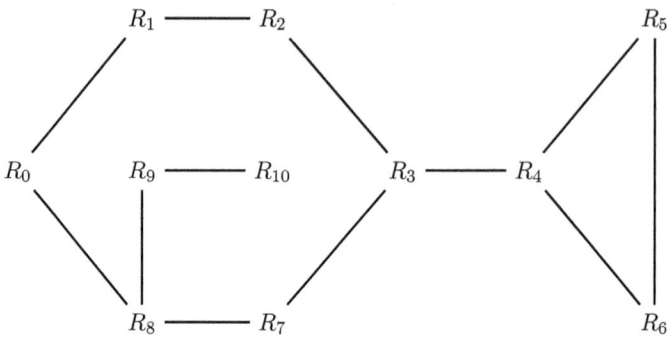

Figure 2.1.: Graph of eleven relations, five biconnected components $G^{BCC}_{|\{R_0,R_1,R_2,R_3,R_7,R_8\}}$, $G^{BCC}_{|\{R_3,R_4\}}$, $G^{BCC}_{|\{R_4,R_5,R_6\}}$, $G^{BCC}_{|\{R_8,R_9\}}$ and $G^{BCC}_{|\{R_9,R_{10}\}}$ and four articulation vertices R_3, R_4, R_8, R_9.

We make the following observation:

Observation 2.1.19. *Let $G = (V, E)$ be a connected undirected graph with k biconnected components. Then the edge set E can be divided into equivalence classes $E_1, E_2, ...E_k$ such that each subset E_i spans one of the k biconnected components $G^{BCC}_i = (V_i, E_i)$ of G.*

Furthermore, we observe:

Observation 2.1.20. *Two biconnected components G_i and G_j cannot have more than one vertex in common. If they have one vertex a in common, then a has to be an articulation vertex, and $V_i \cap V_j = \{a\}$ holds.*

We exemplify the notion of biconnected components and articulation vertices in Figure 2.1. The connected undirected graph $G = (V, E)$ with $|V| = 11$ has five biconnected components which are: $G^{BCC}_{|\{R_0,R_1,R_2,R_3,R_7,R_8\}}$, $G^{BCC}_{|\{R_3,R_4\}}$, $G^{BCC}_{|\{R_4,R_5,R_6\}}$, $G^{BCC}_{|\{R_8,R_9\}}$ and $G^{BCC}_{|\{R_9,R_{10}\}}$. There are four articulation vertices: R_3, R_4, R_8, R_9. We can divide the edge set E in five equivalence classes, which are: $E_1 = \{(R_0, R_1), (R_1, R_2), (R_2, R_3), (R_3, R_7), (R_7, R_8), (R_0, R_8)\}$, $E_2 = \{(R_3, R_4)\}$, $E_3 = \{(R_4, R_5), (R_5, R_6), (R_4, R_6)\}$, $E_4 = \{(R_8, R_9)\}$ and $E_5 = \{(R_9, R_{10})\}$.

2.1.2. Query Graphs, Plan Classes and Costs

In this subsection, we introduce the notion of a query graph which serves as an input for our plan generation algorithms. After that, we specify the notion of a plan class. Finally, we define the C_{out} cost function.

The notion of query graph is synonymously used for graphs and hypergraphs. For the definition of a hypergraph, we refer to Section 3.2.1. A *query graph* is defined as follows:

Definition 2.1.21. *Given a query and a set of join predicates and let $\mathcal{R} = \{R_1, R_2..., R_n\}$ be a set of n relations specified by the query, we define the* query graph $G = (V, E)$ representing the query as an undirected graph or undirected hypergraph, where $\mathcal{R}$ is represented by the vertex set V and the set of join predicates by an edge set $E = \{(v, w) \mid v$ and w represent relations that are referenced by a join predicate$\}$.

The result of the algorithms presented here is a *join tree*. A join tree specifies a certain execution order of join operations.

Definition 2.1.22. *A* join tree *is a binary tree whose leaf nodes are the relations specified in a query and whose inner nodes are the join operations. The edges of a join tree represent the input and output relationship.*

An inner node corresponds to a binary join operation which has two subtrees as input. The leaves of a join tree are the disjoint relations specified in the query. A join tree or a join subtree may consist of just one node or, alternatively, is the root of two subtrees.

From a join tree the query evaluation plan can be built. Essentially, the query evaluation plan is an operator tree with physical algebraic operators as nodes. A plan class groups equivalent plans. The plans within a plan class have the same logical properties. An import logical property is the set of relations the plan comprises. Another logical property is the output cardinality of the plans. The optimal plan of a plan class is the cheapest among all members of the class.

The result of all optimization algorithms presented here will be optimal. From all possible optimal plans of the same plan class with the same lowest costs, the optimization algorithms arbitrarily return one optimal solution.

We give the definition of a *connected subgraph and its complement pair*, which we abbreviate with *ccp*.

Definition 2.1.23. *Let $G = (V, E)$ be a connected query graph, (S_1, S_2) is a* connected subgraph and its complement pair *(or ccp for short) if the following holds:*

- $S_1 \cap S_2 = \emptyset$,
- S_1 *with* $S_1 \subset V$ *induces a connected graph* $G_{|S_1}$,
- S_2 *with* $S_2 \subset V$ *induces a connected graph* $G_{|S_2}$, *and*
- $\exists (v_1, v_2) \in E$ *with* $v_1 \in S_1 \wedge v_2 \in S_2$.

The set of all possible *ccps* is denoted by P_{ccp}. We introduce the notion of *ccps* for a set S to specify all those pairs of input sets that result in the same output set S, if joined.

Definition 2.1.24. *Let $G = (V, E)$ be a connected query graph and S a set with $S \subseteq V$ that induces a connected subgraph $G_{|S}$. For $S_1, S_2 \subset V$, (S_1, S_2) is called a ccp for S if (S_1, S_2) is a ccp and $S_1 \cup S_2 = S$ holds.*

We can observe:

Observation 2.1.25. *If (S_1, S_2) is a ccp for S, then (S_1, S_2) is also a partition of S.*

By $P_{ccp}(S)$, we denote the set of all *ccps* for S. Let $G = (V, E)$ be a connected query graph and $\mathcal{P}_{con}(V) = \{S \subseteq V \mid G_{|S} \text{ is connected} \land |S| > 1\}$ be the set of all connected subsets of V with more than one element, then $P_{ccp} = \cup_{S \in \mathcal{P}_{con}(V)} P_{ccp}(S)$ holds.

If (S_1, S_2) is a *ccp*, then (S_2, S_1) is one as well, and we consider them as symmetric pairs. We are interested in the set P_{ccp}^{sym} of all *ccps*, where symmetric pairs are accounted for only once, e.g., $(S_1, S_2) \in P_{ccp}^{sym}$ if $\text{MIN}_{index}(S_1) < \text{MIN}_{index}(S_2)$ holds, or $(S_2, S_1) \in P_{ccp}^{sym}$ otherwise. By $\text{MIN}_{index}(S)$ we specify the minimal index i of all vertices $v_i \in S$ (Definition 2.1.2). We give no constraints for choosing which one of two symmetric pairs should be member of P_{ccp}^{sym}, but leave this as a degree of freedom. Analogously, we denote the set of all *ccps* for a set S containing either (S_1, S_2) or (S_2, S_1) by $P_{ccp}^{sym}(S)$.

With C_{out} we give a simple cost function that sums up the cardinalities of the intermediate results [3]. C_{out} is defined as

$$C_{out}(T) = \begin{cases} 0 & \text{if } T \text{ is a single relation} \\ |T| + C_{out}(T_1) + C_{out}(T_2) & \text{if } T = T_1 \bowtie T_2 \end{cases}$$

2.1.3. Problem Specification

Since there are many different join ordering problems, we want to specify the problem domain which we investigate here. We apply the well-accepted connectivity heuristic [26] by considering the generation of optimal bushy join trees without cross products. Therefore, the query graph has to be connected. Within this chapter, we allow only select-project-join queries with simple join predicates that are not referencing more than two relations. We discard physical properties like sortedness and groupedness and assume that Bellman's Principle of Optimality holds. For each complexity analysis done in this document, we specify the complexity of set operations $\cup, \cap, \setminus$ to be in $O(1)$. When we assume that the word size is unlimited and we represent sets by using bitvectors, the operations $\cup, \cap, \setminus$ can be implemented in a constant (and small) number of instructions.

2.2. Basic Memoization

As an introduction to top-down join enumeration, we give a basic memoization variant called TDBASIC, which we derive by utilizing a generic top-down algorithm that invokes a naive partitioning algorithm. In the first sub-subsection, we present our generic top-down algorithm. Afterwards, we explain the naive partitioning strategy.

2.2.1. Generic Top-Down Join Enumeration

Our generic top-down join enumeration algorithm TDPLANGEN is based on memoization. We present its pseudocode in Figure 2.2. Like dynamic programming, TDPLANGEN initializes the building blocks for atomic relations first (Line 2). Then, in Line 3 the subroutine TDPGSUB is called, which traverses recursively through the search space. As the name implies, top-down enumeration starts with the vertex set V. Hence at the root invocation of TDPGSUB, the vertex set S corresponds to the vertex set V of the query graph. At every recursion step of TDPGSUB, all possible join trees of two optimal subjoin trees that together comprise the relations of S are built through BUILDTREE (Line 3) that we explain later, and the cheapest join tree is kept. We enumerate the optimal subjoin trees by iterating over the elements (S_1, S_2) of $P_{ccp}^{sym}(S)$ in Line 2. This way, we derive the two optimal subjoin trees, each comprising exactly the relations in S_1 or S_2, respectively, by recursive calls to TDPGSUB. Generating $P_{ccp}^{sym}(S)$ is the task of a partitioning algorithm. Depending on the choice of the partitioning strategy, the overall performance of TDPLANGEN can vary by orders of magnitude.

The recursive descent stops when either $|S| = 1$ or TDPGSUB has already been called for that $G_{|S}$. In both cases, the optimal join tree is already known. To prevent TDPGSUB from computing an optimal tree twice, $BestTree[S]$ is checked in Line 1. $BestTree[S]$ yields a reference to an entry in an associative data structure called *memotable*. The data structure "memoizes" the optimal join tree generated for a set S. If $BestTree[S]$ equals NULL, this invocation of TDPGSUB will be the first one with $G_{|S}$ as input, and the optimal join tree of $G_{|S}$ has not been found yet. Otherwise, $BestTree[S]$ will hold an optimal plan for the plan class of S. Note that during the optimization of S the optimal plan for the plan class might not be found yet because there are still *ccps* for S to be considered. This means that during the process of looping over $P_{ccp}^{sym}(S)$ (Line 2) $BestTree[S]$ does not necessarily hold the optimal join tree for S, but the cheapest tree found so far.

TDPLANGEN(G)

  ▷ **Input:** connected G=(V,E), $V = \bigcup_{1 \leq i \leq |V|} \{R_i\}$
  ▷ **Output:** an optimal join tree for G
1   **for** $i \leftarrow 1$ **to** n
2       $BestTree(\{R_i\}) \leftarrow R_i$
3   **return** TDPGSUB(V)

TDPGSUB($G_{|S}$)

  ▷ **Input:** connected sub graph $G_{|S}$
  ▷ **Output:** an optimal join tree for $G_{|S}$
1   **if** $BestTree[S] =$ NULL
2   **for all** $(S_1, S_2) \in P_{ccp}^{sym}(S)$
3   **do** BUILDTREE(S, TDPGSUB($G_{|S_1}$), TDPGSUB($G_{|S_2}$))
4   **return** $BestTree(S)$

Figure 2.2.: Pseudocode for TDPLANGEN

The pseudocode of BUILDTREE is given in Figure 2.3. It is used to compare the cost of the join trees that belong to the same $G_{|S}$. Since the symmetric pairs (S_1, S_2) and (S_2, S_1) (Line 2 of TDPGSUB) are enumerated only once, we have to build two join trees (Line 1 and Line 4) and then compare their costs. We use the method CREATETREE, which takes two disjoint join trees as arguments and combines them to a new join tree. If different join implementations have to be considered, among all alternatives the cheapest join tree has to be built by CREATETREE. If the created join tree (Line 1) is cheaper than $BestTree[S]$, or even no

BUILDTREE($S, Tree_1, Tree_2$)
    ▷ **Input:** connected vertex set S, two sub join trees
1    $CurrentTree \leftarrow$ CREATETREE$(Tree_1, Tree_2)$
2   **if** $BestTree[S] =$ NULL $\vee cost(BestTree[S]) > cost(CurrentTree)$
3        $BestTree[S] \leftarrow CurrentTree$
4    $CurrentTree \leftarrow$ CREATETREE$(Tree_2, Tree_1)$
5   **if** $cost(BestTree[S]) > cost(CurrentTree)$
6        $BestTree[S] \leftarrow CurrentTree$

Figure 2.3.: Pseudocode for BUILDTREE

PARTITION$_{naive}(G_{|S})$
    ▷ **Input:** a connected node induced (sub) graph $G_{|S}$
    ▷ **Output:** $P_{ccp}^{sym}(S)$
1   **for all** $C \subset S \wedge C \neq \emptyset$
2   **if** MIN$_{index}(C) <$ MIN$_{index}(S \setminus C) \wedge$
            ISCONNECTED$(G_{|C}) \wedge$ ISCONNECTED$(G_{|S \setminus C})$
3   emit$(C, S \setminus C)$

Figure 2.4.: Pseudocode for naive partitioning

tree for S has been built yet, $BestTree[S]$ gets registered with the $CurrentTree$. For building the second tree, we just exchange the arguments (Line 4). Again, the costs of the new join tree are compared to the costs of $BestTree[S]$. Only if the new join tree has lower costs, $BestTree[S]$ gets registered with the new join tree. Note that because of Line 3, $BestTree[S]$ in Line 6 cannot be NULL. Estimating the costs of the two possible join trees at the same time rather than separately and comparing them is more efficient, e.g., for cost functions as given in [17], where $card(T_x) \leq card(T_y) \Rightarrow cost(T_x \bowtie T_y) \leq cost(T_y \bowtie T_x)$ holds, with $card$ is the number of tuples or pages and T_x, T_y are (intermediate) relations.

2.2.2. Naive Partitioning

As we have already seen, the generic top-down enumeration algorithm iterates over the elements of $P_{ccp}^{sym}(S)$. Now, we show how the *ccps* for S can be computed by a naive generate-and-test strategy. We call our algorithm PARTITION$_{naive}$ and give its pseudocode in Figure 2.4. In Line 1, all $2^{|S|} - 2$ possible non-empty and proper subsets of S are enumerated. For rapid subset enumeration, the method described in [36] can be used. We demand that from every symmetric pair only one *ccp* is emitted. There are many possible solutions, but we make sure that the relation with the lowest index (Definition 2.1.2) is always contained in C in Line 2. Three conditions have to be met so that a partition $(C, S \setminus C)$ is a *ccp*. We check the connectivity of $G_{|C}$ and $G_{|S \setminus C}$ in Line 2. The third condition that C needs to be connected to $S \setminus C$ is ensured implicitly by the requirement that the graph $G_{|S}$ handed over as input is connected.

ISCONNECTED$(G_{|C})$

▷ **Input:** a node induced subgraph $G_{|C}$
▷ **Output:** TRUE if $G_{|C}$ is connected, FALSE otherwise
1 $T \leftarrow \{$arbitrary element t of $C\}$
2 **while** $(\mathcal{N}(T) \cap C) \neq \emptyset$
3      $T \leftarrow T \cup (\mathcal{N}(T) \cap C)$
4 **return** $T = C$

Figure 2.5.: Pseudocode for ISCONNECTED

To check for connectivity of the node-induced subgraphs, Observation 2.1.12 can be used. The pseudocode follows directly and is given in Fig. 2.5 with ISCONNECTED.

2.2.3. Exemplified Execution of TDBASIC

As already mentioned, we refer to the generic top-down join enumeration algorithm TDPLANGEN instantiated with PARTITION$_{naive}$ as TDBASIC. Now we exemplify the execution of TDBASIC with the query graph of Figure 2.6. In Figure 2.7 we give the selectivities and cardinalities. For the comparison of equivalent join trees we use the C_{out} cost function (Section 2.1.2). Table 2.1 shows the different states during execution. Thereby the first column is the table entry that serves as reference. The second column displays the recursion level, with 0 indicating the root invocation. The input parameter S is shown in the third column and the current ccp that is being processed is displayed by the fourth column. In other words, Table 2.1 shows the order in which the ccps are enumerated. We can observe that the order is not only top-down but also demand-driven.

Table 2.2 shows a different perspective of the enumeration process by listing the order of calls to BUILDTREE. Again, the first column serves as entry of reference. We give the current ccp for that the call to BUILDTREE was made in the second column. With the third column, we reference the corresponding entry of Table 2.1. The fourth column displays the current join tree. Here, we ignore the join tree that we gain by applying commutativity, since it will have the same costs. The cost for cT are given in the fifth column. The sixth column displays the table entry computing the cheapest tree known so far. This entry corresponds to the current value of $BestTree$.

It should not be surprising that Table 2.1 has the same amount of entries as Table 2.2. We can observe that the order in which the (sub) join trees are computed is bottom-up. For this example, the optimal join tree for $V = \{R_0, R_1, R_2, R_3\}$ is $R_0 \bowtie (R_1 \bowtie (R_2 \bowtie R_3))$ with the cost of 21. The most expensive join tree for V is $((R_0 \bowtie R_1) \bowtie R_2) \bowtie R_3$ with the cost of 11001, which is a huge difference. The most expensive join tree with the costs of 110000 is $R_0 \bowtie (R_1 \bowtie R_2)$. We can see that because of memoization, this subtree was not considered when $((R_0 \bowtie R_1) \bowtie R_2) \bowtie R_3$ was computed, because $BestTree[\{R_0, R_1, R_2\}]$ points to $(R_0 \bowtie R_1) \bowtie R_2$, which is only $\frac{1}{10}$ of the costs.

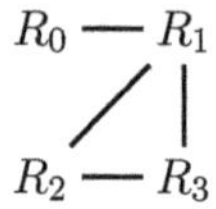

$$R_0 \text{——} R_1$$
$$\diagup \;\;|$$
$$R_2 \text{——} R_3$$

Figure 2.6.: Example graph $G = (V, E)$ with $V = \{R_0, R_1, R_2, R_3\}$ and $E = \{(R_0, R_1), (R_1, R_2), (R_1, R_3), (R_2, R_3)\}$

Relation	Cardinality
R_0	1
R_1	10000
R_2	100
R_3	10

Edge	Selectivity
(R_0, R_1)	0.1
(R_1, R_2)	0.1
(R_1, R_3)	0.001
(R_2, R_3)	0.01

Figure 2.7.: Selectivity and Cardinalities for the Query Graph of Figure 2.6

For the purpose of completeness, we list all *ccp*s in Table 2.3. In particular, we show for every connected subgraph $G_{|S}$ that is considered by TDBASIC the corresponding set $P_{ccp}^{sym}(S)$.

2.2.4. Analysis of TDBASIC

In this section, we give a brief analysis of TDBASIC. Therefore, we count the number of iterations $\#I$ of the loop in Line 1 of PARTITION$_{naive}$ summed up over all invocations of PARTITION$_{naive}$ for all S. Here, the number $\#I$ depends on the shape of the query graph. We analyzed $\#I$ in our experimental studies for different graph shapes and deduced the following formulas:

For chains, we have

$$\#I_{\text{TDBasic}}^{\text{chain}}(|V|) = 2^{|V|+2} - |V|^2 - 3 * |V| - 4.$$

For stars, we have

$$\#I_{\text{TDBasic}}^{\text{star}}(|V|) = 2 * 3^{|V|-1} - 2^{|V|}.$$

For cycles, we have

$$\#I_{\text{TDBasic}}^{\text{cycle}}(|V|) = |V| * 2^{|V|} + 2^{|V|} - 2|V|^2 - 2.$$

For cliques, we have

$$\#I_{\text{TDBasic}}^{\text{cliques}}(|V|) = 3^{|V|} - 2^{|V|+1} + 1.$$

These formulas are identical to Moerkotte's and Neumann's analysis of the dynamic programming variant DPSUB [22].

For analyzing the algorithm's performance, we have to account for the number of times the enumerated partitions pass the test for connectivity. This is equal to the number of times BUILDPLAN is called, which we abbreviate with $\#bP$. Since we avoid to enumerate symmetric partitions twice, this number is half the number of existing *ccp*s.

Entry	L	S	current ccp
1	0	$\{R_0, R_1, R_2, R_3\}$	$(\{R_0\}, \{R_1, R_2, R_3\})$
2	1	$\{R_1, R_2, R_3\}$	$(\{R_1\}, \{R_2, R_3\})$
3	2	$\{R_2, R_3\}$	$(\{R_2\}, \{R_3\})$
4	1	$\{R_1, R_2, R_3\}$	$(\{R_1, R_2\}, \{R_3\})$
5	2	$\{R_1, R_2\}$	$(\{R_1\}, \{R_2\})$
6	1	$\{R_1, R_2, R_3\}$	$(\{R_1, R_3\}, \{R_2\})$
7	2	$\{R_1, R_3\}$	$(\{R_1\}, \{R_3\})$
8	0	$\{R_0, R_1, R_2, R_3\}$	$(\{R_0, R_1\}, \{R_2, R_3\})$
9	1	$\{R_0, R_1\}$	$(\{R_0\}, \{R_1\})$
10	0	$\{R_0, R_1, R_2, R_3\}$	$(\{R_0, R_1, R_2\}, \{R_3\})$
11	1	$\{R_0, R_1, R_2\}$	$(\{R_0\}, \{R_1, R_2\})$
12	1	$\{R_0, R_1, R_2\}$	$(\{R_0, R_1\}, \{R_2\})$
13	1	$\{R_0, R_1, R_2\}$	$(\{R_0, R_1, R_3\}, \{R_2\})$
14	2	$\{R_0, R_1, R_3\}$	$(\{R_0\}, \{R_1, R_3\})$
15	2	$\{R_0, R_1, R_3\}$	$(\{R_0, R_1\}, \{R_3\})$

Table 2.1.: Exemplified execution of TDBASIC for the input graph of Figure 2.6

BT	current ccp	ref Entry	cT	$cost(cT)$	ref BT
1	$(\{R_2\}, \{R_3\})$	3	$R_2 \bowtie R_3$	10	1
2	$(\{R_1\}, \{R_2, R_3\})$	2	$R_1 \bowtie (R_2 \bowtie R_3)$	20	2
3	$(\{R_1\}, \{R_2\})$	5	$R_1 \bowtie R_2$	100000	3
4	$(\{R_1, R_2\}, \{R_3\})$	4	$(R_1 \bowtie R_2) \bowtie R_3$	100010	2
5	$(\{R_1\}, \{R_3\})$	7	$R_1 \bowtie R_3$	100	5
6	$(\{R_1, R_3\}, \{R_2\})$	6	$(R_1 \bowtie R_3) \bowtie R_2$	110	2
7	$(\{R_0\}, \{R_1, R_2, R_3\})$	1	$R_0 \bowtie (R_1 \bowtie (R_2 \bowtie R_3))$	21	7
8	$(\{R_0\}, \{R_1\})$	9	$R_0 \bowtie R_1$	1000	8
9	$(\{R_0, R_1\}, \{R_2, R_3\})$	8	$(R_0 \bowtie R_1) \bowtie (R_2 \bowtie R_3)$	1011	7
10	$(\{R_0\}, \{R_1, R_2\})$	11	$R_0 \bowtie (R_1 \bowtie R_2)$	110000	10
11	$(\{R_0, R_1\}, \{R_2\})$	12	$(R_0 \bowtie R_1) \bowtie R_2$	11000	11
12	$(\{R_0, R_1, R_2\}, \{R_3\})$	10	$((R_0 \bowtie R_1) \bowtie R_2) \bowtie R_3$	11001	7
13	$(\{R_0\}, \{R_1, R_3\})$	14	$R_0 \bowtie (R_1 \bowtie R_3)$	110	13
14	$(\{R_0, R_1\}, \{R_3\})$	15	$(R_0 \bowtie R_1) \bowtie R_3$	1010	13
15	$(\{R_0, R_1, R_3\}, \{R_2\})$	13	$(R_0 \bowtie (R_1 \bowtie R_3)) \bowtie R_2$	111	7

Table 2.2.: Multiple calls to BUILDTREE during the enumeration process for the input graph of Figure 2.6

The numbers again depend on the shape of the query graph but are independent of the partitioning algorithm.

For chains, stars and cliques, we refer to Ono and Lohman [26] and for cycles to Moerkotte and Neumann [22]. We give the formula of [22] for cycles divided by two, since we are only interested in one ccp out of each symmetric pair of ccps.

For chains, we have

$$\#bP^{\text{chain}}(|V|) = \frac{|V|^3 - |V|}{6}.$$

S	$P_{ccp}^{sym}(S)$
$\{R_0,R_1,R_2,R_3\}$	$\{(\{R_0\},\{R_1,R_2,R_3\}),(\{R_0,R_1\},\{R_2,R_3\}),(\{R_0,R_1,R_3\},\{R_2\})\}$
$\{R_1,R_2,R_3\}$	$\{(\{R_1\},\{R_2,R_3\}),(\{R_1,R_2\},\{R_3\}),(\{R_1,R_3\},\{R_2\})\}$
$\{R_2,R_3\}$	$\{(\{R_2\},\{R_3\})\}$
$\{R_1,R_2\}$	$\{(\{R_1\},\{R_2\})\}$
$\{R_1,R_3\}$	$\{(\{R_1\},\{R_3\})\}$
$\{R_0,R_1\}$	$\{(\{R_0\},\{R_1\})\}$
$\{R_0,R_1,R_2\}$	$\{(\{R_0\},\{R_1,R_2\}),(\{R_0,R_1\},\{R_2\})\}$
$\{R_0,R_1,R_3\}$	$\{(\{R_0\},\{R_1,R_3\}),(\{R_0,R_1\},\{R_3\})\}$

Table 2.3.: All connected (sub) sets S and the corresponding $P_{ccp}^{sym}(S)$ during the execution of TDBASIC for the input graph of Figure 2.6

	Chain		Star		Cycle		Clique	
$|V|$	#I	#bP	#I	#bP	#I	#bP	#I	#bP
3	10	4	10	4	12	6	12	6
4	32	10	38	12	46	18	50	25
5	84	20	130	32	140	40	180	90
6	198	35	422	80	374	75	602	301
7	438	56	1330	192	924	126	1932	966
8	932	84	4118	448	2174	196	6050	3025
9	1936	120	12610	1024	4956	288	18660	9330
10	3962	165	38342	2304	11062	405	57002	28501
11	8034	220	116050	5120	24332	550	173052	86524
12	16200	286	350198	11264	52958	726	523250	261625
13	32556	364	1054690	24576	114348	936	1577940	788970
14	65294	455	3172262	53248	245366	1183	4750202	2375101
15	130798	560	9533170	114688	523836	1470	14283372	7141686
16	261836	680	28632278	245760	1113598	1800	42915650	21457825
17	523944	816	85962370	524288	2358716	2176	128878020	64439010
18	1048194	938	258018182	1114112	4980086	2601	386896202	193448101
19	2096730	1140	774316690	2359296	10485036	3078	1161212892	580606446
20	4193840	1330	2323474358	4980736	22019294	3610	3484687250	1742343625

Table 2.4.: Sample values for inner counter and number of calls to BUILDPLAN

For stars, we have

$$\#bP^{\text{star}}(|V|) = (|V|-1) * 2^{|V|-2}.$$

For cycles, we have

$$\#bP^{\text{cycle}}(|V|) = \frac{|V|^3 - 2*|V|^2 + |V|}{2}.$$

For cliques, we have

$$\#bP^{\text{clique}}(|V|) = \frac{3^{|V|} - 2^{|V|+1} + 1}{2}.$$

Table 2.4 compares the number series for the inner counter and the number of calls to BUILDPLAN.

The number of calls to BUILDPLAN $\#bP$ is the lower bound for any join enumeration algorithm, no matter if it works top-down or bottom-up. As half of the enumerated partitions in PARTITION$_{naive}$ are discarded in Line 1, I and $\#bP$ differ at least by a factor of two. Considering the counters for clique queries in Table 2.4, we see that the factor is exactly two because every second partition is discarded through $min_{index}(C) < min_{index}(S \setminus C)$ in Line 2 of TDBASICSUB, but every partition which qualifies passes the two tests for connectivity since in a clique, every vertex is connected to every other vertex.

We can conclude that PARTITION$_{naive}$ has to enumerate all possible subsets C (Line 1), which is more than the number of existing ccps by several orders of magnitude. The only exception to this observation are clique queries and query graphs with many cycles. Thus, TDBASIC is too inefficient to be useful, since the worst case complexity of PARTITION$_{naive}$ is in $O(2^{|V|})$ per emitted ccp. Having that in mind, the question arises whether it is possible to construct a partitioning algorithm that enumerates only the ccps for S and avoids to enumerate symmetric pairs twice. With TDMINCUTLAZY or TDMCL for short, DeHaan and Tompa [5] describe a partitioning algorithm that has a worst case complexity of only $O(|V|^2)$ [8, 9] per emitted ccp. A short description and a subsequent analysis of MINCUTLAZY can be found in Appendix A.

The next three sections describe three new partitioning algorithms. In Section 2.3, we explain how we can improve efficiency of naive partitioning by utilizing a query-graph-aware approach implemented in MINCUTAGAT [9]. Section 2.4 describes how MINCUTCONSERVATIVE [12] further improves upon that basic idea. Section 2.5 introduces MINCUTBRANCH [8] and shows that MINCUTBRANCH has only a complexity of $O(1)$ per emitted ccp for arbitrary acyclic query graphs, cycle und clique queries.

2.3. Advanced Generate and Test

In this section, we describe a novel partitioning algorithm named MINCUTAGAT. MINCUTAGAT was designed by adopting the basic concept of optimistic partitioning [6] that was shown to be incomplete [9].

2.3.1. TDMINCUTAGAT

The pseudo-code for the new partitioning algorithm is given in Figure 2.8. We denote the instantiated generic top-down join enumeration variant by TDMINCUTAGAT or TDMCA for short. Like naive partitioning, MINCUTAGAT relies on a generate-and-test based approach. At the same time, it is also more sophisticated by utilizing adjacency information of the query graph $G = (V, E)$.

The partitioning algorithm is invoked by PARTITION$_{MinCutAGaT}$, which in turn immediately calls the recursive component MINCUTAGAT. The main idea is to successively enlarge a connected set C with one of its neighbors at every recursive iteration. Since only adjacent vertices are added to C, we ensure that C remains connected at any time. Hence, MINCUTAGAT needs to rely on only one connection test, which is to ensure the connectedness of C's complement $S \setminus C$.

The initial set for C consisting of an arbitrary vertex t is handed over in Line 2 of PARTITION$_{MinCutAGaT}$. Since S and $C \subset S$ are connected, for every possible complement $S \setminus C$ there must exist a join edge (v_1, v_2), where $v_1 \in C$ and $v_2 \in (S \setminus C)$ holds. If $S \setminus C$ is connected, then the partition $(C, S \setminus C)$ is a ccp and can be emitted (Line 1 of MINCUTAGAT). As a requirement implied by the definition of $P_{ccp}^{sym}(S)$, (1) duplicate ccps are prohibited and (2) symmetric ccps have to be emitted only once. The latter constraint is ensured automatically because the start vertex t is always element of C so that $t \notin (S \setminus C)$ holds. For the first constraint, we introduce an exclusive filter set X that keeps track of vertices v added to C in different branches of recursion. So once a vertex v is added to X (Line 10) in an ancestor invocation of MINCUTAGAT, it cannot be chosen as a neighbor again and is filtered out (Line 8). If there is only one vertex left in S that is not already a member of C, we can stop our recursive descent because otherwise, C's complement would be empty in the next child invocation. We check for this condition in Line 5 and exit if it is true.

Once an articulation vertex $a \in (S \setminus C)$ which belongs to more than two biconnected components G_i^{BCC}, G_j^{BCC} is added to C, no partition is emitted in the next series of recursive calls of MINCUTAGAT. If k is the number of biconnections G^{BCC} that contain a, then no partition is emitted until C is enlarged with $k-1$ vertex sets V_i, $1 \leq i \leq k$, of $G_i^{BCC} = (V_i, E_i)$ with $a \in V_i$ including the vertex sets of those biconnected components that are directly and indirectly connected with $G_i^{BCC} = (V_i, E_i)$ through paths not containing a. In other words, this means the first partition that is emitted after an articulation vertex a was added to C is produced by a minimal graph cut E_{cut}. Thereby E_{cut} contains only edges (a, x_i) such that $a \in C \wedge x_i \in S \setminus C$ holds.

For MINCUTAGAT, we introduce an improved connection test which we call IS-CONNECTEDIMP (invoked in Line 1). Instead of ensuring that all vertices in a complement $S \setminus (C \cup \{v\})$ are connected to each other, our novel test ensures only that the neighbors $\mathcal{N}(C \cup \{v\})$ are connected to each other within the complement. In other words, we check for a weaker condition that tests if from an arbitrary vertex w with $w \in \mathcal{N}(C \cup \{v\})$ all other vertices u of $\mathcal{N}(C \cup \{v\}) \setminus \{w\}$ are reachable within the complement $S \setminus (C \cup \{v\})$, i.e. if there exists a path for every u connecting w with u, but not containing any vertices of $C \cup \{v\}$. We can even further weaken this condition once we know that the complement $S \setminus C$ is already proven to be connected. In such cases, it is sufficient to check if all elements of $\mathcal{N}(\{v\}) \setminus C$ are connected within $S \setminus (C \cup \{v\})$. On average, ISCONNECTEDIMP is cheaper to execute than a common connection test that was given with ISCONNECTED in Section 2.2.2. In the best case, it is in $O(1)$. The worst case is identical to the complexity of the common connection test, which is in $O(|S \setminus (C \cup \{v\})|)$. We explain ISCONNECTEDIMP in detail in Section 2.3.2.

To decide if it is sufficient to check only the neighbors of v, we introduce the set T. If the current partition $(C, S \setminus C)$ is a ccp (Line 1), then the connection test for the next child invocations needs to check only for the neighbors of the v that is added to C. In that case, the next T is set to $T \leftarrow \emptyset \cup \{v\}$ (Line 3 and Line 9). Otherwise, all neighbors of $C \cup \{v\}$ need to be checked so that the next T is set to $T \leftarrow C \cup \{v\}$ (Lines 4 and 9).

PARTITION$_{MinCutAGaT}(G_{|S})$
> **Input:** a connected (sub)graph $G_{|S}$
> **Output:** $P^{sym}_{ccp}(S)$
1   $t \leftarrow$ arbitrary vertex of S
2   MINCUTAGAT$(G_{|S}, \{t\}, \emptyset, \{t\})$

MINCUTAGAT$(G_{|S}, C, X, T)$
> **Input:** a connected (sub)graph $G_{|S}$, $C \cap X = \emptyset$
> **Output:** *ccp*s for S
1   **if** ISCONNECTEDIMP(S, C, T)
2   emit $(C, S \setminus C)$
3       $T' \leftarrow \emptyset$
4   **else** $T' \leftarrow C$
5   **if** $|C| + 1 \geq |S|$
6   **return**
7   $X' \leftarrow X$
8   **for** $v \in (\mathcal{N}(C) \setminus X)$
9   MINCUTAGAT$(G_{|S}, C \cup \{v\}, X', T' \cup \{v\})$
10      $X' \leftarrow X' \cup \{v\}$

Figure 2.8.: Pseudocode for MINCUTAGAT

ISCONNECTEDIMP$(G_{|S}, C, T)$
> **Input:** (sub)graph $G_{|S}$, $C \subset S$, $T \subseteq C$
> **Output:** if $(S \setminus C)$ is connected TRUE, else FALSE
1   $N \leftarrow (\mathcal{N}(T) \cap S) \setminus C$
2   **if** $|N| \leq 1$
3   **return** TRUE
4   $L \leftarrow \emptyset$
5   $L' \leftarrow \{n\} : n \in N$
6   **while** $L \neq L' \wedge N \nsubseteq L'$
7       $D \leftarrow L' \setminus L$
8       $L \leftarrow L'$
9       $L' \leftarrow L' \cup ((\mathcal{N}(D) \cap S) \setminus C)$
10 **if** $N \subseteq L'$
11   **return** TRUE
12 **else return** FALSE

Figure 2.9.: Pseudocode for ISCONNECTEDIMP

2.3.2. An Improved Connection Test

This section explains the novel connection test ISCONNECTEDIMP used by MIN-CUTAGAT. The pseudo code is given in Figure 2.9.

The purpose of ISCONNECTEDIMP is to check if the neighbors of T that are not in C are connected to each other within $S \backslash C$. In Line 1 of ISCONNECTEDIMP, we compute those neighbors of T as the set N. If N contains only one element, then $S \setminus C$ must be connected and the test returns with a positive result. As a starting point for the test, we choose an arbitrary vertex $n \in N$ (Line 5) and assign it to L'. The loop of Line 6 to 9 computes the indirect neighborhood (Definition 2.1.11) of $\{n\}$. This corresponds to enlarging L' with the neighborhood of L (Line 9) or current L (Line 8). Hereby $\mathcal{N}_i(\{n\}) = \mathcal{N}(L)$ within $G_{|S \backslash C}$ holds. Furthermore, L holds the previous L' (Line 8) and D holds all the new elements of L', which directly corresponds to a generation of neighbors. Note that except for the first iteration of the loop, $\mathcal{N}(L) \cap (S \setminus C) = D$ holds.

Because of $|D| < |L'|$, we compute the next generation of neighbors from D instead of L' (Line 9), which is clearly more efficient.

Once L' contains all vertices of N, the loop is interrupted (Line 6), and it is obvious that all $n \in N$ are reachable within $S \setminus C$ so that TRUE is returned (Line 11). If, on the other hand, L' cannot be enlarged further so that $L = L'$ holds, we have computed all indirect neighbors of $\{n\}$ (within $S \setminus C$) and meet the loop's other stop condition. In that case, we could not reach every element of N, so that $N \setminus L' \neq \emptyset$ must hold and we have to return FALSE (Line 12). Note that those vertices left in $N \setminus L'$ must belong to at least one different connected set that is only adjacent to C and not connected to L'.

2.3.3. Correctness of Advanced Generate and Test

In this subsection, we prove the correctness of MINCUTAGAT. But as a prerequisite, we need to prove the correctness of ISCONNECTEDIMP first.

Correctness of ISCONNECTEDIMP

Lemma 2.3.1. *Algorithm* ISCONNECTEDIMP *terminates if* $G = (V, E)$ *is a connected and finite query graph and* $G_{|S}$ *with* $S \subseteq V$ *a connected (sub)graph.*

Proof. There are two different exit points: (1) an early exit in Line 3 and (2) the exit point at the end of ISCONNECTEDIMP (Lines 11 and 12). If $|(\mathcal{N}(T) \cap S) \setminus C| \leq 1$ holds, the first exit is chosen, and the algorithm terminates. Otherwise, the loop of Lines 6 to 9 is entered. The loop terminates if L' has not been enlarged in the loop's previous iteration or if all neighbors of T — that are in S but not in C — have been added to L' so that $N \subseteq L'$ holds. Let us assume the worst case: D is reassigned with only one one vertex set at a time so that $|D| = 1$ holds. Let us further assume that every time $|((\mathcal{N}(T) \cap S) \setminus C) \setminus L'| = 1$ holds as well. Then there can be only $|S \setminus C| - 1$ number of iterations of the loop. We have to subtract the 1, since $|L'| = 1$ holds when the loop is entered. Therefore, the loop terminates at least after $|S \setminus C| - 1$ iterations and the second exit point is reached. Furthermore, since S is a finite set, every set operation used here, especially the computation of the neighborhood of any subset $D \subset S$, must terminate. Hence, ISCONNECTEDIMP terminates. □

Lemma 2.3.2. *Let* $G = (V, E)$ *be a connected query graph and* $G_{|S}$ *with* $S \subseteq V$ *a connected (sub)graph. Further, let* C *be a non-empty subset of* S *with* $C \subset S$, *then* the complement $S \setminus C$ is connected if all neighbors of C are connected to each other through paths containing only vertices of $S \setminus C$.

Proof. By contradiction. We assume that the set $S \setminus C$ is not connected, although all neighbors of C are connected to each other within $S \setminus C$. Since the neighbors of C are connected through paths containing only vertices in $S \setminus C$, there has to exist a maximally enlarged connected set $A = \bigcup_{0 \leq i \leq |S \setminus C|} (\mathcal{N}_i(C) \setminus C)$ as the union of all i-th gernerations of neighbors of C that are in $\bar{S} \setminus C$. From this follows that $A \subseteq (S \setminus C)$ and $\mathcal{N}(C) \subseteq A$ and $A \cap C = \emptyset$ and $\mathcal{N}(A) \setminus C = \emptyset$ hold. Because A is connected but by assumption $S \setminus C$ is not connected, $A \subset (S \setminus C)$ must hold. Hence, there exists a set of vertices $L = (S \setminus C) \setminus A$ with $L \neq \emptyset$. Because all neighbors of C are contained in A, no vertex in L can be connected to any vertex in C. Furthermore, by the definition of A and L, $(\mathcal{N}(A) \setminus C) \cap L = \emptyset$ holds. But this contradicts the prerequisite that $G_{|S}$ is connected. □

Lemma 2.3.3. *Let $G = (V, E)$ be a connected query graph and $G_{|S}$ with $S \subseteq V$ a connected (sub)graph. Further, let C be a non-empty subset of S with $C \subset S$, then the complement $S \setminus C$ is connected if and only if all neighbors of C are connected to each other through paths containing only vertices of $S \setminus C$.*

Proof. Lemma 2.3.2 shows that if all neighbors of C are connected to each other through paths containing only vertices of $S \setminus C$, then this is a sufficient condition for $G_{|S \setminus C}$ being connected. What is left is to show that it is also a necessary condition. This is proved by contradiction. Let us assume $G_{|S \setminus C}$ is connected but the neighbors of C are not connected to each other. By Definition 2.1.10, the neighborhood of C has to be a subset of $S \setminus C$. But if there are at least two neighbors of C for which no connecting path in $S \setminus C$ exists, then this is by Definition 2.1.7 a contradiction to the connectedness of $G_{|S \setminus C}$. □

Lemma 2.3.4. *Let $G = (V, E)$ be a connected query graph and $G_{|S}$ with $S \subseteq V$ a connected (sub)graph. Further, let C be a non-empty subset of S with $C \subset S \wedge |C| + 2 \leq |S|$ and let $G_{|C}$ and $G_{|S \setminus C}$ be connected subgraphs. Moreover, let v be a vertex so that $v \in S \setminus C \wedge v \in \mathcal{N}(C)$ holds. Then the set $(S \setminus C) \setminus \{v\}$ is connected if and only if all neighbors $\mathcal{N}(\{v\})$ of v are connected to each other within $(S \setminus C) \setminus \{v\}$.*

Proof. Let $G' = (V', E')$ be a connected and finite graph that is identical to the connected subgraph $G_{|S \setminus C}$ of $G = (V, E)$. Then G's vertex set V' is defined by $V' = S \setminus C$, and G's edge set E' is defined by $E' = \{(v_1, v_2) \mid v_1, v_2 \in V' \wedge (v_1, v_2) \in E\}$. Let a set S' be assigned to $S' = V'$ and a set C' be assigned to $C' = \{v\}$ with $v \in V'$. Following from Lemma 2.3.3, $S' \setminus C' = (S \setminus C) \setminus \{v\}$ is connected if and only if the neighbors of $C' = \{v\}$ are connected within $S' \setminus C'$. □

Theorem 2.3.1. *Algorithm* ISCONNECTEDIMP *is correct.*

Proof. The algorithm is either called with the parameter T assigned to a connected vertex set C or to a one vertex set $\{v\}$, while v is the vertex recently added to C. From Lemmas 2.3.3 and 2.3.4, we know that it is sufficient to examine just the connectivity between the vertices that are in $\mathcal{N}(T)$ within $S \setminus C$, which is done in Lines 5 to 9. Lemmas 2.3.3 and 2.3.4 cover also the special case of an early exit in Line 3. Finally, we know that the algorithm must terminate if the query graph is finite through Lemma 2.3.1. □

Correctness of MINCUTAGAT

Lemma 2.3.5. *Algorithm* MINCUTAGAT *terminates if* $G = (V, E)$ *is a connected and finite query graph and* $G_{|S}$ *with* $S \subseteq V$ *a connected (sub)graph.*

Proof. The number of possibilities how the set C can be enlarged in every new invocation is limited by the number of neighbors that are not element of X. The maximal number of neighbors is $|S \setminus C|$. Since $|V|$ is limited, $|S|$ is limited and hence, the number of choices is limited as well. With each recursive invocation, $|C|$ grows by 1, and the complement $|S \setminus C|$ decreases by 1. Therefore, the recursion depth of MIN-CUTAGAT is limited by $|S|$, and the maximal number of choices is asymptotic with an increasing size of C. Because the number of choices is finite, every recursive call must return. This means that the root invocation also has to return and MINCUTAGAT terminates. □

Lemma 2.3.6. *Let* $G = (V, E)$ *be a connected query graph and* $G_{|S}$ *with* $S \subseteq V$ *a connected (sub)graph, then* MINCUTAGAT *enumerates only connected sets and assigns them to* C *where* $C \subset S$ *holds.*

Proof. By induction over the recursion depth n.

Base case: $n = 0$
MINCUTAGAT starts the enumeration with an arbitrary vertex t, which induces a connected subgraph $G_{|\{t\}}$.

Induction hypothesis: recursion depth n enumerates only connected sets of $C \cup \{v\}$ and passes them as parameters to recursion depth $n + 1$.

Induction step: $n \to n + 1$
MINCUTAGAT at recursion level $n + 1$ is called with a connected set C (IH) and considers only vertices that are connected to vertices in C (Definition 2.1.10, Line 8). As any vertex in $\mathcal{N}(C)$ is directly connected to at least one vertex in C, any vertex v can be added to C to form a connected set $C \cup \{v\}$ (Line 9). □

Lemma 2.3.7. *Let* $G = (V, E)$ *be a connected query graph and* $G_{|S}$ *with* $S \subseteq V$ *a connected (sub)graph, then* MINCUTAGAT *enumerates only ccps for* S.

Proof. Because of Lemma 2.3.6, every enumerated set C has to be connected. Since $S \setminus C$ is the complement of C in S, it is disjoint to C, and $C \cup (S \setminus C) = S$ holds. Because of Theorem 2.3.1, every set $V \setminus S$ that passes the test for connectivity must be connected. Since only connected query graphs $G = (V, E)$ or subgraphs $G_{|S}$ are allowed as input, there must exist at least one edge (v_1, v_2) with $v_1 \in C \wedge v_2 \in (S \setminus C)$. Hence, according to Definition 2.1.24, every emitted pair $(C, S \setminus C)$ must be a *ccp* for S. □

Lemma 2.3.8. *Let* $G = (V, E)$ *be a connected query graph and* $G_{|S}$ *with* $S \subseteq V$ *a connected (sub)graph. Further, let* $v \in S$ *be a vertex,* n *a natural number with* $n \geq 0$ *with* $C_n = \cup_{0 \leq i \leq n} \mathcal{N}_i(\{v\})$. *Then* $G_{|C_n}$ *must be a connected subgraph of* $G_{|S}$.

Proof. By induction over n.

Base case: $n = 0$
$C_0 = \mathcal{N}_0(\{v\}) = \{v\}$ (Definition 2.1.11). Thus, G_{C_0} is a connected subgraph of $G_{|S}$.

Induction hypothesis: G_{C_n} is a connected subgraph of $G_{|S}$ for a given, fixed n.

Induction step: $n \to n+1$
For C_{n+1} holds: $C_{n+1} = C_n \cup \mathcal{N}_{n+1}(\{v\})$. We know G_{C_n} is a connected subgraph of $G_{|S}$ (IH), and because $\mathcal{N}_n(\{v\}) \subseteq C_n$, all vertices in $\mathcal{N}_{n+1}(\{v\})$ have to be connected to at least one vertex in C_n. It follows that $G_{|C_{n+1}}$ is a connected subgraph of $G_{|S}$. □

Lemma 2.3.9. *Let $G = (V, E)$ be a connected query graph and $G_{|S}$ with $S \subseteq V$ a connected (sub)graph and v be an arbitrary vertex with $v \in S$. Then the following holds: $\exists n \geq 0$ such that $\forall_{0 \leq i \leq n} \mathcal{N}_i(\{v\}) \neq \emptyset$ and $\forall_{i > n} \mathcal{N}_i(\{v\}) = \emptyset$.*

Proof. According to Definition 2.1.11 for a given $\mathcal{N}_i(\{v\}) = \emptyset$, $\mathcal{N}_{i+1}(\{v\}) = \emptyset$ follows. Besides, since $\mathcal{N}_0(\{v\}) \neq \emptyset$, $\forall_i \mathcal{N}_i(\{v\}) \subseteq V$, and $\forall_{j < i} \mathcal{N}_i(\{v\}) \cap \mathcal{N}_j(\{v\}) = \emptyset$ holds, $\mathcal{N}_{|V|}(\{v\}) = \emptyset$ for a $n \in [0, |V|[$ must hold as well. □

Lemma 2.3.10. *Let $G = (V, E)$ be a connected query graph and $G_{|S}$ with $S \subseteq V$ a connected (sub)graph. If $G_{|C}$ with $|C| > 1 \wedge C \subseteq S$ is a connected subgraph of $G_{|S}$, then $\exists v \in C$ such that $G_{|C \setminus \{v\}}$ is a connected subgraph of $G_{|C}$.*

Proof. In the following, we consider G_C as connected and as the basis for computing $\mathcal{N}(\{v\})$ and $\mathcal{N}_i(\{v\})$, i.e., we consider only the reduced edge set E_C with $E_C = \{(v_0, v_1) \mid (v_0, v_1) \in E \wedge v_0, v_1 \in C\}$. Let us determine for an arbitrary $v_i \in C$ a natural number n such that $\mathcal{N}_n(v_i) \neq \emptyset \wedge \mathcal{N}_{n+1}(v_i) = \emptyset$ holds. According to Lemma 2.3.9, we always can find such a number with $n > 0$ and $\cup_{0 \leq i \leq n} \mathcal{N}_i(v_i) = C$ holds. Following from Lemma 2.3.8, $\cup_{0 \leq i < n} \mathcal{N}_i(\{v_i\})$ induces a connected subgraph of $G_{|C}$. Furthermore, all vertices in $\mathcal{N}_n(\{v_i\})$ are connected to at least one vertex in $\mathcal{N}_{n-1}(\{v_i\})$. This implies that any $v_j \in \mathcal{N}_n(\{v_i\})$ can be removed. Since $n > 0$ and $\mathcal{N}_n(\{v_i\}) \neq \emptyset$ holds, it follows that for any $v_j \in \mathcal{N}_n(\{v_i\})$ the corresponding subgraph $G_{|S \setminus \{v_j\}}$ has to be a connected subgraph of $G_{|C}$. □

Lemma 2.3.11. *Algorithm MINCUTAGAT enumerates only one set C that consists of a single vertex. This instance of C must be connected.*

Proof. The root invocation of MINCUTAGAT is called with $C = \{t\}$, where $t \in S$ holds. This is the only time that C contains just one element. Any recursive self invocation adds another $v \in S$ to the C previously handed over. Since any one-element vertex set is connected, the only instance of C that contains only one vertex must be connected as well. □

Lemma 2.3.12. *In every invocation of MINCUTAGAT, $C \cap X = \emptyset$ holds.*

Proof. By induction over the recursion depth n.

Base Case: $n = 0$
In the root invocation, $C = \{t\}$ with $t \in S$ and $X = \emptyset$ holds. Thus, $C \cap T = \emptyset$ holds.

Induction hypothesis: C and X are disjoint for a given, fixed recursion depth n.

Induction step: $n \to n+1$
We only have to show that in every iteration of Line 9 the sets $C \cup \{v\}$ and X' are disjoint. For every value of v (Line 8) $v \notin C$ and $v \notin X$ holds. Since $C \cap X = \emptyset$ (IH) and $X' \subseteq (X \cup \mathcal{N}(C))$ holds, we can conclude that for all possible values of X' during the loop in Lines 8 to 10, $X' \cap C = \emptyset$ must hold. This is because the new v is added to X' in Line 10, i.e. $C \cup \{v\}$ and X' must still be disjoint in Line 9. □

Lemma 2.3.13. *Algorithm* MINCUTAGAT *enumerates all sets C contained in the powerset of S that are connected and that contain the start vertex t.*

Proof. By contradiction. We assume that not all connected sets containing t are enumerated and assigned to C. Thus, $\exists C \subseteq S \wedge S \neq \emptyset$ such that $G_{|C}$ is a connected subgraph, and C is not enumerated. If several such C exist, we choose C such that $|C|$ is minimal. Lemma 2.3.11 implies that $|C| > 1$. Lemma 2.3.10 implies that $\exists v \in C : G_{C \setminus \{v\}}$ is a connected subgraph. As C is chosen to be minimal, the set $C'' = C \setminus \{v\}$ is enumerated.
  Case 1: v appears in $\mathcal{N}(C'') \setminus X$ during the enumeration of $C \setminus \{v'\}$. This is a contradiction to the assumption that C was not enumerated (Line 9).
  Case 2: v does not appear in $\mathcal{N}(C'') \setminus X$ during the enumeration of C'''. Since v is connected to C'', it must have been excluded, i.e. $v \in X$. We know that in one of the parent or ancestor invocations of MINCUTAGAT with a $C' \subset C''$ and $X' \subset X$ with $v \in \mathcal{N}(C')$, v has been added to X'. But right before v has been added to X', MINCUTAGAT must have been invoked with $C' \cup \{v\}$. That means that in one of those child invocations C has already been enumerated because according to Lemma 2.3.12 $C'' \cap (X' \setminus \{v\}) = \emptyset$ must hold. □

Lemma 2.3.14. *Let $G = (V, E)$ be a connected query graph and $G_{|S}$ with $S \subseteq V$ a connected (sub)graph. Algorithm* MINCUTAGAT *enumerates all ccps $(C, S \setminus C)$ for S where in all sets C the start vertex t is contained.*

Proof. According to Lemma 2.3.7, MINCUTAGAT enumerates only ccps for C. Because of Lemma 2.3.13, all possible connected sets C that contain the start vertex t are enumerated. Thus, Algorithm MINCUTAGAT must enumerate all possible ccps $(C, S \setminus C)$ for S where the condition $t \in C$ holds. □

Lemma 2.3.15. *Let $G = (V, E)$ be a connected query graph and $G_{|S}$ with $S \subseteq V$ a connected (sub)graph. Algorithm* MINCUTAGAT *enumerates all connected sets C that belong to the power set of S containing the start vertex $t \in S$ only once.*

Proof. By contradiction. We assume that $\exists C \subseteq S$, which is enumerated at least twice. If multiple such C exist, we choose C such that $|C|$ is minimal.
Case 1: $|C| = 1$. As discussed in Lemma 2.3.11, MINCUTAGAT enumerates only one set consisting of a single vertex in the root invocation. Thus, $|C| = 1$ is not produced twice, as it is not enumerated in any recursive self invocation.

Case 2: $|C| > 1$. C cannot be enumerated by two different invocations of MINCUTA-GAT with the same parameters, as $|C|$ is minimal (otherwise, a smaller $|C|$ must exist that also has to be enumerated twice). Thus, there must be two different enumeration paths producing C. As both paths start with the same vertex t, they are identical at the beginning (Lemma 2.3.11) in enlarging a set C' where $C' \subset C$ holds. At some point, the common path must fork and two vertices $v_1, v_2 \in \mathcal{N}(C')$ with $v_1 \neq v_2$ and $v_1, v_2 \in C$ must exist. Thus, there are two child invocations, the first one with $C' \cup \{v_1\}$ for the parameter C, and the second one with $C' \cup \{v_2\}$ for the parameter C. They cannot both have identical sets for the parameter X, because for the later child invocation, $\{v_1\}$ is added. But since $v_1 \notin C'$, the vertex must be added later during the recursive descent, but this is impossible, since v_1 is already included in the set X. □

Lemma 2.3.16. *Let* $G = (V, E)$ *be a connected query graph and* $G_{|S}$ *with* $S \subseteq V$ *a connected (sub)graph. Algorithm* MINCUTAGAT *enumerates all ccps* $(C, S \setminus C)$ *for S where all sets C contain the start vertex t only once.*

Proof. As Lemma 2.3.15 clarifies, all connected sets C containing the start vertex t are enumerated only once. Since the set $S \setminus C$ is the complement of C in S and there exists just one complement per set C in S, MINCUTAGAT enumerates all *ccps* $(C, S \setminus C)$ for S only once and $t \in C$ always holds. □

Lemma 2.3.17. *Let* $G = (V, E)$ *be a connected query graph and* $G_{|S}$ *with* $S \subseteq V$ *a connected (sub)graph. Let a partition* $(C, S \setminus C)$ *be a ccp with an arbitrary C such that $C \subset S$ holds. Then,* MINCUTAGAT *emits either* $(C, S \setminus C)$ *or its symmetric counter pair* $(S \setminus C, C)$, *but never both ccps.*

Proof. Algorithm MINCUTAGAT emits the *ccps* always in the form of $(C, S \setminus C)$ but never in the form of $(S \setminus C, C)$ (Line 2 of MINCUTAGAT). Since the start vertex t is always part of C and never element of the complement $S \setminus C$ from two possible symmetric pairs, only one *ccp* for S is emitted. Because Lemma 2.3.14 and Lemma 2.3.16 hold, MINCUTAGAT enumerates all symmetric *ccps* for S only once. □

Theorem 2.3.2. *Algorithm* MINCUTAGAT *is correct.*

Proof. The theorem follows immediately from Lemma 2.3.5, Lemma 2.3.7, Lemma 2.3.14, Lemma 2.3.15, and Lemma 2.3.17. □

2.4. Conservative Graph Partitioning

This section presents a partitioning algorithm named conservative partitioning, which we denote by MINCUTCONSERVATIVE [12]. It is an improvement of the advanced generate-and-test approach presented in Section 2.3. The algorithm emits all *ccps* for a connected vertex set S for which $S \subseteq V$ holds and where V is the vertex set of the query graph $G = (V, E)$. We denote the instantiated top-down memoization variant (Section 2.2.1) by TDMINCUTCONSERVATIVE or TDMCC for short. Its pseudo-code is given in Figure 2.10.

Conservative partitioning is invoked by PARTITION$_{MinCutConservative}$, which in turn immediately calls its recursive component MINCUTCONSERVATIVE. The basic idea of conservative partitioning is similar to the advanced-generate-and-test approach: to successively enhance a connected set C by members of its neighborhood $\mathcal{N}(C)$ at every recursive iteration. For query graphs with many biconnected components, MINCUTAGAT does not perform optimally. The reason is that enhancing C in a way that every graph cut is minimal cannot always be done by just removing one vertex v from $S \setminus C$. As mentioned in Section 2.3, this can happen when v is an articulation vertex a. In the majority of these cases, MINCUTAGAT is not able to emit a ccp in every iteration, which increases the amortized costs per minimal cut. MINCUTCONSERVATIVE is designed to overcome this disadvantage with a conservative approach. In fact, conservative partitioning emits a ccp at the start of every invocation except for the root invocation.

Like MINCUTAGAT, the process of enhancing C starts with a single vertex $t \in S$. For MINCUTCONSERVATIVE, this is done through a redefinition of $\mathcal{N}(\emptyset) = \{t\}$. MINCUTCONSERVATIVE ensures that while C is enlarged it remains connected at any time. Since S and $C \subset S$ are connected, for every possible complement $S \setminus C$ there must exist a join edge (v_1, v_2), where $v_1 \in C$ and $v_2 \in (S \setminus C)$ holds. If at some point of enlarging C its complement $S \setminus C$ in S is connected as well, the algorithm has found a ccp for S.

2.4.1. Correctness Constraints

Besides, the connectivity of C's complement conservative partitioning has to meet some more constraints before emitting a ccp: (1) Symmetric ccps are emitted once, (2) the emission of duplicates has to be avoided, and (3) all ccps for S have to be computed as long as they comply with constraint (1).

Constraint (1) is ensured because the start vertex t is always contained in C and, therefore, can never be part of its complement $S \setminus C$. For the second constraint, the algorithm uses a filter set X of neighbors to exclude from processing. And for constraint (3), it is sufficient to ensure that all possible connected subsets of S that have a connected complement $S \setminus C$ are considered when enlarging C.

2.4.2. The Algorithm in Detail

There are certain scenarios, e.g., when star queries are considered, where constructing every possible connected subset C of S produces an exponential overhead because most of the complements $S \setminus C$ are not connected and the partitions $(C, S \setminus C)$ computed this way are not valid ccps. Therefore, the algorithm follows a *conservative* approach by enhancing C in such a way that the complement must be connected as well. Before we explain this technique, we have to make some observations. From the recursive process of enlarging C, we know that the number of members in C must increase by at least one in every iteration. Furthermore, if a partition $(C, S \setminus C)$ is not a ccp for S, then $S \setminus C$ consists of $k \geq 2$ connected subsets $O_1, O_2, ..., O_k \subset (S \setminus C)$ that are disjoint and not connected to each other. Hence, those subsets $O_1, O_2, ...O_k$ can only be adjacent to C. Let $v_1, v_2, ..., v_l$ be all the members of C's neighborhood $\mathcal{N}(C)$. Then every O_i where $1 \leq i \leq k$ must contain at least one such v_j where $1 \leq j \leq l$ and $k \leq l$ holds. The first ccp after recursively enlarging C by members of $S \setminus C$ would be generated when all subsets O_i with $1 \leq i \leq k$ but one are joined to C.

PARTITION$_{MinCutConservative}(G_{|S})$
    ▷ **Input:** a connected (sub)graph $G_{|S}$, arbitrary vertex $t \in S$
    ▷ **Output:** $P_{ccp}^{sym}(S)$
1   MINCUTCONSERVATIVE$(S, \emptyset, \emptyset)$

MINCUTCONSERVATIVE$(G_{|S}, C, X)$
    ▷ **Input:** a connected (sub)graph $G_{|S}$, $C \cap X = \emptyset$
    ▷ **Output:** *ccps* for S
1   **if** $C = S \vee C \cap X \neq \emptyset$
2   **return**
3   **if** $C \neq \emptyset$
4   emit $(C, S \setminus C)$
5   $X' \leftarrow X$
6   **for** $v \in ((\mathcal{N}(C) \cap S) \setminus X)$
7      $O = $ GETCONNECTEDCOMPONENTS$(G_{|S}, C \cup \{v\}, \{v\})$
8   **for all** $O_i \in O$
9   MINCUTCONSERVATIVE$(G_{|S}, S \setminus O_i, X')$
10     $X' \leftarrow X' \cup \{v\}$
    ▷ $\mathcal{N}(\emptyset) = \{$arbitrary element of $t \in S\}$

Figure 2.10.: Pseudocode for MINCUTCONSERVATIVE

Hence, in order to ensure that at every recursive iteration of MINCUTCONSERVATIVE the complement $S \setminus C$ is connected as well, it does not always suffice to enlarge C by only one of its neighbors but by a larger subset $\cup_{i \neq h} O_i$ with $1 \leq h \leq k$ of its direct and indirect neighborhood. For the computation of all subsets O_i with $1 \leq i \leq k$, MINCUTCONSERVATIVE invokes GETCONNECTEDCOMPONENTS in Line 7, which calculates an output set O containing all subsets O_i. If the complement $S \setminus C$ is connected, the returned O contains only one O_i with $O_i = O_1 = S \setminus C$. Section 2.4.3 explains GETCONNECTEDCOMPONENTS in detail.

Once $O = \{O_1, O_2, ..., O_k\}$ is returned, MINCUTCONSERVATIVE invokes itself for k different times with a corresponding new $C' = S \setminus O_i$, while $1 \leq i \leq k$ holds. Note that if the old $S \setminus C$ is connected, there is only one branch of recursions with a new $C' = S \setminus O_1 = C \cup \{v\}$. The *ccp* corresponding to $S \setminus O_i$ is emitted in Line 4 during the corresponding child invocation. The recursive descent stops once the last neighbor $v \in \mathcal{N}(C)$ was added to C so that for the successive child invocation the condition of Line 1 holds.

As mentioned for meeting constraint (2), conservative partitioning makes use of the filter set X. Therefore, the current v is added to X' (Line 10) after MINCUTCONSERVATIVE has returned from the k recursive calls of Line 9. This ensures that in all other recursive descents invoked with the remaining $v \in \mathcal{N}(C)$ yet to be processed, the current v cannot be chosen as a neighbor again and is excluded from further consideration (Line 6).

2.4.3. Exploring Connected Components

This section explains how GETCONNECTEDCOMPONENTS works. For performance reasons, the computation of the connected components is implemented as a twofold strategy. The first part of GETCONNECTEDCOMPONENTS adopts the improved connection test ISCONNECTEDIMP (Section 2.3.2), and the second part is only executed if the connection test fails. The pseudo code is given in Figure 2.11.

When comparing the first part of GETCONNECTEDCOMPONENTS (Lines 1 to 12) to ISCONNECTEDIMP, the only difference can be found in Lines 3, 11 and 12. This is because ISCONNECTEDIMP returns a Boolean result and GETCONNECTEDCOMPONENTS a set O of sets O_i. In case that $S \setminus C$ is connected, we have to return $C's$ whole complement as the only O_i either in Line 3 or in Line 11. For a detailed explanation of Lines 1 to 12, we refer to Section 2.3.2.

In case $S \setminus C$ is not connected, we are not able to reach all neighbors of T that are elements of $S \setminus C$. Therefore, the condition in Line 10 will not evaluate to TRUE. Hence, L equals our first O_i (Line 12). For the computation of the remaining O_j, we have to execute the second part of GETCONNECTEDCOMPONENTS.

Therefore, we introduce a set U and assign it with all neighbours of T that are not in C and are not element of L (Line 13). We use U to indicate whether there is any other O_j left to compute. This way, U serves as an abort criteria for the loop of Lines 14 to 22. The inner loop of Lines 17 to 20 resembles the loop of our first part (Lines 6 to 9). But this time we cannot implement the second stop condition, as we have done in Line 6 by checking $N \not\subseteq L'$. The second condition was added as an optimization to discover as early as possible that all neighbors of $T = \{v\}$ are connected to each other. This cannot be done here, since the sole purpose of this inner loop is to compute the remaining O_j.

2.5. Branch Partitioning

With the advanced-generate-and-test approach, we improved the naive portioning algorithm by successively enlarging a connected set C. But for graphs with many biconnected components, this technique alone was not efficient enough, since in several invocations of MINCUTAGAT no *ccps* could be emitted. This is because C enlarged only by one vertex at a time does not always result in a connected complement. As a result, we proposed the conservative partitioning approach. Therefore, we transformed the connection test into a computation of the connected and maximally enlarged sets of C's complement. This section presents branch partitioning, a further improved partitioning strategy where the effort of discovering the connected sets O_i within C's complement are avoided.

2.5.1. Branch Partitioning - An Overview

We denote the branch partitioning algorithm by MINCUTBRANCH. The algorithm is invoked by TDPGSUB to compute for a given vertex set S of a connected (sub)graph $G_{|S}$ all possible partitions into two disjoint interconnected sets (S_1, S_2) that are *ccps* for S. The output of branch partitioning is the set $P_{ccp}^{sym}(S)$ so that symmetric *ccps* are emitted only once. In the Figures 2.12 and 2.13, we give the algorithm's pseudocode

GETCONNECTEDCOMPONENTS $(G_{|S}, C, T)$
    ▷ **Input:** (sub)graph $G_{|S}, C \subset S, T \subseteq C$
    ▷ **Output:** set O of connected disjoint sets O_i
    $\forall_{O_i, O_j \in O, i \neq j} \; O_i \subseteq (S \setminus C) \wedge O_i \cap O_j = \emptyset$
1 $N \leftarrow (\mathcal{N}(T) \cap S) \setminus C$
2 **if** $|N| \leq 1$
3   **return** $\{S \setminus C\}$
4 $L \leftarrow \emptyset$
5 $L' \leftarrow \{n\} : n \in N$
6 **while** $L \neq L' \wedge N \not\subseteq L'$
7      $D \leftarrow (L' \setminus L)$
8      $L \leftarrow L'$
9      $L' \leftarrow L' \cup \mathcal{N}(D) \setminus C$
10 **if** $N \subseteq L'$
11   **return** $\{S \setminus C\}$
12 **else** $O \cup \{L\}$
    ▷ now explore all other to C adjacent subsets
13 $U \leftarrow N \setminus L$
14 **while** $U \neq \emptyset$
15     $L \leftarrow \emptyset$
16     $L' \leftarrow \{n\} : n \in U$
17   **while** $L \neq L'$
18         $D \leftarrow (L' \setminus L)$
19         $L \leftarrow L'$
20         $L' \leftarrow L' \cup \mathcal{N}(D) \setminus C$
21     $U \leftarrow U \setminus L$
22     $O \cup \{L\}$
23 **return** O

Figure 2.11.: Pseudocode for GETCONNECTEDCOMPONENTS

with PARTITION$_{MinCutBranch}$ and MINCUTBRANCH. We call the instantiated generic memoization variant TDMINCUTBRANCH, with a TD as a prefix to indicate the top-down join enumeration algorithm that is based on branch partitioning.

The algorithm's approach adopts the idea of MINCUTAGAT: to recursively enlarge a set C by members of its neighborhood $\mathcal{N}(C)$, starting with a single vertex $t \in S$. This way, we ensure that at every instance of the algorithm's execution C is connected. If at some point of enlarging C its complement $S \setminus C$ in S is connected as well, the algorithm has found a *ccp* for S. Besides, the connectivity of C's complement branch partitioning has to meet some more constraints before emitting a *ccp*: (1) Symmetric *ccp*s are emitted once, (2) the emission of duplicates has to be avoided, and (3) all *ccp*s for S have to be computed as long as they comply with constraint (1).

Constraint (1) is ensured because the start vertex t - arbitrarily chosen during the initialization of the partitioning algorithm in Line 1 of PARTITION$_{MinCutBranch}$ - is always contained in C and, therefore, can never be part of its complement. For the second constraint, the algorithm uses a filter set X of neighbors to exclude from processing. After every recursive self-invocation of the algorithm, the neighbor $v \in \mathcal{N}(C)$ that was used to enlarge C is added to X. Later, we will see in detail how this works. For constraint (3), it is sufficient to ensure that all possible connected subsets of S are considered when enlarging C.

Checking for the connectivity of the complement set adds a linear overhead per test. Furthermore, there are certain scenarios, e.g., when star queries are considered, where constructing every possible connected subset C of S produces an exponential overhead because most of the complements $S \setminus C$ are not connected and the partitions $(C, S \setminus C)$ computed this way are not valid ccps. For branch partitioning, we propose a novel technique which ensures that no partitions are generated that are not a ccp at the same time. As a positive side effect, the additional check for connectivity or the discovery of connected components as needed by MINCUTAGAT and MINCUTCONSERVATIVE can be eliminated.

Before we explain our technique, we repeat important observations of Section 2.4.2. From the recursive process of enlarging C, we know that the number of members in C must increase by one in every iteration. Furthermore, if a partition $(C, S \setminus C)$ is not a ccp for S, then $S \setminus C$ consists of $k \geq 2$ connected subsets $O_1, O_2, ..., O_k \subset (S \setminus C)$ that are disjoint and not connected to each other. Hence, those subsets $O_1, O_2, ...O_k$ can only be adjacent to C. Let $v_1, v_2, ..., v_l$ be all the members of C's neighborhood $\mathcal{N}(C)$. Then every O_i with $1 \leq i \leq k$ must contain at least one such v_j with $1 \leq j \leq l$ and $k \leq l$ holds. The first ccp after enlarging C by members of $S \setminus C$ would be generated when all subsets O_i with $1 \leq i \leq k$ but one are joined to C.

Having made these observations, we are ready to explain our basic idea. The key principle is to exploit information about how $S \setminus C$ is connected from all of MIN-CUTLAZY's child invocations. Therefore, we introduce a new input parameter L and a result set R. The one-element set L contains the last vertex v that was added to C through the parent invocation. The result set R of a child invocation contains the maximally enlarged and connected set O_i such that $L \subseteq R$ holds. We compute R by combining the result sets R_{tmp} from the child invocations with L. But we have to be careful to include only those R_{tmp} that are adjacent to L. Hence, we need to distinguish between $\mathcal{N}(L)$ and $(\mathcal{N}(C) \setminus \mathcal{N}(L))$: only those R_{tmp} can be joined to R where $\mathcal{N}(L) \cap R_{tmp} \neq \emptyset$ holds.

To make use of the connected sets R_{tmp} that are adjacent to v, we postpone the emission of ccps towards the end. Instead of enlarging C with all but one R_{tmp} when the complement $S \setminus C$ is not connected, we introduce an optimization which simply emits $(S \setminus R_{tmp}, R_{tmp})$ right away. Note that if $S \setminus C$ is connected, there exists only one R_{tmp} with $R_{tmp} = S \setminus C$ and $(S \setminus R_{tmp}, R_{tmp}) = (C, S \setminus C)$ holds. In case $S \setminus C$ is not connected, $C \subset (S \setminus R_{tmp})$ must hold. We have said that due to constraint (3), all connected subsets of S have to be considered as values for the set C. Through the optimization certain connected sets $S \setminus R_{tmp}$ are skipped. Because we avoid only those $S \setminus R_{tmp}$ where the complement $S \setminus (S \setminus R_{tmp}) = R_{tmp}$ is not a connected set, our optimization is still sufficient to meet constraint (3).

2.5.2. The Algorithm in Detail

In the following, we take a closer look at the pseudocode given in Figures 2.12 and 2.13. PARTITION$_{MinCutBranch}$ calls MINCUTBRANCH the first time with $C = L =$

$\{t\}$, where $t \in S$ is an arbitrary vertex. This ensures constraint (1) because the complement R_{tmp} cannot contain t at any instance of MINCUTBRANCH's execution. In Line 1 and Line 2, the result sets R and R_{tmp} are initialized.

When processing the neighbors of C, the primary interest lies on the neighbors of the recently added vertex $v \in L$ because they are important for the computation of the return value. Therefore, in Line 3 the set N_L is introduced to store all the neighbors that certainly need to be processed, i.e., all neighbors of L that are not in X. The other neighbors of C which, at the same time, are not neighbors of L, are only explored if they belong to the result set R_{tmp} of one of the child invocations called with a neighbor of L. We store the neighbors of this category in the set N_B that holds all neighbors of C but not those that are in $\mathcal{N}(C)$ and, additionally, are not in X (Line 5). Special care has to be taken before processing neighbors of L that are also elements of X, whereas the set X holds former neighbors that have been processed in an ancestor invocation. Now, only those neighbors of L that are also element of X and are not contained in one of the result sets R_{tmp} need to be processed. We compute those candidates in Line 4 and store them into N_X. Whether the other neighbors that are contained by the last two sets N_B and N_X are processed or not is decided dynamically during the loop in Lines 6 to 29.

The loop (Lines 6 to 29) consists of three cases. To understand these cases, we have to learn about the additional requirement that exists due to our duplicate avoidance technique. As already mentioned, we use the filter set X to exclude its members from being processed as a new L in a child invocation of MINCUTBRANCH. Moreover, if a complement $S \setminus R_{tmp}$ is not disjoint with X, then $(S \setminus R_{tmp}, R_{tmp})$ is a duplicate and has already been emitted. For explaining this fact, we denote by v_{old} a member of $S \setminus (R_{tmp} \cap X)$. We know that $v_{old} \in \mathcal{N}(C)$ must hold, because v_{old} being a member of X implies that v_{old} was processed as a v in an ancestor invocation of MINCUTBRANCH as a neighbor of a C_{old}. As we will see later, v_{old} must be connected to v within $S \setminus C_{old}$ with $C_{old} \subset C$. Hence, a recursive descent started from a child invocation with a $C = C_{old} \cup \{v_{old}\}$ and an $L = \{v_{old}\}$ must have returned at one point with the same R_{tmp} as our current value. Therefore, the partition $(S \setminus R_{tmp}, R_{tmp})$ has already been emitted. We implement the test for duplicates in Line 24 and emit the *ccp* in Line 27.

Let us now consider the chain query of Figure 2.15. We choose R_0 as the initial C. In the root invocation of MINCUTBRANCH, we first process R_1. When the child invocation returns, R_{tmp} equals $\{R_1, R_3\}$. Before processing R_2 as the second neighbor, we add R_0 to X'. In the next child invocation of MINCUTBRANCH with $C = \{R_0, R_2\}$, $L = \{R_2\}$, and $X = \{R_0\}$, a further recursive call with $C = \{R_0, R_2, R_4\}$, $L = \{R_4\}$, and $X = \{R_0\}$ would return a $R = \{R_4\}$. But instead of emitting the *ccp* $(\{R_4\}, \{R_0, R_1, R_2, R_3\})$, we would falsely assume that it is a duplicate because $(S \setminus R_{tmp}) \cap X \neq \emptyset$ holds. To solve this problem, a X' needs to be reset to X once a new neighbor v is chosen that is not part of R yet (Line 12).

As a consequence, we specify the processing order of the three sets N_L, N_B and N_X dynamically and define three cases: Case (1) is checked in Line 7. It is true if a child invocation has started with a $v_x \in N_L$ (case (2)) or a $v_x \in N_X$ (case (3)) and a $v_y \in N_L$ or $v_y \in N_B$ is part of the returned R_{tmp}. Since the next invocation which we start with $L = \{v_y\}$ must return the same R_{tmp}, we do not have to save its return value and have no partition to emit, since it is already emitted. Note that the child

PARTITION$_{MinCutBranch}(G_{|S})$
    ▷ **Input:** a connected (sub)graph $G_{|S}$, arbitrary vertex $t \in S$
    ▷ **Output:** $P_{ccp}^{sym}(S)$
1    $t \leftarrow$ arbitrary vertex of S
2   MINCUTBRANCH$(G_{|S}, \{t\}, \emptyset, \{t\})$

Figure 2.12.: Pseudocode for PARTITION$_{MinCutBranch}$

invocation's excluded filter set is set to X', which in turn we must have set or reset to our own X in Line 12 by processing case (2) or (3) before. After processing v_y, we delete it from its originating set, which is either N_L (Line 10) or N_B (Line 11).

Lines 13 to 16 cover case (2). If the condition of case (1) is not valid and there are elements of N_L left, we have to consider case (2). That means N_L is not empty and either R_{tmp} is empty and no neighbor has been processed yet or no other $v \in N_L$ is part of the current R_{tmp}. As explained for our duplicate avoidance technique, we have to set or reset the new input parameter X' to our current input parameter X. Because this also needs to be done for case (3), we move this task to Line 12. Once the child invocation returns, we save the result in R_{tmp}. Note that $R_{tmp} \cap R = \emptyset$ holds. Later in Line 28, R_{tmp} is joined with R. Having processed the current v, it is subtracted from N_L in Line 16.

Case (3) ensures that all those neighbors $v \in N_X$ are processed that are not part of any returned R_{tmp}. A child invocation started with such an $L = \{v\}$ could not emit any further *ccp*s because of the condition in Line 24. As we only have to compute R_{tmp}, we use REACHABLE (Section 2.5.4). Because it is constructed solely for this task, it is a simpler and, therefore, more efficient method. With the instruction of Line 19, we avoid further unnecessary calls to REACHABLE. Note that the results of case (2) are also used to minimize N_X.

Lines 20 to 26 will be explained in Section 2.5.3. Before we return the call, we join L to the final result set R.

2.5.3. Two Optimization Techniques

Lines 20 to 26 specify two optimization techniques that are not a requirement for the branch partitioning algorithm. The first technique considers cases where R_{tmp} contains elements of X. In that case, all other invocations of MINCUTBRANCH and their child invocations with neighbors of C that are disjoint from R_{tmp} cannot emit any partitions because the R'_{tmp} that they produce must be disjoint with R_{tmp} so that $S \setminus R'_{tmp}$ cannot be disjoint with X (Line 24) any more. But as we need to ensure that R is correctly computed, we have to add those neighbors for which we want to avoid unnecessary calls to MINCUTBRANCH to N_X (Line 20).

The second optimization technique avoids exploring all the other neighbors of C which are also elements of R_{tmp} if the complement $S \setminus R_{tmp}$ is not disjoint with X. As already mentioned, if these neighbors were not subtracted from N_L and N_B, they would be processed in the next iterations of the loop, and the condition of Line 8 would qualify. Hence, all resulting child invocations of MINCUTBRANCH in Line 9 could not be avoided, although they would not have emitted any *ccp*s.

MINCUTBRANCH$(G_{|S}, C, X, L)$
▷ **Input:** a connected (sub)graph $G_{|S}, C, X \subset S, |L| = 1$
▷ **Output:** *ccp*s for S
1   $R \leftarrow \emptyset$
2   $R_{tmp} \leftarrow \emptyset$
3   $N_L \leftarrow ((\mathcal{N}(L) \cap S) \setminus C) \setminus X$
4   $N_X \leftarrow ((\mathcal{N}(L) \cap S) \setminus C) \cap X$
5   $N_B \leftarrow (((\mathcal{N}(C) \cap S) \setminus C) \setminus N_L) \setminus X$
6   **while** $N_L \neq \emptyset \vee N_X \neq \emptyset \vee N_B \cap R_{tmp} \neq \emptyset$
7   **if** $(N_B \cup N_L) \cap R_{tmp} \neq \emptyset$ ▷ case (1)
8          $v \leftarrow$ a element of $((N_B \cup N_L) \cap R_{tmp})$
9   MINCUTBRANCH$(G_{|S}, C \cup \{v\}, X', \{v\})$
10         $N_L \leftarrow N_L \setminus \{v\}$
11         $N_B \leftarrow N_B \setminus \{v\}$
12   **else** $X' \leftarrow X$
13   **if** $N_L \neq \emptyset$ ▷ case (2)
14           $v \leftarrow$ a element of N_L
15           $R_{tmp} \leftarrow$ MINCUTBRANCH$(G_{|S}, C \cup \{v\}, X', \{v\})$
16           $N_L \leftarrow N_L \setminus \{v\}$
17   **else** $v \leftarrow$ a element of N_X ▷ case (3)
18           $R_{tmp} \leftarrow$ REACHABLE$(G_{|S}, C \cup \{v\}, \{v\})$
19      $N_X \leftarrow N_X \setminus R_{tmp}$
20   **if** $R_{tmp} \cap X \neq \emptyset$
21          $N_X \leftarrow N_X \cup (N_L \setminus R_{tmp})$
22          $N_L \leftarrow N_L \cap R_{tmp}$
23          $N_B \leftarrow N_B \cap R_{tmp}$
24   **if** $(S \setminus R_{tmp}) \cap X \neq \emptyset$
25          $N_L \leftarrow N_L \setminus R_{tmp}$
26          $N_B \leftarrow N_B \setminus R_{tmp}$
27   **else** emit $(S \setminus R_{tmp}, R_{tmp})$
28      $R \leftarrow R \cup R_{tmp}$
29   $X' \leftarrow X' \cup \{v\}$
30   **return** $R \cup L$

Figure 2.13.: Pseudocode for MINCUTBRANCH

2.5.4. Exploring Restricted Neighbors

Finally, we explain REACHABLE as given in Figure 2.14. As already mentioned, it is its aim to return the maximally enlarged and connected set containing $L = \{v\}$ adjacent to C. In Line 1 of REACHABLE, the result set R is initialized with the one-element set L. Enlarging R starts with the set of neighbors of L that are disjoint to C and lie within S (Line 3). During the while loop in Lines 4 to 6, all the neighbors of the neighbors from the previous iteration of the loop that are disjoint with C (Line 6) are added to R (Line 5). The loop is exited once no vertex is left to be added.

REACHABLE$(G_{|S}, C, L)$
    ▷ **Input:** (sub)graph $G_{|S}$, $C \subseteq S$, $L \subseteq C$, $|L| = 1$
    ▷ **Output:** connected set R adjacent to C
1    $R \leftarrow L$
2    $I \leftarrow S \setminus C$
3    $N \leftarrow (\mathcal{N}(L) \cap I)$
4   **while** $N \neq \emptyset$
5        $R \leftarrow R \cup N$
6        $N \leftarrow ((\mathcal{N}(N) \cap I) \setminus R)$
7   **return** R

Figure 2.14.: Pseudocode for REACHABLE

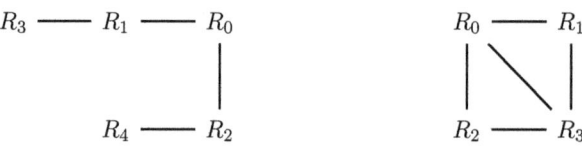

Figure 2.15.: Chain Query   Figure 2.16.: Cyclic Query

2.5.5. Two Examples

We illustrate the execution of MINCUTBRANCH by two examples. Tables 2.5 and 2.6 show the execution steps when the chain query of Figure 2.15 or, respectively, the cyclic query of Figure 2.16 is given as input. The first column named *level* keeps track of the recursion level. The root invocation is indicated with a 0. Column two shows which *case* in the parent invocation has initiated the current call. We omit invocations where $N_L = N_X = N_B = \emptyset$, because they return immediately to the parent invocation by avoiding the loop of Lines 6 to 29.

For all acyclic graphs, MINCUTBRANCH has only case 2 to consider. Table 2.5 confirms this for chain graphs. The maximal recursion depth depends on the position of the start vertex t (Line 1 of PARTITION$_{MinCutBranch}$). Here, we have chosen $t = R_0$ as the start vertex. Therefore, the recursion depth is 2, but this is not shown, because the recursions with $L = \{R_3\}$ and $L = \{R_4\}$ are omitted. For the graph of Figure 2.16, we have a recursion depth of 3 and again $t = R_0$ as the start vertex. Note that the invocation with $L = \{R_2\}$, following the third entry in Table 2.6, is left out. As can be seen for this example at the last three entries of Table 2.6, there is a recursive invocation of MINCUTBRANCH with $C = \{R_0, R_3\}$ and $X = \{R_1, R_2\}$ that does not emit any further *ccp*s. Unfortunately, this is an execution overhead that cannot be avoided easily.

2.5.6. Complexity of Branch Partitioning

We determine the complexity of MINCUTBRANCH to emit successive *ccp*s by $O(\frac{i+r+l}{|P_{ccp}^{sym}(S)|})$, where i is the number of iterations of the loop in Line 6, r is the number

level	case	C	L	X	N_L	N_X	N_B
0	-	$\{R_0\}$	$\{R_0\}$	$\emptyset$	$\{R_1, R_2\}$	$\emptyset$	$\emptyset$
1	2	$\{R_0, R_1\}$	$\{R_1\}$	$\emptyset$	$\{R_3\}$	$\emptyset$	$\emptyset$
1		MCB. returns $\{R_3\}$ $\to$ emitting $(\{R_3\}, \{R_0, R_1, R_2, R_4\})$						
0		MCB. returns $\{R_3, R_1\}$ $\to$ emitting $(\{R_1, R_3\}, \{R_0, R_2, R_4\})$						
1	2	$\{R_0, R_2\}$	$\{R_2\}$	$\emptyset$	$\{R_4\}$	$\emptyset$	$\emptyset$
1		MCB. returns $\{R_4\}$ $\to$ emitting $(\{R_4\}, \{R_0, R_1, R_2, R_3\})$						
0		MCB. returns $\{R_4, R_2\}$ $\to$ emitting $(\{R_2, R_4\}, \{R_0, R_1, R_3\})$						

Table 2.5.: Exemplified execution of MINCUTBRANCH for the graph of Figure 2.15

level	case	C	L	X	N_L	N_X	N_B
0	-	$\{R_0\}$	$\{R_0\}$	$\emptyset$	$\{R_1, R_2, R_3\}$	$\emptyset$	$\emptyset$
1	2	$\{R_0, R_1\}$	$\{R_1\}$	$\emptyset$	$\{R_3\}$	$\emptyset$	$\{R_2\}$
2	2	$\{R_0, R_1, R_3\}$	$\{R_3\}$	$\emptyset$	$\{R_2\}$	$\emptyset$	$\emptyset$
2		MCB. returns $\{R_2\}$ $\to$ emitting $(\{R_2\}, \{R_0, R_1, R_3\})$						
1		MCB. returns $\{R_2, R_3\}$ $\to$ emitting $(\{R_2, R_3\}, \{R_0, R_1\})$						
2	1	$\{R_0, R_1, R_2\}$	$\{R_2\}$	$\{R_3\}$	$\emptyset$	$\{R_3\}$	$\emptyset$
2		REACHABLE returns $\{R_3\}$ $\to$ emitting $(\{R_3\}, \{R_0, R_1, R_2\})$						
0		MCB. returns $\{R_2, R_3, R_1\}$ $\to$ emitting $(\{R_1, R_2, R_3\}, \{R_0\})$						
1	1	$\{R_0, R_2\}$	$\{R_2\}$	$\{R_1\}$	$\{R_3\}$	$\emptyset$	$\emptyset$
2	2	$\{R_0, R_2, R_3\}$	$\{R_3\}$	$\{R_1\}$	$\emptyset$	$\{R_1\}$	$\emptyset$
2		REACHABLE returns $\{R_1\}$ $\to$ emitting $(\{R_1\}, \{R_0, R_2, R_3\})$						
1		MCB. returns $\{R_1, R_3\}$ $\to$ emitting $(\{R_1, R_3\}, \{R_0, R_2\})$						
1	1	$\{R_0, R_3\}$	$\{R_3\}$	$\{R_1, R_2\}$	$\emptyset$	$\{R_1, R_2\}$	$\emptyset$
1		REACHABLE returns $\{R_1\}$ $\to$ not emitting emitting duplicate						
1		REACHABLE returns $\{R_2\}$ $\to$ not emitting emitting duplicate						
0		MCB. returns $\{R_1, R_2, R_3\}$						

Table 2.6.: Exemplified execution of MINCUTBRANCH for the graph of Figure 2.16

of all invocations of REACHABLE and l is the number of all iterations of the loop in Line 4 of REACHABLE.

For acyclic graphs, we know that $|P_{ccp}^{sym}(S)| = |S| - 1$ holds. Furthermore, no $v \in N_B \cup N_X$ will be processed. Therefore, $i = |S| - 1$ and $r = l = 0$ holds, since there is no call to REACHABLE. Hence, the complexity of MINCUTBRANCH to emit a ccp for acyclic graphs is in $O(1)$.

A cycle query has $|P_{ccp}^{sym}(S)| = \frac{1}{2}|S|^2 \setminus \frac{1}{2}|S|$ symmetric $ccps$ for S. Each of the first $|S| - 1$ invocations processes a neighbor taken from the set N_L. That recursive descent is always initiated through Line 15. There are $|S| - 2$ second invocations of the loop of Line 6 calling MINCUTBRANCH from Line 9. Those invocations process further $\sum_{k=1}^{|S|-2} k$ neighbors in total. Altogether, there are $|S| - 1 + |S| - 2| + \sum_{k=1}^{|S|-2} k = \frac{1}{2}|S|^2 + 12|S| - 2 = i$ neighbors processed. REACHABLE is called $r = |S| - 2$ times, and the loop of Line 4 never iterates, so that $l = 0$ holds. Therefore, the total complexity per emitted ccp is $\frac{|S|^2+3|S|-8}{|S|(|S|-1)}$, which decreases asymptotically to 1, so that the complexity is $O(1)$.

Considering clique queries, we know that $|P_{ccp}^{sym}(S)| = 2^{|S|-1} - 1$ holds. There are $2^{|S|-1}$ neighbors processed that are element of N_L. Furthermore, there are $2^{|S|-2} - 1$ neighbors processed that are element of N_X. Therefore, $i = 2^{|S|-1} + 2^{|S|-2} \setminus 1 = \frac{3}{4}2^{|S|} - 1$ and $r = 2^{|S|-2} - 1$ holds. The number of iterations through the loop of Line 4 must be $|S| - 2$ times less than there are calls to REACHABLE, so that $l = 2^{|S|-2} - |S| - 3$ holds. To emit all symmetric $ccps$, the complexity is $\frac{5}{4}2^{|S|} - |S| - 5$. Per emitted ccp the complexity increases asymptotically to $\frac{5}{2}$. Hence, the complexity for clique queries is in $O(1)$.

2.6. Evaluation

This section summarizes our experimental findings. We start by briefly describing our setup. Then we give an organizational overview (Section 2.6.2) and present our results (Section 2.6.3).

2.6.1. Experimental Setup

For all plan generators, no matter whether they work top-down or bottom-up, a shared optimizer infrastructure was established. It contains the common functions to instantiate, fill, and lookup the memotable, initialize and use plan classes, estimate cardinalities, calculate costs, and compare plans. Thus, the different plan generators differ only in those parts of the code responsible for enumerating $ccps$. Except for PARTITION$_{naive}$ all partitioning algorithms are implemented as an iteratator. Appendix B.1 shows the C++ Code for MINCUTCONSERVATIVE and B.2 the C++ Code for MINCUTBRANCH. We store the pre-calculated ancestors, descendants (Section A.1, required by MINCUTLAZY) and neighbors of a vertex in an array of size $|V|$.

Since, due to the fact that we ignore pruning, the cost calculation is immaterial for our investigation, we simply use C_{out} (Section 2.1.2). To generate our workload, we have implemented a generic query graph generator. In a first step, it generates chain, star, cycle, and clique queries as well as random acyclic and cyclic graphs. For the latter, edges are randomly added by selecting two relation's indices using uniformly distributed random numbers. In a second step, cardinalities and selectivities are attached using a random generator with a Gaussian distribution. Since we do not apply branch-and-bound pruning techniques (Chapter 4), these numbers do not influence the search space of the plan generators.

2.6.2. Organizational Overview

In our empirical analysis, we compare basic memoization, denoted by TDBASIC, based on naive partitioning and TDMCL with the novel memoization variants: TDMCL$_{Imp}$, TDMCA, TDMCC and TDMCB. Table 2.6.2 shows an overview over the different top-down join enumeration algorithms. To put all six top-down plan generation algorithms in perspective, we include the results of Moerkotte's and Neumann's DPCCP [22] as a very efficient bottom-up join enumeration algorithm via dynamic programming.

Name	Abb. Name	Partitioning Strategy	Remarks
TDBASIC	TDBASIC	PARTITION$_{naive}$	Sec. 2.2.2
TDMINCUTLAZY	TDMCL	MINCUTLAZY	Sec. A.2
TDMINCUTLAZY$_{Imp}$	TDMCL$_{Imp}$	MINCUTLAZY	Sec. A.5.1
TDMINCUTAGAT	TDMCA	MINCUTAGAT	Sec. 2.3
TDMINCUTCONSERVATIVE	TDMCC	MINCUTCONSERVATIVE	Sec. 2.4
TDMINCUTBRANCH	TDMCB	MINCUTBRANCH	Sec. 2.5

Table 2.7.: Names and abbreviated names of different plan generation algorithms with different partitioning strategies.

For our experiments, we measured the execution time of the six different plan generators on the same workload. To minimize measurement errors, we computed the average for every algorithm run for a given input. For fixed query shapes that are chains, stars, cycles, and cliques, and for random acyclic graphs, we give the number of vertices on the abscissa and the execution time in log scale on the ordinate. We draw lines to connect the averaged execution times.

Since for randomly generated cyclic queries the algorithms' performance results deviate significantly for the same number of vertices, we show the results for different numbers of vertices separately. At the abscissa, we choose to display the number of edges and again the execution time in log scale on the ordinate. We do not present the exact results, which still can deviate strongly, but results smoothed by Bezier curves.

As we will see, apart from some minor exceptions, Moerkotte's and Neumann's DPCCP is the algorithm which performs best. Therefore, it is interesting to evaluate the results in terms of the quotient of the algorithm's execution time and the execution time of DPCCP. For the following discussion, we refer to that quotient as the normed time.

We include only those query graphs in our evaluation that all plan generators could process in less than 100 seconds. Our workload consists of 25.500 query graphs. The number of vertices and edges for our random cyclic queries are uniformly distributed. We conducted all our experiments on an Intel Pentium D with 3.4 GHz, 2 Mbyte second level cache and 3 Gbyte of RAM that runs openSUSE 11.0. We used the Intel C++ compiler with the O3 compiler option set.

2.6.3. Experiments

This section summarizes our experimental findings. First, we give a short evaluation of the partitioning costs between lazy minimal cut partitioning and branch partitioning. Then, we follow with an evaluation of acyclic query graphs and present the results for cyclic graphs at the end.

Partitioning Costs

We have analyzed the complexity of lazy minimal cut partitioning (MINCUTLAZY in Appendix A.4) and branch partitioning (MINCUTBRANCH in Section 2.5.6) for chain, star, cycle and clique queries. For both partitioning strategies, the complexity is in $O(1)$ for chain, star and cycle queries per emitted ccp. But when clique queries are

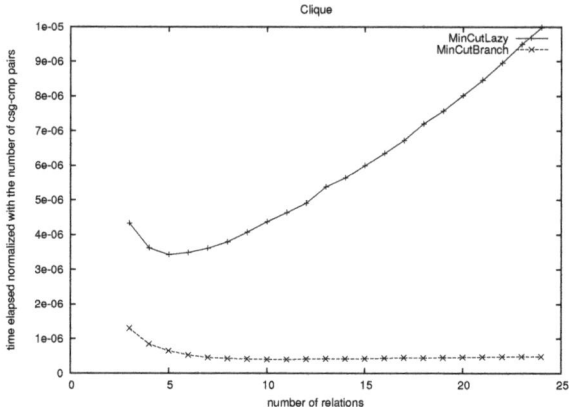

Figure 2.17.: Cost per emitted *ccp* of MINCUTLAZY and MINCUTBRANCH for clique queries.

considered, MINCUTLAZY has a complexity in $O(|S|^2)$, whereas MINCUTBRANCH is still in $O(1)$ per emitted *ccp*. Therefore, we have measured the partitioning costs and discuss them here for clique queries. Figure 2.17 shows our results with the number of vertices on the abscissa and the execution time per emitted *ccp* on the ordinate.

The costs per emitted *ccp* are decreasing for a small number of vertices. But with five and more vertices, the costs for lazy minimal cut partitioning are increasing again. The increase is quadratic. For MINCUTBRANCH, the costs are dropping for less than ten vertices. After that, they are slightly increasing. The decrease at the start of both curves is due to some instantiation overhead that becomes negligible compared to the other processing costs, when a higher number of vertices is considered. Our results support a quadratic increase as proven by our complexity analysis, but this effect is rather weak for the number of vertices considered here. Note that the effect was weakened by our implementations, since we have used inline assembler instructions to minimize the accessing cost of the data structure MINCUTLAZY relies on.

For MINCUTBRANCH, we have proven that the complexity is increasing asymptotically to a constant factor. Our results show a very weak increase. This is caused by an increasing number of cache misses for an increasing number of vertices.

In summary, our results show that the performance differences between the two algorithms for clique queries are strongly increasing with a higher number of vertices.

For the other three graph shapes, MINCUTBRANCH clearly dominates MINCUTLAZY, but the differences are not as strong as for clique queries, because both algorithms have only a constant overhead in those scenarios.

Cost of Plan Generation for Acyclic Query Graphs

We give the results for chain queries in Figure 2.18, for star queries in Figure 2.19 and for random acyclic graphs that are neither chain nor star queries in Figure 2.20. For all different acyclic graphs, the normed runtimes of TDBASIC and TDMCA show an exponential increase, although the effect is much weaker for TDMCA. With a maximal normed runtime of almost 47000 (Table 2.8) for chain queries, TDBASIC is a terrible choice for acyclic graphs. DeHaan's and Tompa's TDMCL performs on a mediocre level with a maximal factor of 3.5 for star queries (Table 2.8). Since TDMCL$_{Imp}$ needs much fewer biconnection tree buildings when acyclic graphs are considered, as our derived formulas (Section A.5.2) show, it is distinctly faster than TDMCL (maximal factor of 1.8 for star queries). TDMCC performs quite well and is only dominated by TDMCB in every acyclic scenario. Except for star queries, where we have more cache misses with an increasing number of vertices, TDMCB performs even better than the state-of-the-art in dynamic programming for graphs DPCCP. The lowest factor we could determine for TDMCB was at 0.66 for random acyclic queries.

Cost of Plan Generation for Cyclic Query Graphs

Cycle and clique queries belong to the same group of cyclic graphs, but in terms of the number of *ccp*s, they belong to two opposite sides of the spectrum. Cycles have the lowest number of edges that is possible for cyclic graphs, removing one edge would result in a chain query. We present their results in Figure 2.21. Cliques have the maximal number of edges possible. The results for clique queries can been found in Figure 2.22. Table 2.9 summarizes the normed runtimes for all evaluated algorithms.

As expected, the results for cycle queries look more similar to those for chain queries than to the results for clique queries. From Table 2.9 we can see only for TDBASIC and TDMCA the averaged normed runtime has increased compared to the results for chain queries. Again, TDMCB is the fastest algorithm, closely followed by TDMCC.

When looking at cliques, the picture changes completely. Now TDBASIC dominates TDMCL and TDMCL$_{Imp}$. TDMCA performs better than TDBASIC, since it relies only on one connection test per emitted *ccp*. This time, TDMCB performs second best and is only dominated by DPCCP. Again, TDMCC is only slightly slower than TDMCB.

When we consider random cyclic graphs, we can trace the performance shift between cycle and clique queries. We display our results for 8 and 16 vertices in Figure 2.23 and 2.24. The trends of the normed runtimes of TDMCA and TDBASIC compared to the trends of TDMCL and TDMCL$_{Imp}$, respectively, are oppositional. Whereas the normed runtime of TDMCA and TDBASIC is decreasing with an increasing number of edges for a fixed number of vertices, TDMCL's and TDMCL$_{Imp}$'s normed runtime is increasing. For a fixed number of vertices and a relatively small number of edges, the differences between TDMCL and TDMCL$_{Imp}$ are distinctive, but for a number of edges lying in the median span, the differences become indistinctive. Independent of the number of edges or vertices, TDMCL$_{Imp}$ dominates TDMCL.

One can clearly see that TDMCA dominates TDBASIC and TDMCL and its improved version with some minor exceptions of TDMCL$_{Imp}$ at the beginning of the spectrum.

Once more, all top-down join enumeration algorithms except for TDMCC are outperformed by TDMCB. Although TDMCC's average normed runtime is by 0.8% lower, its minimum and maximum normed runtimes are higher. With an averaged normed runtime of 1.1 for random cyclic queries, TDMCB is almost as efficient as DPCCP, which performs best. We can contrast the worst relative factor of 1.47 with a factor of

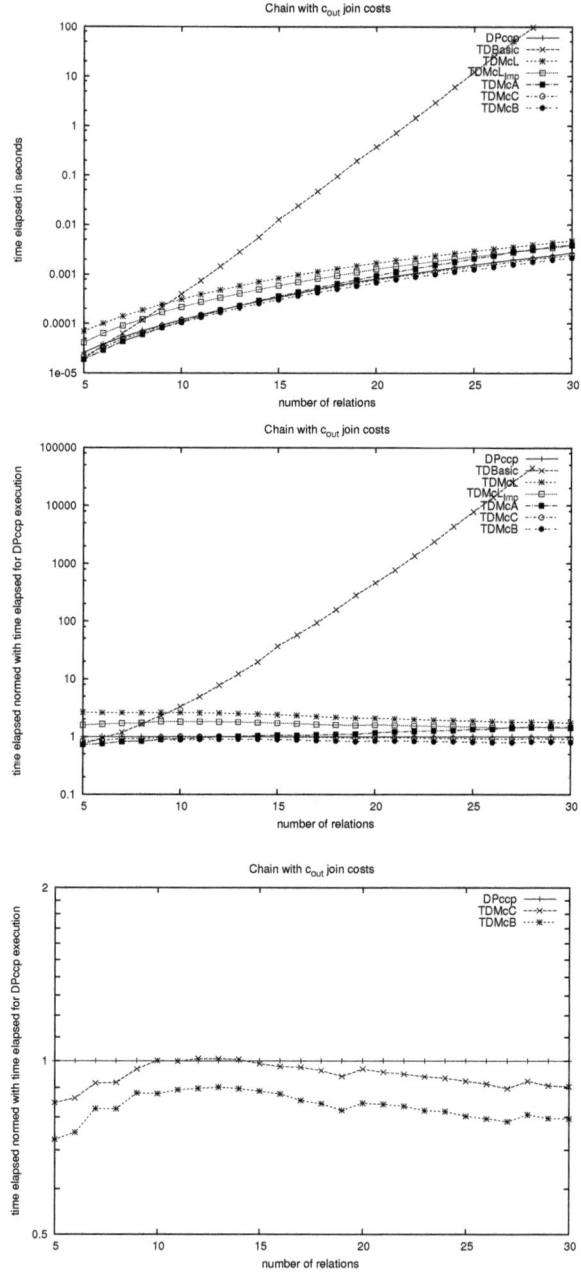

Figure 2.18.: Absolute and normed runtime results for chain queries.

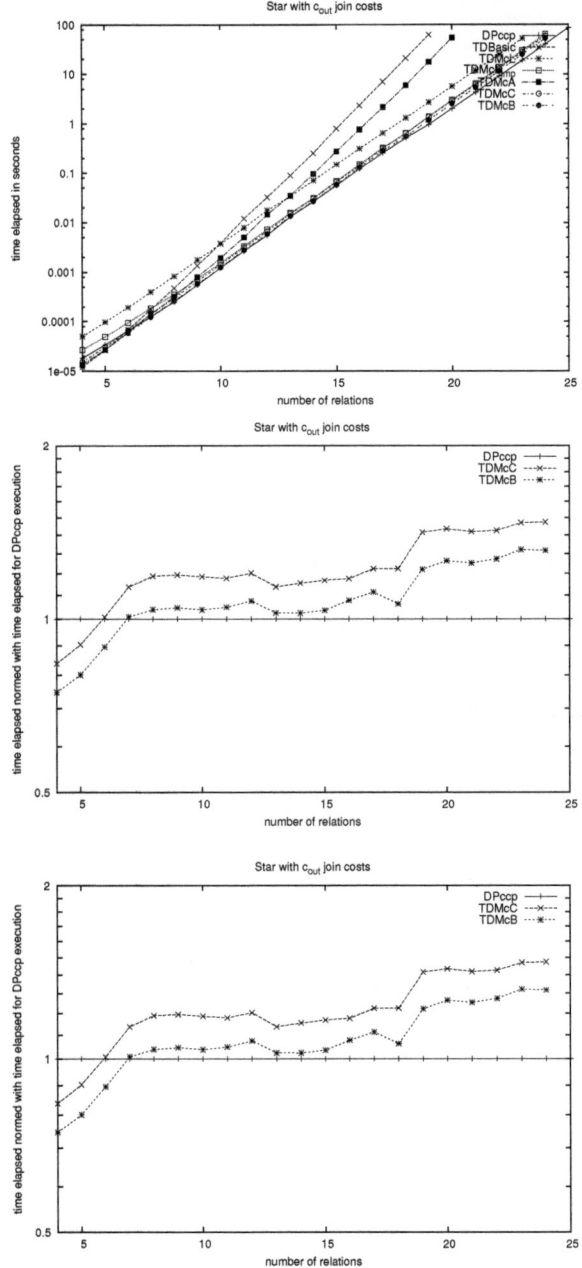

Figure 2.19.: Absolute and normed runtime results for star queries.

Algorithm	Chain			Star			Acyclic		
	min	max	avg	min	max	avg	min	max	avg
DPCCP	0.00 s	0.00 s	0.00 s	0.00 s	2.02 s	0.11 s	0.00 s	0.26 s	0.01 s
TDBASIC	1.06	46827	1569	0.89	77	11.88	0.94	5646	151
TDMCL	1.69	2.85	2.27	2.19	3.50	2.93	1.48	3.22	2.23
TDMCL$_{Imp}$	1.22	2.35	1.64	0.90	1.77	1.34	0.82	2.35	1.20
TDMCA	0.65	1.66	1.11	0.76	30	4.02	0.62	9.77	1.88
TDMCC	0.78	1.09	0.96	0.87	1.49	1.17	0.79	1.18	0.98
TDMCB	0.74	0.98	0.85	0.77	1.30	1.04	0.66	1.03	0.85

Table 2.8.: Minimum, maximum and average of the normalized runtimes for chain, star and random acyclic queries.

Algorithm	Cycle			Clique			Cyclic		
	min	max	avg	min	max	avg	min	max	avg
DPCCP	0.00 s	0.00 s	0.00 s	0.00 s	7.75 s	0.97 s	0.00 s	15.68 s	1.64 s
TDBASIC	0.77	22951	3631	0.49	1.96	1.46	1.10	201	5.76
TDMCL	1.37	3.95	2.59	2.40	8.48	6.35	2.13	8.00	5.63
TDMCL$_{Imp}$	1.07	2.33	1.55	3.23	7.75	5.82	1.24	7.41	5.43
TDMCA	0.63	1.79	1.38	0.72	1.41	1.15	0.80	5.58	1.30
TDMCC	0.84	1.09	0.94	0.72	1.26	1.09	0.81	1.54	1.12
TDMCB	0.74	0.98	0.84	0.74	1.29	1.06	0.78	1.47	1.13

Table 2.9.: Minimum, maximum and average of the normalized runtimes for cycle, clique and random cyclic queries.

$\frac{1}{0.78} = 1.28$ in the best case, being faster than DPCCP, although no branch-and-bound pruning is put in place.

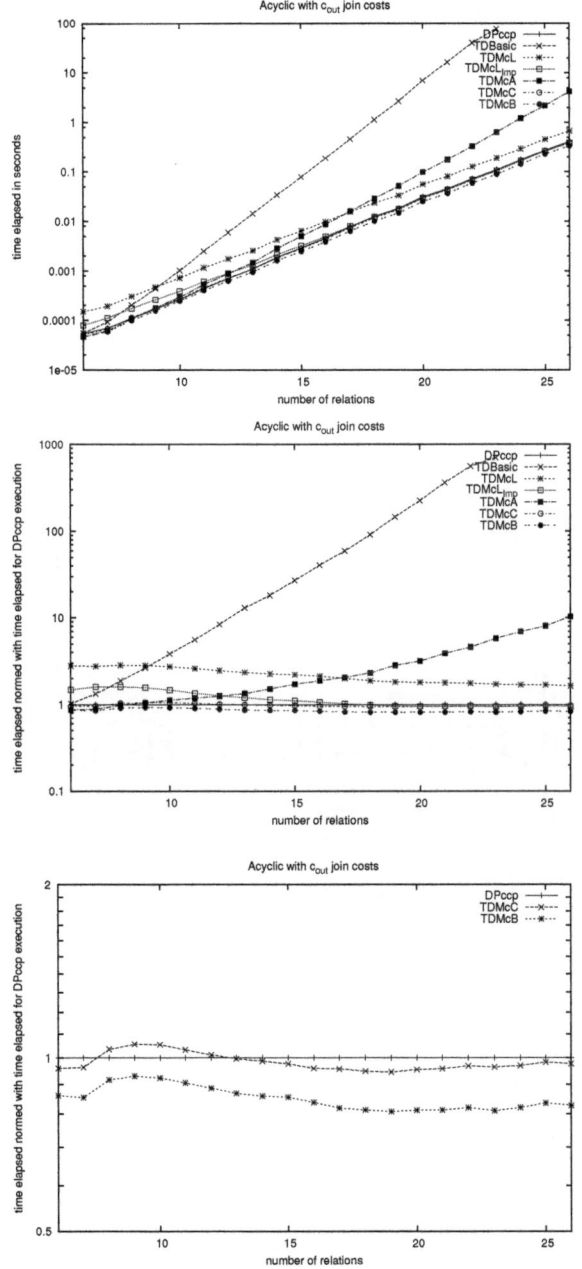

Figure 2.20.: Absolute and normed runtime results for random acyclic queries that are neither chain nor star queries.

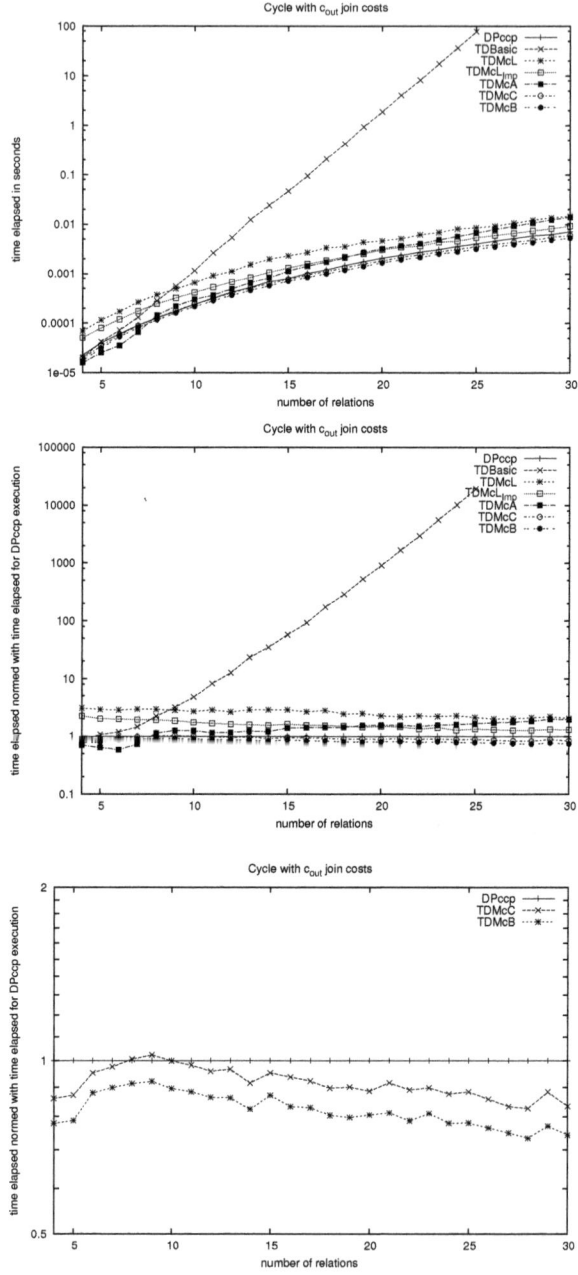

Figure 2.21.: Absolute and normed runtime results for cycle queries.

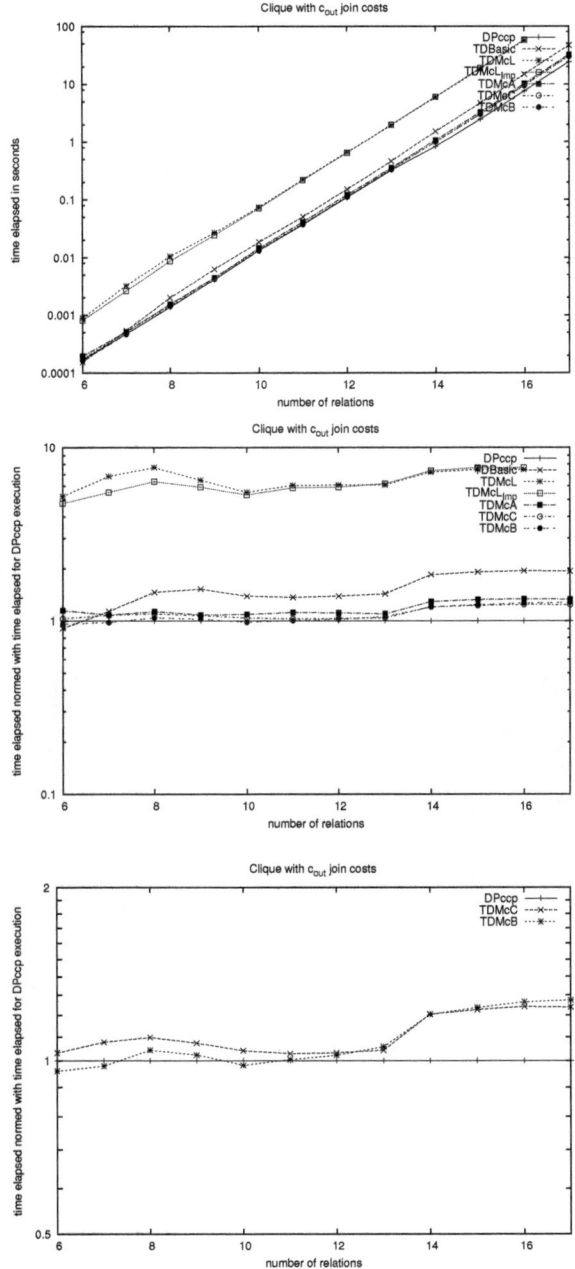

Figure 2.22.: Absolute and normed runtime results for clique queries.

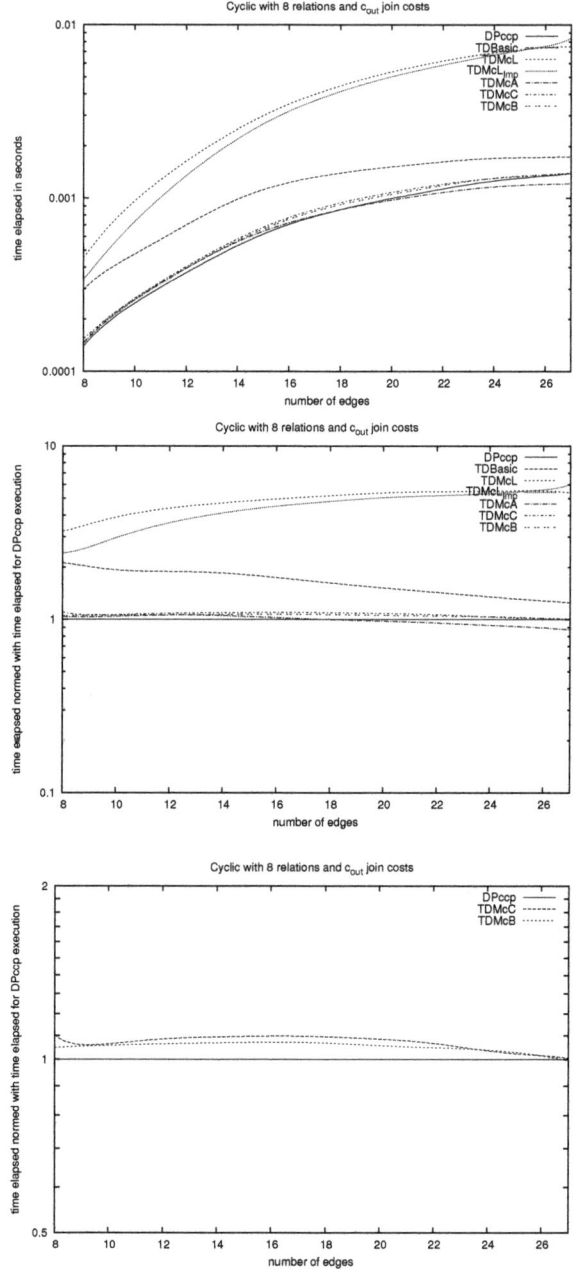

Figure 2.23.: Absolute and normed runtime results for cyclic queries with 8 vertices.

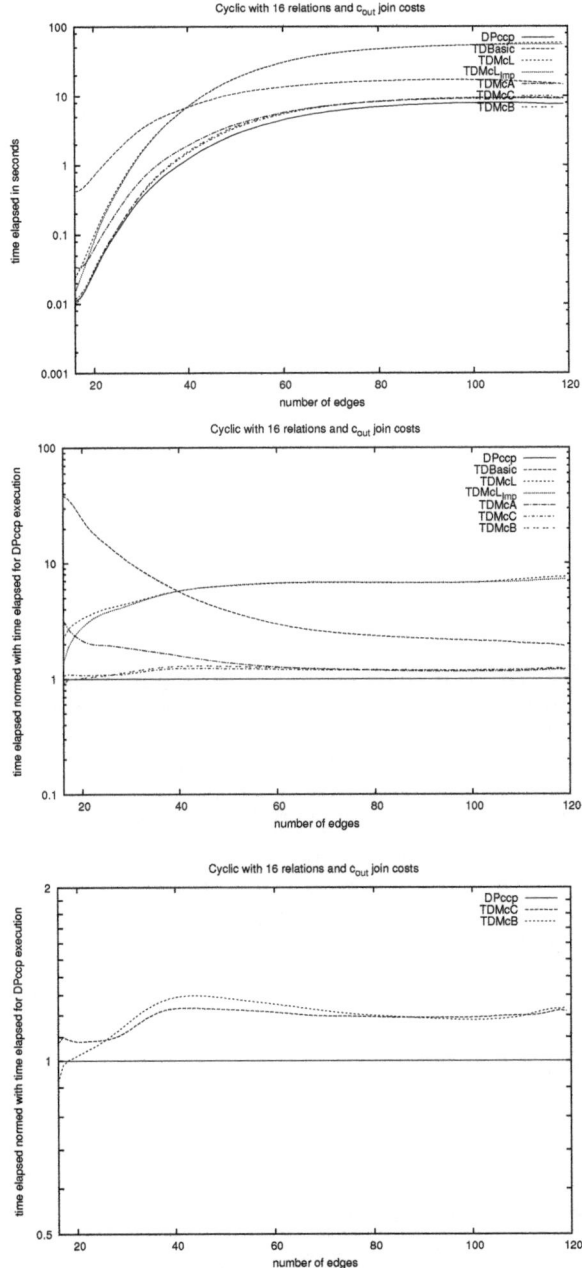

Figure 2.24.: Absolute and normed runtime results for cyclic queries with 16 vertices.

3. Hypergraph-Aware Join Enumeration Algorithms

3.1. Motivation

In the last chapter, we introduced different top-down join enumeration algorithms that generate optimal plans. However, for all of them the type of input queries was limited to:

1. only inner joins,

2. only simple join predicates referencing two relations, and

3. no cross products were allowed.

If a query falls into this category, it can be represented by a query graph that is a simple undirected connected graph. There are three reasons why the simple graph model for this type of queries suffices:

1. Inner joins can be freely reordered, since they are commutative and associative. Thus, every plan generated by the plan generator is a valid plan, i.e., produces the same result as the initial plan specified by the query.

2. Simple join predicates reference two relations only. Therefore, each such join predicate can be represented by a graph edge that connects two vertices. Those two vertices in turn represent the two referenced relations of the predicate.

3. If no cross products are allowed, the mapping of join predicates to graph edges will produce a connected graph.

However, in practice real-world queries often do not meet all three restrictions at the same time. If other operators like left outer joins, full outer joins, antijoins, semijoins, and groupjoins are considered in a query, then no longer are all plans valid. In other words: There might be certain operator reorderings gained by applying commutativity and associativity that result in an invalid plan, i.e., a plan that produces the wrong query result.

Consider the query

Select * From (R0 Left Outer Join R1 On R0.A = R1.B)
              Full Outer Join R2 On R1.C = R2.D

The query can be translated into an initial operator tree:

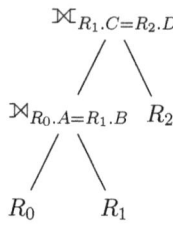

For this query, no valid reordering is possible. To prevent invalid reorderings, conflicts need to be detected and represented. Moerkotte et al. [20] presented three different conflict detectors that can be used by dynamic programming-based or memoization-based join enumeration algorithms in order to prevent invalid plans.

Without going into details, at the core of their conflict presentation is a set of relations, called TES, associated with each operator in the initial operator tree [21, 27, 20]. The intuition behind it is rather simple: before an operator can be applied to join two subplans, all relations in TES must be present in the two subplans. For our example, we have $\text{TES}(\bowtie_{R_0.A=R_1.B}) = \{R_0, R_1\}$ and $\text{TES}(\bowtie_{R_1.C=R_2.D}) = \{R_0, R_1, R_2\}$. Since non-commutative operators might be considered, the conflict detectors generally distinguish between the relations contained in the left and right branch of the initial operator tree. Intersection of the TES with the set of relations contained in the left and right branch of the operator tree gives a pair (L-TES, R-TES) of sets of relations. For $\bowtie_{p_{1,2}}$, this pair is $(\{R_0, R_1\}, \{R_2\})$. As [21, 20] shows, instead of modeling the predicate $R_1.C = R_2.D$ as a simple graph edge (R_1, R_2), a complex hyperedge $(\{R_0, R_1\}, \{R_2\})$ is introduced. As shown in [20] for the conflict detector CD-A, the join enumerator can be limited to valid orderings by utilizing complex hyperedges.

Because of the second limitation, any graph-aware plan generator should be able to handle hypergraphs [2, 27, 35]. This is because any complex join predicate references more than two relations. Thus, a complex join predicate cannot be mapped to a simple edge, but to a complex hyperedge only.

Apart from non-inner joins and complex join predicates, cross products might be specified in a query. As will be explained later, we can use complex hyperedges to encapsulate cross products and transform them into join operators with a selectivity of one.

As we have argued, in practice we need to deal with hypergraphs. Hence, to overcome the three limitations, we need hypergraph-aware plan generators. Consequently, Moerkotte and Neumann [21] extended DPCCP to DPHYP to handle hypergraphs. Since DPHYP is a bottom-up join enumeration algorithm, it cannot benefit from branch-and-bound pruning. On the other hand, branch-and-bound pruning can significantly speed up plan generation [5, 12], while still guaranteeing plan optimality.

In this chapter, we present a novel algorithm called TDMCCHYP (short for TD-MINCUTCONSERVATIVEHYP) as an advancement of TDMINCUTCONSERVATIVE. TDMCCHYP is the first available plan generation algorithm which works top-down and is able to deal with hypergraphs. Furthermore, we propose a generic framework that can be used by any existing partitioning algorithm for simple graphs to efficiently partition hypergraphs. We show how the novel framework can by utilized by any existing graph-aware top-down join enumeration algorithm.

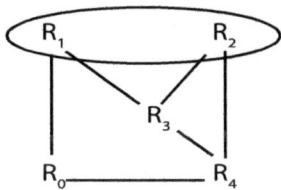

Figure 3.1.: Hypergraph $H(V,E) = (\{R_0, R_1, R_2, R_3, R_4\}, \{(\{R_0\}, \{R_1, R_2\}), (\{R_0\}, \{R_4\}), (\{R_1\}, \{R_3\}), (\{R_2\}, \{R_3\}), (\{R_2\}, \{R_4\}), (\{R_3\}, \{R_4\})\})$

This chapter is organized as follows. Section 3.2 explains some preliminaries. In Section 3.3, we continue with a naive approach for top-down plan generation. Section 3.4 introduces TDMCCHYP [11]. In Section 3.5, a novel framework as a generic approach [10] is presented. Section 3.6 concludes this chapter with an evaluation.

3.2. Preliminaries

3.2.1. Hypergraphs

Let us begin with the definition of *hypergraphs*.

Definition 3.2.1. *A hypergraph is a pair $H = (V, E)$ such that*

1. *V is a non-empty set of nodes, and*
2. *E is a set of hyperedges, where a hyperedge is an unordered pair (v, w) of non-empty subsets of V ($v \subset V$ and $w \subset V$) with the additional condition that $v \cap w = \emptyset$.*

We call any non-empty subset of V a hypernode. We assume that the nodes in V are totally ordered via an (arbitrary) relation $\prec$.

A hyperedge (v, w) is simple *if $|v| = |w| = 1$. A hypergraph is* simple *if all its hyperedges are simple. We call all non-simple hyperedges* complex *hyperedges and all non-simple hypergraphs* complex *hypergraphs.*

As explained in [20] (Section 3.1), the conflict detector CD-A computes the hyperedges of a hypergraph by considering the L-TES and R-TES of a given join operator. Note that here it does not matter if the hyperedge is computed as (L-TES, R-TES) or (R-TES, L-TES). Important for the differentiation between L-TES and R-TES is a certain node-ordering $\prec$ of the hypergraph. More specifically, we order the relations from the left to right in the initial operator tree as gained from the SQL query [21]. That is, if R and S are two leaves in the initial operator tree and R occurs left of S, then $R \prec S$ must hold.

Take a look at the complex hypergraph $H(V, E)$ depicted in Figure 3.1 with $V = \{R_0, R_1, R_2, R_3, R_4\}$ and $E = E_{simple} \cup E_{complex}$. The graph H has five simple edges with $E_{simple} = \{(\{R_0\}, \{R_4\}), (\{R_1\}, \{R_3\}), (\{R_2\}, \{R_3\}), (\{R_2\}, \{R_4\}), (\{R_3\}, \{R_4\})\}$ and one complex hyperedge with $E_{complex} = \{(\{R_0\}, \{R_1, R_2\})\}$.

The next definition is an adoption of Definition 2.1.2. It specifies what we mean by an *index* of a vertex.

Definition 3.2.2. *Let $H = (V, E)$ be a hypergraph and v_i a vertex with $v_i \in V$. Further, let $\prec$ be a binary relation specifying the total order of the vertices of V. We say i is the* index *of v_i with $i = |\{w \prec v_i | w \in V\}|$.*

To decompose a join-ordering problem represented as a hypergraph into smaller problems, we need the notion of *subgraph*. More specifically, we only deal with *node-induced subgraphs*.

Definition 3.2.3. *Let $H = (V, E)$ be a hypergraph and $V' \subseteq V$ a subset of nodes. The* node-induced subgraph *$H|_{V'}$ of H is defined as $H|_{V'} = (V', E')$ with $E' = \{(v, w) | (v, w) \in E, v \subseteq V', w \subseteq V'\}$. The node ordering on V' is the restriction of the node ordering of V.*

The node-induced subgraph $H|_{V'}$ of the hypergraph H as given in Figure 3.1 with $V' = \{R_0, R_2, R_4\}$ has an edge set $E' = \{(\{R_0\}, \{R_4\}), (\{R_2\}, \{R_4\})\}$ that consists only of simple edges. Hence, $H|_{V'}$ is a simple hypergraph. Next, we define *connectedness*.

Definition 3.2.4. *Let $H = (V, E)$ be a hypergraph. H is* connected *if $|V| = 1$ or if there exists a partitioning V', V'' of V and a hyperedge $(v, w) \in E$ such that $v \subseteq V'$, $w \subseteq V''$, and both $H|_{V'}$ and $H|_{V''}$ are connected.*

The node-induced subgraph $H|_{\{R_0, R_1, R_2, R_3\}}$ gained from the connected hypergraph of Figure 3.1 is connected, whereas $H|_{\{R_0, R_1, R_2\}}$ is not.

If $H = (V, E)$ is a hypergraph and $V' \subseteq V$ is a subset of the nodes such that the node-induced subgraph $H|_{V'}$ is connected, we call V' a *connected subgraph* or *csg* for short. The number of connected subgraphs is important: it directly corresponds to the number of entries in the memotable.

We assume that all hypergraphs used as input for our algorithms are connected. This way, we can make sure that no cross products are needed. However, when dealing with hypergraphs, this condition can easily be assured by adding according hyperedges: for every pair of connected components, we can add a hyperedge whose hypernodes contain exactly the relations of the connected components. By considering these hyperedges as ⋈ operators with selectivity 1, we get an equivalent connected hypergraph, i.e., one that describes the same query.

We now specify what we mean by a path between vertices x and y in $H = (V, E)$.

Definition 3.2.5. *Let $H = (V, E)$ be a hypergraph, then a* path *$x \rightarrow^* y$ with length l between vertices $x \in V$ and $y \in V$ is defined as a sequence of hypernodes $\langle v_0, v_1, v_2, ..., v_l \rangle$ with $x \in v_0 \land y \in v_l$ and $\forall_{0 \leq i \leq l} v_i \subset V$ and $(v_{i-1}, v_i) \in E$ for $i = 1, 2, ...l$. The length l of the path is the number of hyperedges $(v_0, v_1), (v_1, v_2), ..., (v_{l-1}, v_l)$ in the path.*

With the definition of a path, we are able to give the notion of a *cycle*.

Definition 3.2.6. *Let $H = (V, E)$ be an undirected graph, then a* cycle *is a path $\langle v_0, v_1, v_2, ..., v_l \rangle$ with $\forall_{0 \leq i \leq l} v_i \subset V$ where $v_0 \cap v_l \neq \emptyset$ holds.*

We introduce the notion of an *articulation hyperedge* and give its definition:

Definition 3.2.7. *Let $H = (V, E)$ be a connected hypergraph. Then we call a hyperedge (v, w) an articulation hyperedge if removing (v, w) from E disconnects the graph H.*

The hypergraph shown in Figure 3.1 has only one articulation hyperedge: $(\{R_1\}, \{R_3\})$. We observe that an articulation hyperedge cannot be part of any cycle. Hence, we call a hypergraph whose complex hyperedges are all articulation hyperedges a complex cycle-free hypergraph. The hypergraph of Figure 3.1 is not a complex cycle-free graph since the complex hyperedge $(\{R_0\}, \{R_1, R_2\})$ is not an articulation hyperedge.

As has been previously mentioned, invalid operator reorderings can be prevented by transforming simple edges into hyperedges [2, 21, 20]. Complex hypergraphs that are the result of those transformations can be mainly categorized as complex cycle-free hypergraphs. We strongly believe that among all complex query graphs that can be found in real-world scenarios, the majority belongs to this category. The only common exception will be graphs that contain complex hyperedges originating from complex predicates.

For the purpose of completeness, we adopt Definition 2.1.23 and 2.1.24 for hypergraphs:

Definition 3.2.8. *Let $H = (V, E)$ be a connected hypergraph, (S_1, S_2) is a connected subgraph and its complement pair (or ccp for short) if the following holds:*

- *S_1 with $S_1 \subset V$ induces a connected graph $H_{|S_1}$,*
- *S_2 with $S_2 \subset V$ induces a connected graph $H_{|S_2}$,*
- *$S_1 \cap S_2 = \emptyset$, and*
- *$\exists (v, w) \in E \mid v \subseteq S_1 \wedge w \subseteq S_2$.*

The set of all possible *ccps* is denoted by $\mathcal{P}_{ccp}$. We introduce the notion of *ccp for a set* to specify all those pairs of input sets that result in the same output set, if joined.

Definition 3.2.9. *Let $H = (V, E)$ be a connected hypergraph and S a set with $S \subseteq V$ that induces a connected subgraph $H_{|S}$. For $S_1, S_2 \subset V$, (S_1, S_2) is called a ccp for S if (S_1, S_2) is a ccp and $S_1 \cup S_2 = S$ holds.*

By $\mathcal{P}_{ccp}(S)$, we denote the set of all *ccps* for S. Let $\mathcal{P}_{con}(V) = \{S \subseteq V \mid H_{|S} \text{ is connected} \wedge |S| > 1\}$ be the set of all connected subsets of V with more than one element, then $\mathcal{P}_{ccp} = \cup_{S \in \mathcal{P}_{con}(V)} \mathcal{P}_{ccp}(S)$ holds.

Note that if (S_1, S_2) is a ccp for S, then (S_2, S_1) is one as well. We call them symmetric pairs.

Next, we define a *compound vertex*:

Definition 3.2.10. *Let $H = (V, E)$ be a hypergraph. A compound vertex c represents a set of vertices $V' = \{v_0, v_1, ...v_n\}$, where $V' \subset V \wedge c \notin V$ holds.*

In practice, vertex sets are represented as bitvectors, i.e., by utilizing $uint32\_t$ or $uint64\_t$ types. Thereby two advantages can be combined: The vertex set representation becomes very space efficient, and set operations on the bitvector(s) can be computed in a few processor cycles only. Since a vertex is represented through a bit in the

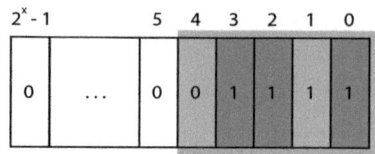

Figure 3.2.: A bitvector with 2^x bits where the first five bits are reserved for representing subsets of $V = \{v_0, v_1, v_2, v_3, v_4\}$. With the first four bits the vertex set $S = \{v_0, v_1, v_2, v_3\}$ is represented.

bitvector and the bitvector is limited by the word size, the question arises how to represent a compound vertex within the same bitvector. Therefore, take a look at Figure 3.2, where a bitvector with 2^x bits is shown. We use the first five bits with a light gray background to represent arbitrary subsets of the vertex set $V = \{v_0, v_1, v_2, v_3, v_4\}$. Let us assume we want to represent a vertex set $S = \{v_0, v_1, v_2, v_3\}$. Then the first four of the five bits are set. The fifth bit is reserved, but not set. Further, assume we want to introduce a compound vertex c that represents the vertices $\{v_0, v_2, v_3\}$. We indicated this in Figure 3.2 by the bits with the dark gray background, i.e., the first bit (index 0), the third (index 2) and fourth bit (index 3). Thus, we can unset the first, the third and the fourth bit. But in exchange, we have to encode the presence of the compound vertex c by a bit. Hence, we have two possibilities: Either we assign a new and additional index, e.g. index 5 since $c \notin V$ holds, or we reuse an index, e.g. index 0, 2 or 3. Therefore, we differentiate between two kinds of compound vertices which we call: *index-introducing compound vertices* and *index-reusing compound vertices*.

3.2.2. Graphs vs. Hypergraphs

We need the next definitions in order to explain some principle ideas of our generic framework. We start by defining an embedding g that maps a graph $G = (V_G, E_G)$ to a hypergraph $H = (V_H, E_H)$.

Definition 3.2.11. *Let $\mathbb{G}$ be the set of all graphs and $\mathbb{H}$ the set of all hypergraphs. Further, let $\mathbb{E}_\mathbb{G}$ be the set of all graph edges and $\mathbb{E}_\mathbb{H}$ the set of all hyperedges. We define $g : \mathbb{G} \to \mathbb{H}$ as an embedding that maps an undirected graph $G = (V, E_G)$ to an undirected hypergraph $H = (V, E_H)$, where $g(G(V, E_G)) = H(V, g_e(E_G))$ holds. Thereby g_e with $g_e : \mathbb{E}_\mathbb{G} \to \mathbb{E}_\mathbb{H}$ that maps a set of graph edges E_G to a set of hyperedges E_H is defined such that $g_e(E_G) = \{(\{u\}, \{v\}) \mid (u, v) \in E_G\}$ holds.*

Next, we define the reverse mapping g^{-1}:

Definition 3.2.12. *Let $\mathbb{G}$ be the set of all graphs and $\mathbb{H}$ the set of all hypergraphs. Further, let $\mathbb{E}_\mathbb{G}$ be the set of all graph edges and $\mathbb{E}_\mathbb{H}$ the set of all hyperedges. We define $g^{-1} : \mathbb{H} \to \mathbb{G}$ as a mapping with $g : \mathbb{H} \to \mathbb{G}$ that maps an undirected hypergraph $H = (V, E_H)$ to an undirected graph $G = (V, E_G)$, where $g^{-1}(H(V, E_H)) = G(V, g_e^{-1}(E_H))$ holds. We define g_e^{-1} with $g_e^{-1} : \mathbb{E}_\mathbb{H} \to \mathbb{E}_\mathbb{G}$ that maps a set of simple hyperedges E_H to a set of graph edges E_G such that $g_e(E_H) = \{(u, v) \mid (\{u\}, \{v\}) \in E_H\}$ holds.*

We give the notion of *restrictedness* for hypergraphs:

Definition 3.2.13. *Let* $H_i = (V, E_i)$ *and* $H_j = (V, E_j)$ *be two undirected connected hypergraphs. Further, let* P^i_{ccp} *be the set of ccps computed for* H_i *and* P^j_{ccp} *the set of ccps computed for* H_j. *We say that* H_i *is* less restrictive *than* H_j *if* $P^i_{ccp} \supset P^j_{ccp}$ *holds, and* more restrictive *if* $P^i_{ccp} \subset P^j_{ccp}$ *holds.*

3.2.3. Neighborhood

The main idea for generating *ccp*s efficiently is to incrementally expand connected subgraphs by considering new nodes in the *neighborhood* of a subgraph.

We start with the definition of a *simple neighborhood* that relies only on simple edges and returns one set of vertices.

Definition 3.2.14. *Let* $H = (V, E)$ *be a connected hypergraph and* C *be a subset of* V. *Then, the* simple neighborhood *of* $C \subseteq V$ *is defined as:*

$$\mathcal{N}_{simple}(C) = \{x \mid x \in v \wedge (u,v) \in E \wedge u \subset C \wedge \\ v \subset (V \setminus C) \wedge |u| = 1 \wedge |v| = 1\}.$$

We now give the definition of *neighborhood* for all edges, including complex hyperedges. We further restrict the neighborhood by some set of X of forbidden nodes. As we will see, this is necessary in order to avoid the generation of *ccp*s more than once.

Definition 3.2.15. *Let* $H = (V, E)$ *be a connected hypergraph, S a set of nodes* $(S \subseteq V)$ *such that* $H_{|S}$ *is connected, and* $X \subseteq V$ *a set of excluded nodes. Then, the* neighborhood *of* $C \subset S$ *excluding* X *is defined as:*

$$\mathcal{N}(S, C, X) = \{v \mid (u,v) \in E \wedge u \subseteq C \wedge v \subseteq S \setminus C \wedge \\ v \cap X = \emptyset\}.$$

For our approach, we need the notion of *minimal neighborhood*, where all subsumed hypernodes $v \in \mathcal{N}(S, C, X)$ are eliminated. Again, this is necessary to avoid duplicate generation of *ccp*s.

Definition 3.2.16. *Let* $S \subseteq V$, $C \subseteq V$, $X \subseteq V$ *be sets of nodes with* $C \subset S$ *and* $H_{|S}$ *connected. Then, we define the* minimal neighborhood *of* $C \subset S$ *excluding* X *as:*

$$\mathcal{N}\downarrow(S, C, X) = \{v \mid v \in N(S, C, X) \wedge \\ \nexists u \in N(S, C, X) : u \subset v\}.$$

Thus, the minimal neighborhood only retains those hypernodes which are not proper supersets of others.

Let us exemplify Definitions 3.2.14, 3.2.15 and 3.2.16 by the hypergraph of Figure 3.1: $\mathcal{N}_{simple}(\{R_0\}) = \{R_4\}$, $\mathcal{N}_{simple}(\{R_0, R_4\}) = \{R_2, R_3\}$, $\mathcal{N}(V, \{R_0, R_4\}, \emptyset) = \{\{R_1, R_2\}, \{R_2\}, \{R_3\}\}$, $\mathcal{N}\downarrow(V, \{R_0, R_4\}, \emptyset) = \{\{R_2\}, \{R_3\}\}$ and $\mathcal{N}\downarrow(V, \{R_0\}, \emptyset) = \{\{R_1, R_2\}, \{R_4\}\}$.

3.3. Basic Memoization for Hypergraphs

The basic variant of top-down join enumeration through memoization for inner-join operations and simple join predicates has been discussed in Section 2.2. We adapt it here for the use of complex predicates with inner and non-inner join operations [10, 20]. Thereby, TDBASICHYP is an instantiation of the generic top-down join enumeration algorithm TDPLANGENHYP with the naive generate-and-test strategy PARTITION$_{naiveHyp}$.

In Section 3.3.1, we explain the generic top-down join enumeration algorithm TDPLANGENHYP. Section 3.3.2 describes PARTITION$_{naiveHyp}$ and Section 3.3.3 a suitable test for the connectedness of hypergraphs or node-induced subgraphs.

3.3.1. Generic Top-Down Join Enumeration for Hypergraphs

Our generic top-down join enumeration algorithm TDPLANGENHYP is based on memoization [5]. We present its pseudocode in Figure 3.3. As input, TDPLANGENHYP takes a hypergraph H and a set of (join) operators O. Both inputs are derived from some SQL query. For more information on how a query is transformed into a set of operators O and a hypergraph, we refer to [20].

Like dynamic programming, TDPLANGENHYP first initializes the building blocks for single relations and adds them to the lookup table *BestTree*. It then calls the recursive routine TDPGHYPSUB in Line 3 of TDPLANGENHYP for the whole set V of nodes. TDPGHYPSUB checks for the presence of an already derived best plan for any input set of nodes S. If such a plan does not exist, TDPGHYPSUB iterates over all ccps (S_1, S_2) for S (Line 2). If an operator is applicable [20] (Line 4), the subroutine BUILDTREE is invoked. The applicability test (Line 4) includes L-TES $\subseteq S_1 \wedge$ R-TES $\subseteq S_2$ and ensures correctness of the generated plan [20].

Whereas Line 2 declaratively specifies the set of ccps for S to be considered, any real implementation must provide a procedure to generate them explicitly. This is the task of a partitioning algorithm and the only exchangeable part of our generic algorithm TDPLANGENHYP. In Section 3.3.2, we will describe with PARTITION$_{naiveHyp}$ a naive method for computing $P_{ccp}(S)$.

Remember that for TDPLANGEN as described in Section 2.2.1, we only considered symmetric pairs once and, therefore, had to compute $P_{ccp}^{sym}(S)$ only where $|P_{ccp}^{sym}(S)| * 2 = |P_{ccp}(S)|$ holds. This was possible since we only considered inner joins and thus did not rely on an applicability test. But for the conflict detection approach of [20] to work properly, we have to make sure that all ccps for S are considered in Line 4. This is because at least one ccp of each symmetric pair, i.e. either (S_1, S_2) or (S_2, S_1), will fail the applicability test APPLICABLE for the matching o. Hence, we still have to handle commutativity explicitly within BUILDTREE.

The pseudocode of BUILDTREE is given in Figure 3.4. It is used to compare the cost of the join trees that belong to the same $H_{|S}$. The basic functionality is already described in Section 2.2.1. New, however, is the handling of commutativity. Therefore, the (join) operator o is passed to BUILDTREE. Only if o has the commutative property [20], commutativity can be applied (Lines 5 to 7). Interesting orders should be handled as proposed in [25, 23].

TDPLANGENHYP(H, O)
  ▷ **Input:** connected $H = (V, E)$, O set of operators ∘
  ▷ **Output:** an optimal join tree for H
1 **for** $i \leftarrow 1$ **to** $|V|$
2      $BestTree[\{R_i\}] \leftarrow R_i$
3 **return** TDPGHYPSUB(H)

TDPGHYPSUB($H_{|S}, O$)
  ▷ **Input:** connected $H_{|S}$, O set of operators ∘
  ▷ **Output:** an optimal join tree for $H_{|S}$
1 **if** $BestTree[S] = $ NULL
2   **for all** $(S_1, S_2) \in P_{ccp}(S)$
3   **for** ∘ $\in O$
4   **if** APPLICABLE(∘,S_1,S_2)
5   BUILDTREE(∘, S, TDPGHYPSUB(S_1), TDPGHYPSUB(S_2))
6 **return** $BestTree[S]$

Figure 3.3.: Pseudocode for TDPLANGENHYP

BUILDTREE(∘, $S, Tree_1, Tree_2$)
  ▷ **Input:** (join) operator ∘, vertex set S, two optimal join trees
1 $CurrentTree \leftarrow$ CREATETREE($Tree_1, Tree_2$)
2 **if** $BestTree[S] = $ NULL $\lor$
      $cost(BestTree[S]) > cost(CurrentTree)$
3      $BestTree[S] \leftarrow CurrentTree$
4 **if** ∘ is commutative
5      $CurrentTree \leftarrow$ CREATETREE($Tree_2, Tree_1$)
6   **if** $cost(BestTree[S]) > cost(CurrentTree)$
7          $BestTree[S] \leftarrow CurrentTree$

Figure 3.4.: Pseudocode for BUILDTREE

3.3.2. Naive Partitioning of Hypergraphs

As we have seen, the generic top-down enumeration algorithm iterates over the elements of $P_{ccp}(S)$. One way of computing the *ccp*s for S is adopting the naive generate-and-test strategy PARTITION$_{naive}$, as presented in Section 2.2.2. We call the resulting naive partitioning algorithm PARTITION$_{naiveHyp}$ and give its pseudocode in Figure 3.5. In Line 1, all $2^{|S|} - 2$ possible non-empty and proper subsets of S are enumerated. Three conditions have to be met so that a partition $(C, S \setminus C)$ is a *ccp*. We check the connectivity of $H_{|C}$ and $H_{|S \setminus C}$ in Line 2. We give a test for connectedness in Section 3.3.3. The third condition that C needs to be connected to $S \setminus C$ is ensured implicitly by the requirement that the (sub) graph handed over as input is connected.

3.3.3. Test for Connectedness of Hypergraphs

Whereas the test for connectedness for query graphs with simple edges as described in Section 2.2.2 is cheap ($O(|V|)$) and straightforward to implement, the test for con-

PARTITION$_{naiveHyp}(H_{|S})$
   ▷ **Input:** a connected (sub) graph $H_{|S}$
   ▷ **Output:** $P_{ccp}(S)$
1 **for all** $C \subset S \wedge C \neq \emptyset$
2   **if** ISCONNECTEDHYP($H_{|C}$) ∧ ISCONNECTEDHYP($H_{|S \setminus C}$)
3   emit($C, S \setminus C$)

Figure 3.5.: Pseudocode for naive partitioning for hypergraphs

nectedness of complex hypergraphs is more expensive ($O(|V|*|E|)$) and more delicate. Therefore, we explain it here in length. We give the pseudocode with ISCONNECTEDHYP in a modularized fashion (Figures 3.6, 3.7 and 3.8). This enables us to reuse some parts later on.

The basic idea of ISCONNECTEDHYP is to start with a set of single disjoint vertex sets $O_i \subset C$ with $|O_i| = 1$. Since each vertex set contains only one vertex at a time, each vertex set O_i itself must be connected. Then, these sets are merged by finding connecting hyperedges. Consider a hyperedge (u,v) and two disjoint vertex sets O_i, O_j. If $u \subseteq O_i \wedge v \subseteq O_j$ holds, then the two vertex sets O_i, O_j are connected. We have to iterate over the set of hyperedges several times until only a single vertex set is left. Otherwise, we fail to merge some vertex sets O_i, O_j. If there is only a single vertex set left at the end, the (sub) hypergraph must be connected.

For performance reasons, our approach works in two steps. The first step merges vertex sets O_i, O_j by considering simple edges only. We do so by calling GETSIMPLECOMPONENTS in Line 1 of ISCONNECTEDHYP. GETSIMPLECOMPONENTS chooses an arbitrary vertex in Line 4 to start with and assigns it to L', which then gets enlarged by adding adjacent singleton vertex sets within the loop in Lines 5 to 8. Note that instead of iterating over all simple edges, we exploit the precomputed simple neighborhood $\mathcal{N}_{simple}$ (Def. 3.2.14), which is much more efficient (Line 8). If the vertex set L' cannot be enlarged further (Line 5), we choose another new vertex $i \in I$ (Line 4) as the new L'. The newness is ensured in Line 9. The loop starts over with the new L'. We return from the call to ISCONNECTEDHYP with a set O_{set} of merged vertex sets O_i once we have considered all single vertex sets $i \in I$ that have not been previously merged.

In Line 3 of ISCONNECTEDHYP, we implemented an early exit that only checks if O_{set} contains only one vertex set O_i. If so, it is obvious that all vertices in C must be connected. Otherwise, we have to consider the complex hyperedges in order to determine if all $O_j \in O_{set}$ could be merged to one O_i. This is done by calling MERGECOMPONENTS in Line 7 of ISCONNECTEDHYP as the second step of our approach. MERGECOMPONENTS maintains two sets of vertex sets: O_{set} and O'_{set}. O'_{set} was initialized with an arbitrary element $T \in O_{set}$ (Lines 4, 6 of ISCONNECTEDHYP) which was deleted from O_{set} (Line 5 of ISCONNECTEDHYP) before the call. Now, MERGECOMPONENTS considers one vertex set $O_i \in O_{set}$ at a time (Line 1) and tries to merge it with some vertex sets O_j (Line 7) already added to O'_{set}. Therefore, we need to consider hyperedges that can connect O_i with O_j. Instead of iterating over the list of complex hyperedges, we make use of the neighborhood $\mathcal{N}$ (Def. 3.2.15) in Line 6. If two candidates O_i, O_j can be merged, we have to make sure that the now combined vertex set T cannot be further enlarged with other elements of O'_{set}. This is

ISCONNECTEDHYP($H_{|C}$)
> ▷ **Input:** a node induced subgraph $H_{|C}$
> ▷ **Output:** TRUE if $H_{|C}$ is connected, FALSE otherwise

1. $O_{set} \leftarrow$ GETSIMPLECOMPONENTS($H_{|C}, C, \emptyset$)
2.   **if** $|O_{set}| \leq 1$
3.   **return** TRUE
4. $T \leftarrow O_i \in O_{set}$
5. $O_{set} \leftarrow O_{set} \setminus \{T\}$
6. $O'_{set} \leftarrow \{T\}$
7. $O'_{set} \leftarrow$ MERGECOMPONENTS($H_{|C}, \emptyset, O_{set}, O'_{set}$)
8.   **return** $|O'_{set}| \leq 1$

Figure 3.6.: Pseudocode for ISCONNECTEDHYP

GETSIMPLECOMPONENTS($H_{|S}, I, X$)
> ▷ **Input:** $I \cup X = S, X \cap I = \emptyset$
> ▷ **Output:** O_{set} a set<connected sets>
> $\forall_{O_i, O_j \in O_{set}} O_i, O_j \subseteq I \wedge O_i \cap O_j = \emptyset$

1. $O_{set} \leftarrow \emptyset$
2.   **while** $I \neq \emptyset$
3. $L \leftarrow \emptyset$
4. $L' \leftarrow i \in I$
5.   **while** $L \neq L'$
6. $D \leftarrow L' \setminus L$
7. $L \leftarrow L'$
8. $L' \leftarrow L' \cup ((\mathcal{N}_{simple}(D) \cap S) \setminus X)$
9. $I \leftarrow I \setminus L'$
10. $O_{set} \leftarrow O_{set} \cup \{L'\}$
11.   **return** O_{set}

Figure 3.7.: Pseudocode for GETSIMPLECOMPONENTS

necessary because for the combined set T, other hyperedges might qualify where one of their two hypernodes can contain nodes from O_i and O_j at the same time. Therefore, the loop of Line 4 is put in place. When T cannot be enlarged any further, we add it to O'_{set} in Line 11. Note that all vertex sets O_j used for the enlargement of T have been deleted from O'_{set} before (Line 9). Once all O_i of O_{set} have been considered, we know that no element O_j of O'_{set} can be merged with any other $O_k \in O'_{set}$.

When the call is returned, we check how many elements are contained in O'_{set}. We know that C can only be connected if O'_{set} has just one element. Since we define an empty set to be connected as well, we check for $|O'_{set}| \leq 1$ and return the result of this test (Line 8).

3.4. Conservative Partitioning for Hypergraphs

In Section 2.4 and 2.5 MINCUTBRANCH [8, 9] and MINCUTCONSERVATIVE [12] have been presented. Both partitioning algorithms are very efficient, but do not accept hypergraphs as input. PARTITION$_{naiveHyp}$, on the other hand, can handle hypergraphs,

```
MERGECOMPONENTS(H_S, X, O_set, O'_set)
    ▷ Input: S ∩ X = ∅, O_set, O'_set sets<connected sets>
    ▷ Output: O'_set a set<connected sets>
    ∀_{O_i,O_j ∈ O'_set} O_i, O_j ⊆ (S \ X) ∧ O_i ∩ O_j = ∅
 1  for all O_i ∈ O_set
 2      T ← O_i
 3      t ← 0
 4      while t ≠ |T|
 5          t ← |T|
 6          N_set ← N(S, T, X)
 7          for all O_j ∈ O'_set
 8              if ∃v ∈ N_set : v ⊆ O_j
 9                  O'_set ← O'_set \ {O_j}
10                  T ← T ∪ O_j
11      O'_set ← O'_set ∪ {T}
12  return O'_set
```

Figure 3.8.: Pseudocode for MERGECOMPONENTS

but is too expensive to execute and, thus, should not be used in practice, as Section 3.6 will show.

In this section, we present with MINCUTCONSERVATIVEHYP [11] a partitioning algorithm that performs much better when enumerating all *ccp*s for a given S and a given hypergraph. The name was chosen because we adopted and extended a principle idea of MINCUTCONSERVATIVE. Since MINCUTCONSERVATIVEHYP is a partitioning algorithm, it can be used to instantiate the generic top-down join enumeration algorithm (Section 3.3.1). We denote the instantiated top-down memoization variant by TDMCCHYP (short for TDMINCUTCONSERVATIVEHYP). The pseudocode for MINCUTCONSERVATIVEHYP is given in Figure 3.10.

3.4.1. Overview of MINCUTCONSERVATIVEHYP

Before we present the algorithm in detail, we explain its basic idea. The goal of a partitioning algorithm is to compute the set $P_{ccp}(S)$ for a connected vertex set S. As we will show in Section 3.6, the generate-and-test approach of TDBASICHYP is not practical at all, because the majority of generated partitions is rejected by either one of the tests for connectedness in Line 2 of PARTITION$_{naiveHyp}$. In certain scenarios (e.g., chain queries), this adds an exponential overhead for each emitted *ccp*. Clearly, this has to be avoided.

Let C be a set of vertices. For the time being, assume that C is initialized with an arbitrary single vertex $t \in S$. The general idea of MINCUTCONSERVATIVEHYP is to recursively enlarge a connected set C of vertices by adding members of its neighborhood $\mathcal{N}$. If at some point during the enlargement of C its complement $S \setminus C$ in S is connected as well, the algorithm has found a *ccp* for S. We ensure that at (almost) every instance of the algorithm's execution C is connected. Sometimes there are exceptions, and their handling is described below.

Besides, the connectedness of C's complement $S \setminus C$ MINCUTCONSERVATIVEHYP has to meet some more constraints before emitting a *ccp*: (1) Only one of two symmetric *ccps* is computed, (2) the emission of duplicates has to be avoided, and (3) all *ccps* for S have to be computed as long as they comply with constraint (1).

We demand constraint (1) purely out of performance reasons. This is if a *ccp* is found and emitted, we can emit its symmetric counterpart right away and do not need to bother to compute it later on. We can easily ensure constraint (1) because the start vertex t – arbitrarily chosen as the initial neighborhood – is always contained in C and, therefore, can never be part of its complement. For the second constraint, the algorithm uses a filter set X of neighbors to exclude from processing. After every recursive self-invocation of the algorithm, the adjacent hypernode v that was used to enlarge C is added to X. The presence of cycles in the hypergraph that involve complex hyperedges requires some additional precautions. Therefore, we introduce X_{map}, which is a mapping between vertices and vertex sets, and helps us to prevent duplicates. Later, we will see in detail how this ties in. For constraint (3), it is sufficient to ensure that all possible connected subsets of S that contain the start vertex t are considered when enlarging C.

There are certain scenarios, e.g., when simple hypergraphs like star queries are considered, where constructing every possible connected subset C of S produces an exponential overhead. This is because most of the produced complements $S \setminus C$ are not connected and the partitions $(C, S \setminus C)$ computed this way are not valid *ccps*. Therefore, the algorithm follows a *conservative* approach by enhancing C in such a way that the complement must be connected as well.

To explain this approach, we have to make some observations. From the recursive process of enlarging C, we know that the number of members in C must increase by at least one in every iteration. Furthermore, if a partition $(C, S \setminus C)$ is not a *ccp* for S, then $S \setminus C$ consists of $k \geq 2$ connected subsets $O_1, O_2, ..., O_k \subset (S \setminus C)$ that are disjoint and not connected to each other. Hence, those subsets $O_1, O_2, ...O_k$ can only be adjacent to C. Let $v_1, v_2, ..., v_l$ be hypernodes that are all the members of C's neighborhood $\mathcal{N}(S, C, \emptyset)$. Then every O_i with $1 \leq i \leq k$ must contain at least one such v_y where $1 \leq y \leq l$ and $k \leq l$ holds. The first *ccp* after recursively enlarging C by members of $S \setminus C$ would be generated when all subsets O_i with $1 \leq i \leq k$ but one are joined to C. Hence, in order to ensure that at every recursive iteration of MINCUTCONSERVATIVEHYP the complement $S \setminus C$ is connected as well, it does not always suffice to enlarge C by only one of its adjacent hypernodes, but by a larger subset $\cup_{O_j}$ of its direct and indirect neighborhood. Section 3.4.4 will explain how the subsets $O_1, O_2, ...O_k$ are computed with GETCONNECTEDCOMPONENTS.

Let C be a connected set of vertices and (u, v) a complex hyperedge with $|v| > 1 \wedge u \subseteq C$. Then, if C is enlarged by v to $C' := C \cup v$, the new C' is not necessarily connected. For an example, we refer to Figure 3.1. If C is set to $\{R_0\}$ and $v = \{R_1, R_2\}$, the new $C' = \{R_0, R_1, R_2\}$ is not connected any more. Hence, we have to check every time whether C' is connected. DPHYP deals with this problem by exploiting its bottom-up processing nature (see ENUMERATECMPREC in [21]): C' is connected if and only if there exists an entry for C' in the dynamic programming table ($BestTree[C']$). We cannot rely on such a trick because TDMINCUTCONSERVATIVEHYP works top-down. Moreover, it is not sufficient to precompute the connectedness of certain subsets of V, e.g. all complex complex hypernodes of V. In fact, we would have to consider all $2^{|V|} - 2$ possible subsets of V or at least all connected non-empty subsets of V. Therefore, we have chosen a different approach.

We introduce a set of vertex sets C_{set}. C_{set} keeps track of the connected components (maximally enlarged subsets) of C that are not connected to each other. To check if C is connected, we only have to ensure that C_{set} contains just one vertex set (which would be equal to C). Since the majority of the hypernodes of all hyperedges will be connected, maintaing C_{set} will be cheap. In the worst case, it is in $O(|C_{set}|^2)$, which is still cheaper than a call to ISCONNECTED ($O(|C|^2)$). MAINTAINCSET takes care of this task and is explained in Section 3.4.5.

3.4.2. The Algorithm in Detail

Now we take a closer look at the pseudocode of MINCUTCONSERVATIVEHYP in Figure 3.10. PARTITION$_{MinCutConservativeHyp}$ invokes MINCUTCONSERVATIVEHYP with $C = X = F = \emptyset$. C_{set} as well as X_{map} are also empty. With the exception of F, the intention behind every parameter of MINCUTCONSERVATIVEHYP has already been explained. F is used as an optimization technique in form of a filter set to speed up duplicate avoidance and is discussed in Section 3.4.3.

Remember that S is the set for which we want to create ccps $(C, S \setminus C)$. MINCUTCONSERVATIVEHYP recursively enlarges C until the stop criterium with $|C| = |S| - 1$ (Line 3) is met. C is enlarged by hypernodes that are members of its minimal neighborhood (Definition 3.2.16, Line 8). To avoid duplicate ccps, vertices that have been added to C in previous invocations are excluded here and in further child invocations. In the root invocation, C is set to be empty, which means that its minimal neighborhood would be empty as well. To deal with the initial empty C, we redefine the minimal neighborhood of the empty set to be the singleton set containing solely an arbitrary start vertex $t \in S$.

The loop in Lines 8 to 20 iterates over all adjacent hypernodes v, where $v \in \mathcal{N} \downarrow (S, C, X) \wedge C \cup v \neq S$ holds. The condition $C \cup v \neq S$ ensures that the new C for the next child invocation is not equal to S, which would not give rise to any more ccps.

As has been discussed, we need to take special care of how we enlarge C such that the complement $S \setminus (C \cup v)$ is connected as well. Therefore, we have to determine if $S \setminus (C \cup v)$ consists of subsets $O_1, O_2, ... O_k$ that are disjoint and not interconnected to each other. Thus, we calculate $O := O_1, O_2, ... O_k$ by a call to GETCONNECTEDCOMPONENTS (explained in Section 3.4.4). Following from the discussion in Section 3.4.1, the next ccp is only emitted when all but one subset O_i with $1 \leq i \leq k$ are merged with the current C. As a consequence, we compute the next C simply by assigning O_i's complement in S to C' (Line 11). All different O_i are then considered by processing the loop consisting of Lines 10 to 15.

Referring to Section 3.4.1, a merge of an adjacent hypernode with C might not result in a connected C' anymore. This still might be true if even all but one of the connected subsets $O_1, O_2, ... O_k$ are merged with C', i.e. $C' = S \setminus O_i$. We exemplify this fact with the complex hypergraph of Figure 3.9. Therefore, assume that the initial C is set to $\{R_0\}$. The next step enlarges the initial C with $v = \{R_1, R_3\}$. Then, the connected components of the complement $S \setminus (C \cup v) = \{R_2, R_4\}$ are computed by invoking GETCONNECTEDCOMPONENTS. Since R_2 is not connected to R_4 two components are returned by GETCONNECTEDCOMPONENTS. For the first connected component R_2, the new C' is computed as $\{R_0, R_1, R_3, R_4\}$. But the new C' is not connected.

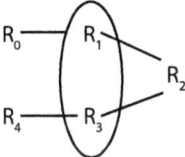

Figure 3.9.: Hypergraph with five relation and a disconnected hypernode.

Therefore, MAINTAINCSET (explained in Section 3.4.5) manages the set of connected subsets of C by adding and merging $C' \setminus C$ with the elements of C_{set}. In Line 15, MINCUTCONSERVATIVEHYP invokes itself. Before the next child invocation emits a partition $(C, S \setminus C)$, the condition of Line 1 is checked. Here, we ensure that C is connected by checking the cardinality of C_{set}. Furthermore, we ensure that $S \setminus C$ is not empty.

The next section explains our duplicate avoidance technique.

3.4.3. Avoiding Duplicates

In the following, we present two alternative approaches: Our first approach is more efficient, but produces false negatives. Our second approach produces no false negatives, but has higher processing costs.

Duplicate Avoidance with False Negatives

To prevent the emission of duplicate *ccps*, MINCUTCONSERVATIVEHYP distinguishes between two cases: the simple case and the complex case.

The first case occurs if solely a single vertex r is added to C, i.e., $|C'\setminus C| = 1$. In this case, we can apply the duplicate avoidance technique of MINCUTCONSERVATIVE [12] (Section 2.4), which we now briefly review. The new node r is added to the excluded set X' (Line 17). As a consequence, r cannot be chosen again from the neighborhood (Line 8) in any further child invocation. Additionally, we have to check that X' is disjoint with C' (Line 12). To see this, imagine a vertex set v with $|v| = 1$ was merged with X, and in a later iteration of the loop in Line 8, another vertex set u with $|u| = 1$ is chosen to be merged with C'. Assume that the call to GETCONNECTEDCOMPONENTS yields $O = \{O_1, O_2, ...O_k\}$. Then, u must be part of some O_i ($1 \leq i \leq k$). Now, if the previously chosen v is also part of O_i at some recursive call, then only *ccps* are emitted that have been emitted before. The check $X' \cap C' \neq \emptyset$ prevents this.

The second case is much more complex. We proceed in several steps. In step 1, let us observe that it is easy to generate duplicate *ccps*. Consider the hypergraph in Figure 3.11 with $S = \{R_0, R_1, R_2, R_3, R_4, R_5\}$. Let us forward to the point of the algorithm's execution where $C = \{R_0, R_1\}$ holds. To continue, we have to recursively enlarge C with its neighbors. Hence, we have to walk the cycle in the direction $C \to v \to w$, which generates $C, C \cup v, C \cup v \cup w$. The opposite direction gives us $C \cup w$, $C \cup w \cup v$. Thus, it is easy to generate duplicate connected components, and because $C \cup v \cup w$ would be generated twice, the corresponding *ccp* $(C \cup v \cup w, x)$ would be emitted twice.

PARTITION$_{MinCutConservativeHyp}(H_{|S})$
  ▷ **Input:** a connected (sub) hypergraph $H_{|S}$
  ▷ **Output:** all *ccp* for S
1 **for all** $r \in S$
2    $X_{map}[\{r\}] \leftarrow \emptyset$
3 MINCUTCONSERVATIVEHYP($H_{|S}, \emptyset, \emptyset, \emptyset, X_{map}, \emptyset$)

MINCUTCONSERVATIVEHYP($H_{|S}, C, C_{set}, X, X_{map}, F$)
  ▷ **Input:** connected set S, $C \cap X = \emptyset$, $F \subseteq C$
    C_{set} a set<connected sets>
    X_{map} a map<vertex, set of vertices>
  ▷ **Output:** *ccp*s for S
1 **if** $|C_{set}| = 1 \wedge C \neq S$
2   emit $(C, S \setminus C)$ and $(S \setminus C, C)$
3 **if** $|C| = |S| - 1$
4   **return**
5 $X' \leftarrow X$
6 $X'_{map} \leftarrow X_{map}$
7 $F' \leftarrow F$
  ▷ $\mathcal{N} \downarrow (S, \emptyset, \emptyset) = \{$arbitrary element of $t \in S\}$
8 **for all** $v \in \mathcal{N} \downarrow (S, C, X) : C \cup v \neq S$
9    $O \leftarrow$ GETCONNECTEDCOMPONENTS($H_{|S}, C \cup v$)
10   **for all** $O_i \in O$
11     $C' \leftarrow S \setminus O_i$
12   **if** $X' \cap C' \neq \emptyset \vee ((C' \setminus C) \cap F' \neq \emptyset \wedge \neg$CHECKXMAP$(C', F', X'_{map}))$
13   **continue**
14     $C'_{set} \leftarrow$ MAINTAINCSET($H_{|S}, C, C', C_{set}$)
15   MINCUTCONSERVATIVEHYP($H_{|S}, C', C'_{set}, X', X'_{map}, F'$)
16   **if** $|v| = 1$
17     $X' \leftarrow X' \cup v$
18   **else**
19     $F' \leftarrow F' \cup v$
20     $X'_{map} \leftarrow$ MAINTAINXMAP(v, X'_{map})

Figure 3.10.: Pseudocode for MINCUTCONSERVATIVEHYP

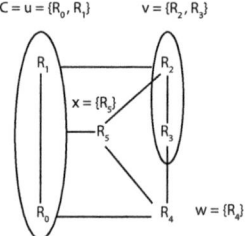

Figure 3.11.: Sample Hypergraph

In step 2, we convince ourselves that the duplicate avoidance technique of MIN-CUTCONSERVATIVE does not help here. Imagine we have to partition the hypergraph in Figure 3.11 with $S = \{R_0, R_1, R_2, R_3, R_4, R_5\}$. Then the minimal neighborhood

$\mathcal{N} \downarrow (S, C, X)$ with $C = \{R_0, R_1\}$ contains $v = \{R_2, R_3\}$. Once v is chosen in Line 8, v is added to C. Assume we apply the technique used in MINCUTCONSERVATIVE. Then we have to add all members of v to X'. Because of $R_3 \in v$, that would imply that we cannot generate $C \cup w \cup \{R_3\}$ with $w = \{R_4\}$ later on, which breaks our correctness constraint (3) (Section 3.4.1).

In step 3, we present our duplicate avoidance strategy. Therefore, we introduce X_{map} that represents a mapping between vertices and vertex sets. The mapping is managed by MAINTAINXMAP presented in Figure 3.12. Now, instead of adding all vertices of the hypernode v to X' (case 1), we alter X_{map}. We register for every member of v either (1) the whole hypernode $A = v$ (Line 3 of MAINTAINXMAP), or (2) merge v with an already registered vertex set (Line 5 of MAINTAINXMAP).

To check if we are allowed to add $\{R_3\}$ to C (Figure 3.11), we have to consult our X_{map}. This is done by a call to CHECKXMAP (Line 12 of MINCUTCONSERVATIVE-HYP). Figure 3.13 shows the pseudocode. CHECKXMAP checks for all vertices $r \in v$ that are added to C if their mapping $X_{map}[r]$ is (1) either empty or (2) does not overlap completely with the new C so that $X_{map}[r] \not\subseteq C$ holds (Line 2 of CHECKXMAP). Let us explain the intuition behind the latter by referring to our example scenario. When we enlarged $C = u$ with v, we set $X_{map}[R_2] = v$ and $X_{map}[R_3] = v$ after returning from the child invocation. In the next iteration of the loop (8 of MINCUTCONSERVATIVEHYP), we merge $C = u$ with w. If we now want to add R_3 to $C = u \cup w$, CHECKXMAP allows this because $X_{map}[R_3] = v$ and $v \setminus C \neq \emptyset$ holds. In general, any combination of vertices in v is allowed to be added to C, as long as not all elements of v are added to C. At that point where we try to add the last member r of v to C as well, $X_{map}[r]$ returns v, and since $v \subset C$ holds, CHECKXMAP returns FALSE. Since CHECKXMAP ensures that not all members of $X_{map}[r]$ are included into C', we have to pay attention during the maintenance of X_{map} in the case the value of a given entry $X_{map}[r]$ is already assigned with. Before we enlarge $X_{map}[r]$ (Line 5 of MAINTAINXMAP) we have to ensure that $X_{map}[r]$ does not already contain A (second part of the condition in Line 2). For those cases, we have to curtail $X_{map}[r]$ (Line 3) instead of enlarging it. Thus, we allow only for proper subsets of A (and not for the superset $X_{map}[r]$ of A) to be added to C in later recursions of MINCUTCONSERVATIVEHYP.

Iterating over all members of C in Line 1 of CHECKXMAP is relatively expensive. Therefore, we introduce a vertex filter set F. In Line 19 of MINCUTCONSERVATIVE-HYP, we add all elements of a hypernode v to F. It is easy to see that we only need to consider the vertices of C that are also element of F in Line 1 of CHECKXMAP. Furthermore, we can even avoid the whole effort of evaluating CHECKXMAP if all the vertices in $C' \setminus C$ with which C is going to be enlarged are disjoint to F (Line 12 of MINCUTCONSERVATIVEHYP). If we assume that the majority of complex hyperedges are introduced because of non-inner join conflict encodings, the majority of hypergraphs will not have any cycles involving a complex hyperedge and can be categorized as complex cycle-free hypergraphs. In those cases, $(C' \setminus C) \cap F' = \emptyset$ holds, and CHECKXMAP is never called.

As has been said, this approach produces false negatives. Hence, duplicate *ccps* might be emitted. But these cases are rare. Nevertheless, they result in a performance penalty because of two reasons: First, further unnecessary subcalls to MINCUTCONSERVATIVEHYP might be made, which can cause the emission of further false *ccps*.

MAINTAINXMAP(A, X_{map})
  ▷ **Input:** set A of vertices, X_{map} a map<vertex, set of vertices>
  ▷ **Output:** modified X_{map}
1 **for all** $r \in A$
2   **if** $X_{map}[r] = \emptyset \vee A \subseteq X_{map}[r]$
3        $X_{map}[r] \leftarrow A$
4   **else**
5        $X_{map}[r] \leftarrow X_{map}[r] \cup A$
6 **return** X_{map}

Figure 3.12.: Pseudocode for MAINTAINXMAP

CHECKXMAP(C, F, X_{map})
  ▷ **Input:** set C, F, X_{map} a map<vertex, set of vertices>
  ▷ **Output:** FALSE if duplicate *ccp*s have to be avoided
1 **for all** $r \in (C \cap F)$
2   **if** $X_{map}[r] \neq \emptyset$ and $X_{map}[r] \setminus C = \emptyset$
3   **return** FALSE
4 **return** TRUE

Figure 3.13.: Pseudocode for CHECKXMAP

And second, false *ccp*s increase the number of iterations of the loop in Lines 2 to 5 of TDPGHYPSUB. Which in turn results in two additional subcalls of TDPGHYP-SUB for every duplicate *ccp*. Note that those two invocations will return immediately because the condition of Line 1 of TDPGHYPSUB evaluates to FALSE. With the complex hypergraph of Figure 3.14 as input, we give an example where a duplicate *ccp* is produced through a false negative. Table 3.1 lists all input parameters for each invocation of MINCUTCONSERVATIVEHYP except for $H_{|S}$ and C_{set}. In this example, S will be set to $S = \{R_0, R_1, R_2, R_3, R_4, R_5\}$. The first column of Table 3.1 just serves as entry number for reference. Although C is a vertex set, we display the order of insertion instead of using a set notation (Column 3). For the given S, MINCUT-CONSERVATIVEHYP emits 19 *ccp*s (symmetric counter pairs not counted), including one duplicate *ccp*. Thereby $(\{R_0, R_1, R_2, R_5\}, \{R_3, R_4\})$ is emitted twice, right after Entry 10 and Entry 19. The call to $R_0 \to R_1 \to R_2 \to R_5$ should have been avoided (Entry 19). The problem here is that the X_{map} entries of R_2 and R_5 have each be enlarged by a second hypernode. $X_{map}[R_2]$ was enlarged by R_5 after the returned call of Entry 12 and $X_{map}[R_5]$ by R_4 after the returned call of Entry 15. Thus CHECKXMAP$(C = \{R_0, R_1, R_2, R_5\}, F = \{R_2, R_3, R_4, R_5\}, X_{map})$ produced a false negative and Entry 19 was not prevented.

Next, we present our duplicate avoidance technique that is free of false negatives.

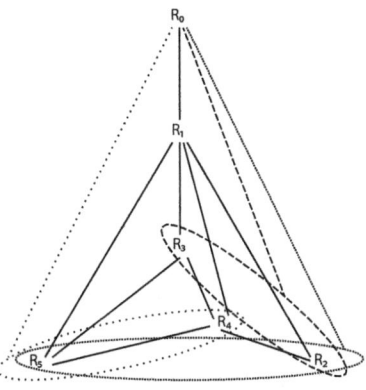

Figure 3.14.: Hypergraph $H(V, E) = (\{R_0, R_1, R_2, R_3, R_4\}, \{(\{R_0\}, \{R_1\}), (\{R_1\},$
$\{R_2\}), (\{R_1\}, \{R_3\}), (\{R_1\}, \{R_4\}), (\{R_1\}, \{R_5\}), (\{R_2\}, \{R_4\}),$
$(\{R_3\}, \{R_4\}), (\{R_3\}, \{R_5\}), (\{R_4\}, \{R_5\}), (\{R_0\}, \{R_2, R_3\}), (\{R_0\},$
$\{R_2, R_5\}), (\{R_0\}, \{R_4, R_5\})\})$

Duplicate Avoidance without False Negatives

As we have seen, the previous technique produces false negatives in some unlikely scenarios. Let us discuss a simple alternative. Therefore, we do not modify the technique as used in MINCUTCONSERVATIVE for the simple cases where $|v| = 1$ (Line 8 of MINCUTCONSERVATIVEHYP) holds. But we modify the handling of the complex cases with $|v| > 1$. Instead of maintaining a vertex set for every vertex to which we have referred as X_{map}, we introduce a set of hypernodes X_{set}. In case a v with $|v| > 1$ was processed (Line 8 of MINCUTCONSERVATIVEHYP) we simple add v to X_{set}. Now in order to detect duplicates and avoid unnecessary calls to MINCUTCONSERVATIVE-HYP, we check if $C' \cap X' = \emptyset$ holds. This is done as before and covers only the simple case. For the complex case, we iterate over all entries of $h \in X_{set}$ and ensure that $C' \cap h = \emptyset$ holds.

Unfortunately, this can become relatively expensive. Therefore, we refine our method. The intuition behind this is that we want to skip the iteration and subsequent checking of complex hypernodes that cannot cause duplicate *ccp*s anyway. We achieve this by adopting our idea of X_{map}. This time, X_{map} will contain sets of complex hypernodes. Now once a complex hypernode v is processed, we add v to $X_{map}[x]$, where $x \in v$ holds. We determine x by extracting the vertex with the smallest index in v. This is done by MAINTAINXMAP$_{NoFN}$, as given in Figure 3.15.

In order to decide if a call to MINCUTCONSERVATIVEHYP will produce duplicate *ccp*s and, hence, has to be avoided, we have to modify CHECKXMAP as well. We give the pseudocode for our modified version with CHECKXMAP$_{NoFN}$ in Figure 3.16. Since $X_{map}[r]$ now contains a set of complex hypernodes, we have to check each of them to ensure that none of them is contained in C (Line 3 of CHECKXMAP$_{NoFN}$).

As has been said, duplicate *ccp*s produced by the usage of MAINTAINXMAP and CHECKXMAP are rare. On the other hand, MAINTAINXMAP$_{NoFN}$ and CHECKXMAP $_{NoFN}$ are more expensive to execute. Therefore, we use MINCUTCONSERVATIVE-

	C	X	X_{map}	F
1	R_0	$\emptyset$	empty	$\emptyset$
2	$R_0 \to R_2, R_3$	$\emptyset$	empty	$\emptyset$
3	$R_0 \to R_2, R_3 \to R_1$	$\emptyset$	empty	$\emptyset$
4	$R_0 \to R_2, R_3 \to R_1 \to R_4$	$\emptyset$	empty	$\emptyset$
5	$R_0 \to R_2, R_3 \to R_1 \to R_5$	$\{R_4\}$	empty	$\emptyset$
6	$R_0 \to R_2, R_3 \to R_4$	$\{R_1\}$	empty	$\emptyset$
7	$R_0 \to R_2, R_3 \to R_4 \to R_5$	$\{R_1\}$	empty	$\emptyset$
8	$R_0 \to R_2, R_3 \to R_5$	$\{R_1, R_4\}$	empty	$\emptyset$
9	$R_0 \to R_2, R_5$	$\emptyset$	$R_2{:}\{R_2,R_3\}, R_3{:}\{R_2,R_3\}$	$\{R_2,R_3\}$
10	$R_0 \to R_2, R_5 \to R_1$	$\emptyset$	$R_2{:}\{R_2,R_3\}, R_3{:}\{R_2,R_3\}$	$\{R_2,R_3\}$
	emitting ($\{R_0, R_1, R_2, R_5\}, \{R_3, R_4\}$)			
11	$R_0 \to R_2, R_5 \to R_1 \to R_4$	$\{R_3\}$	$R_2{:}\{R_2,R_3\}, R_3{:}\{R_2,R_3\}$	$\{R_2,R_3\}$
12	$R_0 \to R_2, R_5 \to R_4$	$\{R_1, R_3\}$	$R_2{:}\{R_2,R_3\}, R_3{:}\{R_2,R_3\}$	$\{R_2,R_3\}$
13	$R_0 \to R_4, R_5$	$\emptyset$	$R_2{:}\{R_2,R_3,R_5\}, R_3{:}\{R_2,R_3\}, R_5{:}\{R_2,R_5\}$	$\{R_2,R_3,R_5\}$
14	$R_0 \to R_4, R_5 \to R_1, R_3$	$\emptyset$	$R_2{:}\{R_2,R_3,R_5\}, R_3{:}\{R_2,R_3\}, R_5{:}\{R_2,R_5\}$	$\{R_2,R_3,R_5\}$
15	$R_0 \to R_4, R_5 \to R_3$	$\{R_1, R_2\}$	$R_2{:}\{R_2,R_3,R_5\}, R_3{:}\{R_2,R_3\}, R_5{:}\{R_2,R_5\}$	$\{R_2,R_3,R_5\}$
16	$R_0 \to R_1$	$\emptyset$	$R_2{:}\{R_2,R_3,R_5\}, R_3{:}\{R_2,R_3\}, R_4{:}\{R_4,R_5\}, R_5{:}\{R_2,R_4,R_5\}$	$\{R_2,R_3,R_4,R_5\}$
17	$R_0 \to R_1 \to R_2$	$\emptyset$	$R_2{:}\{R_2,R_3,R_5\}, R_3{:}\{R_2,R_3\}, R_4{:}\{R_4,R_5\}, R_5{:}\{R_2,R_4,R_5\}$	$\{R_2,R_3,R_4,R_5\}$
18	$R_0 \to R_1 \to R_2 \to R_4$	$\{R_3\}$	$R_2{:}\{R_2,R_3,R_5\}, R_3{:}\{R_2,R_3\}, R_4{:}\{R_4,R_5\}, R_5{:}\{R_2,R_4,R_5\}$	$\{R_2,R_3,R_4,R_5\}$
19	$R_0 \to R_1 \to R_2 \to R_5$	$\{R_3, R_4\}$	$R_2{:}\{R_2,R_3,R_5\}, R_3{:}\{R_2,R_3\}, R_4{:}\{R_4,R_5\}, R_5{:}\{R_2,R_4,R_5\}$	$\{R_2,R_3,R_4,R_5\}$
	emitting ($\{R_0, R_1, R_2, R_5\}, \{R_3, R_4\}$)			
20	$R_0 \to R_1 \to R_3$	$\{R_2\}$	$R_2{:}\{R_2,R_3,R_5\}, R_3{:}\{R_2,R_3\}, R_4{:}\{R_4,R_5\}, R_5{:}\{R_2,R_4,R_5\}$	$\{R_2,R_3,R_4,R_5\}$
21	$R_0 \to R_1 \to R_3 \to R_5$	$\{R_2, R_4\}$	$R_2{:}\{R_2,R_3,R_5\}, R_3{:}\{R_2,R_3\}, R_4{:}\{R_4,R_5\}, R_5{:}\{R_2,R_4,R_5\}$	$\{R_2,R_3,R_4,R_5\}$
22	$R_0 \to R_1 \to R_5$	$\{R_2, R_3, R_4\}$	$R_2{:}\{R_2,R_3,R_5\}, R_3{:}\{R_2,R_3\}, R_4{:}\{R_4,R_5\}, R_5{:}\{R_2,R_4,R_5\}$	$\{R_2,R_3,R_4,R_5\}$

Table 3.1.: MINCUTCONSERVATIVEHYP emits a duplicate *ccp* with input of Figure 3.14 and $S = \{R_0, R_1, R_2, R_3, R_4, R_5\}$

HYP only with the former technique and presented the latter only for reasons of completeness.

3.4.4. GETCONNECTEDCOMPONENTS

The pseudocode for GETCONNECTEDCOMPONENTS is given in Figure 3.17. As has been said, GETCONNECTEDCOMPONENTS is designed to compute all disjoint, con-

MAINTAINXMAP$_{NoFN}(A, X_{map})$
    ▷ **Input:** set A of relations, X_{map} a map<vertex, set of complex hypernodes>
    ▷ **Output:** modified X_{map}
1    $i \leftarrow \text{MIN}_{index}(A)$
2    $v \leftarrow v_i \in A$
3    $X_{map}[v] \leftarrow X_{map}[v] \cup A$
4   **return** X_{map}

Figure 3.15.: Pseudocode for MAINTAINXMAP$_{NoFN}$

CHECKXMAP$_{NoFN}(C, F, X_{map})$
    ▷ **Input:** set C, F, X_{map} a map<vertex, set of complex hypernodes>
    ▷ **Output:** FALSE if duplicate *ccp*s have to be avoided
1   **for all** $r \in (C \cap F)$
2   **if** $X_{map}[r] \neq \emptyset$
3   **for all** $h \in X_{map}[r]$
4   **if** $h \setminus C = \emptyset$
5   **return** FALSE
6   **return** TRUE

Figure 3.16.: Pseudocode for CHECKXMAP$_{NoFN}$

nected but not interconnected subsets $O_1, O_2, ...O_k$ of C's complement in S. The main idea of GETCONNECTEDCOMPONENTS is similar to the one used in ISCONNECTEDHYP (Section 3.3.3). In Line 1, we call GETSIMPLECOMPONENTS (explained in Section 3.3.3) to compute all the subsets of $S \setminus C$ that induce disjoint connected hypergraphs consisting of simple edges only.

The result of that call is stored into O_{set}. Now, we only need to check whether the simple connected components can be merged further by considering complex hyperedges. This task is delegated to MERGECOMPONENTS (Section 3.3.3) in Line 5 of GETCONNECTEDCOMPONENTS. For more details, we refer to Section 3.3.3.

3.4.5. MAINTAINCSET

The purpose of MAINTAINCSET is to speed up the test for connectedness of C. The result of the test is needed in order to determine if a partition $(C, S \setminus C)$ is a valid *ccp* (Line 1 of MINCUTCONSERVATIVEHYP). The pseudocode is shown in Figure 3.18. As the name implies, MAINTAINCSET manages C_{set}, which contains all disjoint, connected but not interconnected subsets of C. If C_{set} contains only one vertex set, this means that C consists only of one connected subset and must therefore be connected. Besides the C_{set} also S, C and C' are handed over. The latter two input parameters are used to determine all vertices that were added to C. We assign the result to the vertex set I (Line 1).

GETCONNECTEDCOMPONENTS$(H_{|S}, C)$
    ▷ **Input:** $C \subset S$ a connected set
    ▷ **Output:** O'_{set} a set<connected sets>
    $\forall_{O_i, O_j \in O'_{set}} \; O_i, O_j \subseteq (S \setminus C) \wedge O_i \cap O_j = \emptyset$
1   $O_{set} \leftarrow$ GETSIMPLECOMPONENTS$(H_{|S}, S \setminus C, C)$
2   $T \leftarrow O_i \in O_{set}$
3   $O_{set} \leftarrow O_{set} \setminus \{T\}$
4   $O'_{set} \leftarrow \{T\}$
5   $O'_{set} \leftarrow$ MERGECOMPONENTS$(H_{|S}, C, O_{set}, O'_{set})$
6   **return** O'_{set}

Figure 3.17.: Pseudocode for GETCONNECTEDSETS

MAINTAINCSET$(H_{|S}, C, C', C_{set})$
    ▷ **Input:** set S of relations, $C' \subseteq S, C \subseteq C'$
              C_{set} a set<connected sets>
    ▷ **Output:** modified C_{set}
1   $I \leftarrow C' \setminus C$
2   $O_{set} \leftarrow$ GETSIMPLECOMPONENTS$(H_{|S}, I, S \setminus I)$
3   $C'_{set} \leftarrow$ MERGECOMPONENTS$(H_{|S}, S \setminus C', O_{set}, C_{set})$
4   **return** C_{set}

Figure 3.18.: Pseudocode for MAINTAINCSET

We utilize GETSIMPLECOMPONENTS (Line 2) to compute all the subsets of I that induce connected hypergraphs consisting only of simple edges. The computed subsets are stored in O_{set} and handed over to MERGECOMPONENTS (Line 3), which merges them with the components of C_{set}. For every subset of O_{set}, there are two possibilities. It can either be merged with one subset of C_{set}, or it combines two or more subsets of C_{set} by forming one unified vertex set. But one member of O_{set} will always be adjacent to at least one connected subset in C_{set}. There is only one exception that occurs when MAINTAINCSET is called from MINCUTCONSERVATIVEHYP's root invocation, then C_{set} will be empty and C'_{set} will be returned containing only $\{t\}$ (a vertex set with the start vertex t).

3.4.6. An Example

We illustrate the execution of MINCUTCONSERVATIVEHYP by an example. Table 3.2 shows the execution steps for the cyclic query given in Figure 3.1. The first column is the table entry number that serves as reference. The second column keeps track of the recursion level. The root invocation is indicated with a 0. Columns $3-6$ show the input parameters of MINCUTCONSERVATIVEHYP. S is set to $\{R_0, R_1, R_2, R_3, R_4\}$ and remains unchanged. The last column displays the result of the minimal neighborhood (Def. 3.2.16) $\mathcal{N} \downarrow (S, C, X)$. The start vertex t is set to R_0. Although C is a vertex set, we display the order of insertion instead of using a set notation (Column 3).

In this example, MINCUTCONSERVATIVE emits six *ccp*s. However, one partition is generated but not emitted because C is not connected at that point (entry no. 11). We have omitted the calls to MAINTAINCSET because its results are implicitly given as a parameter of the next child invocation. MAINTAINXMAP is called only once (entry no. 13). It registers for every member of the hypernode $\{R_1, R_2\}$ the hypernode itself. At the same time, F is enlarged with $\{R_1, R_2\}$. We can see that our filter technique is quite effective, since CHECKXMAP is called only once (entry no. 17). All the other times, $(C' \setminus C) \cap F' \neq \emptyset$ does not hold. There is only one time where the result of GETCONNECTEDCOMPONENTS contains more than one vertex set (entry no. 23). At this instance, v is assigned with $\{R_3\}$ and C is assigned with $\{R_0, R_4\}$. Instead of setting C' to $C \cup v$, it is set to $S \setminus O_i = S \setminus \{R_1\} = \{R_0, R_2, R_3, R_4\}$. Otherwise, the complement $S \setminus C' = \{R_1, R_2\}$ would not be connected during the next child invocation.

3.5. Generic Top-Down Join Enumeration for Hypergraphs

The techniques we used in Section 3.4 to construct MINCUTCONSERVATIVEHYP as a derivative of MINCUTCONSERVATIVE are very specific and cannot be applied to any other graph-partitioning algorithm in order to enable it to handle hypergraphs. Thus, we want to propose a more generic approach. This section describes a generic graph-partitioning framework to which we refer as PARTITION$_X$. It is an improvement of [10]. PARTITION$_X$ enables any existing graph-partitioning algorithm for top-down join enumeration to deal with hypergraphs. In particular, we use PARTITION$_X$ to enhance MINCUTBRANCH, which results in a novel partitioning algorithm that we call MINCUTBRANCHHYP. We call the instantiated top-down join enumeration variant TDMCBHYP. As we will see, the new approach is not only generic, but also more efficient in terms of performance and, thus, superior.

3.5.1. High-Level Overview

To explain our main ideas, let us make four important observations. These will highlight the problems we face and will indicate solutions.

First, assume that we have two simple connected hypergraphs $H_v = (v, E_v)$ and $H_w = (w, E_w)$ with $|v| > 1 \lor |w| > 1$. Now we want to connect both graphs with one edge. We discuss two possible solutions: (1) A connected complex hyperedge (v, w) covering the whole vertex sets v, w on both sides. We refer to the resulting complex hypergraph as $H_{complex}$. (2) Instead of (v, w) we introduce a simple edge $(\{x\}, \{y\})$, where $x \in v \land y \in w$ holds. We refer to this connected simple hypergraph as H_{simple}. According to Definition 3.2.13, $H_{complex}$ is more restrictive than H_{simple}, since partitioning the resulting set $V = v \cup w$ into all possible *ccp*s (Definition 3.2.8) leaves us with much fewer choices if a complex hyperedge ($|P^{ccp}(v \cup w)| = 2$) is introduced (1) instead of a simple edge (2). To exemplify this, consider the disconnected graph $H = (V = v \cup w, E = \{(\{R_0\}, \{R_1\})\})$ with $v = \{R_0, R_1\} \land w = \{R_2\}$. On the one hand, if we connect v and w by the complex hyperedge (v, w), then $P^{ccp}(v \cup w)$ has two *ccp*s: $(\{R_0, R_1\}, \{R_2\})$ and $(\{R_2\}, \{R_0, R_1\})$. On the other hand, if we

	L	C	C_{set}	X	X_{map}	F	$\mathcal{N}\downarrow$
1	0	$\emptyset$	$\emptyset$	$\emptyset$	empty	$\emptyset$	$\{\{t = R_0\}\}$
2	1	R_0	$\{\{R_0\}\}$	$\emptyset$	empty	$\emptyset$	$\{\{R_1, R_2\},\{R_4\}\}$
3	1	\multicolumn{6}{l	}{emitting $(\{R_0\},\{R_1,R_2,R_3,R_4\})$}
4	1	\multicolumn{6}{l	}{$v = \{R_1, R_2\} \rightarrow$ GETCONNECTEDCOMPONENTS$(S, \{R_0, R_1, R_2\}) \rightarrow \{\{R_3, R_4\}\}$}
5	2	$R_0 \rightarrow R_1, R_2$	$\{\{R_0\},\{R_1\},\{R_2\}\}$	$\emptyset$	empty	$\emptyset$	$\{\{R_3\},\{R_4\}\}$
6	2	\multicolumn{6}{l	}{$v = \{R_3\} \rightarrow$ GETCONNECTEDCOMPONENTS$(S, \{R_0, R_1, R_2, R_3\}) \rightarrow \{\{R_4\}\}$}
7	3	$R_0 \rightarrow R_1, R_2 \rightarrow R_3$	$\{\{R_0, R_1, R_2, R_3\}\}$	$\emptyset$	empty	$\emptyset$	$\{\{R_4\}\}$
8	3	\multicolumn{6}{l	}{emitting $(\{R_0, R_1, R_2, R_3\},\{R_4\})$}
9	2	\multicolumn{6}{l	}{$v = \{R_4\} \rightarrow$ GETCONNECTEDCOMPONENTS$(S, \{R_0, R_1, R_2, R_4\}) \rightarrow \{\{R_3\}\}$}
10	3	$R_0 \rightarrow R_1, R_2 \rightarrow R_4$	$\{\{R_0, R_2, R_4\},\{R_1\}\}$	$\{R_3\}$	empty	$\emptyset$	$\emptyset$
11	3	\multicolumn{6}{l	}{no emission of $(\{R_0, R_1, R_2, R_4\},\{R_3\})$ since $	C_{set}	> 1$}
12	1	\multicolumn{6}{l	}{$v = \{R_4\} \rightarrow$ GETCONNECTEDCOMPONENTS$(S, \{R_0, R_4\}) \rightarrow \{\{R_1, R_2, R_3\}\}$}
13	1	\multicolumn{6}{l	}{call to MAINTAINXMAP$(\{R_1, R_2\},$ empty$) \rightarrow R_1 : \{R_1, R_2\}, R_2 : \{R_1, R_2\}$}
14	2	$R_0 \rightarrow R_4$	$\{\{R_0, R_4\}\}$	$\emptyset$	$R_1:\{R_1,R_2\},\{R_1,R_2:\{R_1,R_2\}\, R_2\}$		$\{\{R_2\},\{R_3\}\}$
15	2	\multicolumn{6}{l	}{emitting $(\{R_0, R_4\},\{R_1, R_2, R_3\})$}
16	2	\multicolumn{6}{l	}{$v = \{R_2\} \rightarrow$ GETCONNECTEDCOMPONENTS$(S, \{R_0, R_2, R_4\}) \rightarrow \{\{R_1, R_3\}\}$}
17	2	\multicolumn{6}{l	}{call to CHECKXMAP$(\{R_0, R_2, R_4\},\{R_1,R_2\},R_1:\{R_1,R_2\}, R_2:\{R_1,R_2\}) \rightarrow$ returns TRUE}
18	3	$R_0 \rightarrow R_4 \rightarrow R_2$	$\{\{R_0, R_2, R_4\}\}$	$\emptyset$	$R_1:\{R_1,R_2\},\{R_1,R_2:\{R_1,R_2\}\, R_2\}$		$\{\{R_3\}\}$
19	3	\multicolumn{6}{l	}{emitting $(\{R_0, R_2, R_4\},\{R_1, R_3\})$}
20	3	\multicolumn{6}{l	}{$v = \{R_3\} \rightarrow$ GETCONNECTEDCOMPONENTS$(S, \{R_0, R_2, R_3, R_4\}) \rightarrow \{\{R_1\}\}$}
21	4	$R_0 \rightarrow R_4 \rightarrow R_2 \rightarrow R_3$	$\{\{R_0, R_2, R_3, R_4\}\}$	$\emptyset$	$R_1:\{R_1,R_2\},\{R_1,R_2:\{R_1,R_2\}\, R_2\}$		$\{\{R_1\}\}$
22	4	\multicolumn{6}{l	}{emitting $(\{R_0, R_2, R_3, R_4\},\{R_1\})$}
23	2	\multicolumn{6}{l	}{$v = \{R_3\} \rightarrow$ GETCONNECTEDCOMPONENTS$(S, \{R_0, R_3, R_4\}) \rightarrow \{\{R_1\},\{R_2\}\}$}
24	3	$R_0 \rightarrow R_4 \rightarrow R_1, R_3$	$\{\{R_0, R_1, R_3, R_4\}\}$	$\{R_2\}$	$R_1:\{R_1,R_2\},\{R_1,R_2:\{R_1,R_2\}\, R_2\}$		$\emptyset$
25	3	\multicolumn{6}{l	}{emitting $(\{R_0, R_1, R_3, R_4\},\{R_2\})$}

Table 3.2.: Exemplified execution of MINCUTCONSERVATIVEHYP for the graph of Figure 3.1 with $S = \{R_0, R_1, R_2, R_3, R_4\}$

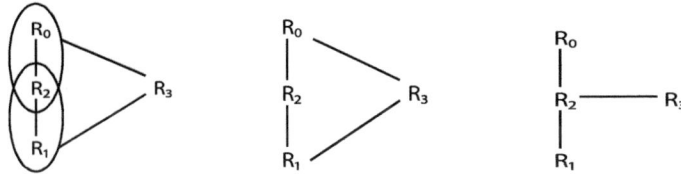

Figure 3.19.: (a) Overlapping hyperedges, (b) and (c) simple graphs

choose ($\{R_0\}, \{R_2\}$), this gives rise to two additional ccps: ($\{R_0, R_2\}, \{R_1\}$) and ($\{R_1\}, \{R_0, R_2\}$). Hence, the latter case is less restrictive.

For the **second** observation, we take a look at the naive partitioning strategy for hypergraphs PARTITION$_{naiveHyp}$ (Figure 3.5). Line 1 of PARTITION$_{naiveHyp}$ enumerates $2^{|v \cup w|} - 2$ subsets of $S = v \cup w$. Considering $H_{complex}$, we observe that only $C = v$ and $C = w$ make it past Line 2. This is clearly inefficient, since all other generated subsets of $S = v \cup w$ are rejected.

Assume that we substitute the complex hyperedge (v, w) of $H_{complex}$ by a simple edge ($\{x\}, \{y\}$) with $x \in v \wedge y \in w$. Then, the complex graph $H_{complex}$ becomes a simple hypergraph to which we refer as $H_{complex \to simple}$. As a consequence, we can utilize the reverse mapping (Definition 3.2.12) $g^{-1}(H_{complex \to simple})$ and reuse a highly efficient graph-aware partitioning algorithm for graphs like MINCUTBRANCH or MINCUTCONSERVATIVE. However, we have to be careful, since complex hyperedges are more restrictive and, thus, by converting hyperedges to simple edges, invalid ccps might be generated. Therefore, we need to check the ccps of the simple graph for connectivity within the original hypergraph. We call partitions of the simple graph that are not valid ccps of the original complex hypergraph *false ccps*. In the example used in the first observation, the false ccps are ($\{R_0, R_2\}, \{R_1\}$) and ($\{R_1\}, \{R_0, R_2\}$).

Third, if we represent a complex hyperedge (v, w) by a simple edge, there are $|v| * |w|$ possibilities to do so. For the graph presented in Figure 3.19(a), the call to PARTITION$_{naiveHyp}(H_{|\{R_0, R_1, R_2, R_3\}})$ generates 14 subsets assigned to C, but only $C = \{R_0\}, \{R_1\}, \{R_0, R_1, R_2\}, \{R_3\}, \{R_0, R_2, R_3\}$ and $\{R_1, R_2, R_3\}$ survive the test in Line 2. Thus, there exist only six valid ccps: $\{(\{R_0\}, \{R_1, R_2, R_3\}), (\{R_0, R_1, R_2\}, \{R_3\}), (\{R_0, R_2, R_3\}, \{R_1\})\}$ (symmetric counter pairs left out). For g^{-1} (Definition 3.2.12) applied on the hypergraph given in Figure 3.19(b), a graph-aware partitioning algorithm generates 12 partitions and, therefore, 6 false ccps. Since the two hyperedges of Figure 3.19(a) overlap, the mapping of Figure 3.19(c) is one of the 4 possible combinations. Here, not a single false ccp is generated when g^{-1} and a graph-aware partitioning algorithm is used. We conclude that in certain cases, there are good (restrictive) and bad (less restrictive) mappings.

We summarize what we have observed so far: Using PARTITION$_{naiveHyp}$ as a partitioning algorithm results in a huge computational overhead. Therefore, we are interested in reusing efficient graph-partitioning algorithms. For simple hypergraphs, we only have to apply our inverse mapping function g^{-1} to gain a graph which can be used as input to any graph-partitioning algorithm. Since the hypergraph is simple, no false ccps will be produced. This is because for any simple hypergraph H_{simple}: $g(g^{-1}(H_{simple})) = H_{simple}$ (Definitions 3.2.11 and 3.2.12) holds. But for complex

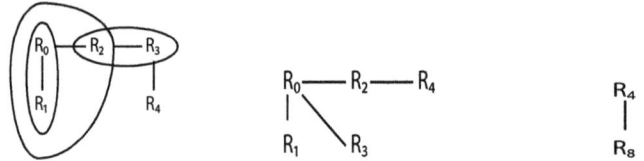
Figure 3.20.: (a) Hypergraph, (b) simple graph and (c) final graph

hypergraphs $H_{complex}$: $H_{complex}$: $g(g^{-1}(H_{complex})) = H_{complex}$ does not hold, since g^{-1} maps only simple hyperedges to graph edges and ignores complex hyperedges.

Thus, we denote by s a function that maps the complex hyperedges of a given hypergraph to simple hyperedges. There are several ways of defining s, but for now we leave s undefined. Let $H_{complex}$ be an arbitrary complex hypergraph. Then we compute the input of our graph-partitioning algorithm as follows: $g^{-1}(s(H_{complex}))$. According to our third observation, there are good (restrictive) and bad (less restrictive) mappings. In other words, by applying s we might loose restrictness so that in many cases $g(g^{-1}(s(H_{complex}))) = H_{complex}$ will not hold. Note that for any simple hypergraph H_{simple}, our mapping s needs to be defined as the identity function such that $g(g^{-1}(s(H_{simple}))) = H_{simple}$ holds. In general, if $s(H) \neq H$ holds, then the simple hypergraph $s(H)$ will be less restrictive and we need connection tests based on H that filter out false $ccps$. In Section 3.5.3, we present COMPUTEADJACENCYINFO as our implementation for the composition of $g^{-1} \circ s$.

Now, take a look at Figure 3.20(a). A call to PARTITION$_{naiveHyp}(H_{|\{R_0,R_1,R_2,R_3,R_4\}})$ results in the generation of 30 subsets assigned to C, where just $C = \{R_0, R_1, R_2, R_3\}$ and $C = \{R_4\}$ make it past Line 2. Invoking COMPUTEADJACENCYINFO (Section 3.5.3) produces the simple graph of Figure 3.20(b). Taking that graph as an input for a call to any graph-aware partitioning algorithm would return four pairs: $(\{R_0, R_1, R_2, R_3\}, \{R_4\})$, $(\{R_0, R_2, R_3, R_4\}, \{R_1\})$, $(\{R_0, R_1, R_3\}, \{R_2, R_4\})$ and $(\{R_0, R_1, R_2, R_4\}, \{R_3\})$ (symmetric counter pairs left out). But only the first partition and its symmetric counter pair are valid $ccps$. Hence, the produced simple graph of Figure 3.20(b) is less restrictive than the original one. In Figure 3.20(a), we can see that R_1 cannot be separated from R_0, since otherwise, the connection to R_2 would be lost. Furthermore, R_2 cannot be separated from R_0, R_1, or the connection to R_3 would be lost. On top of that, R_2 and R_3 have to remain in the same subgraph, or the connection to R_4 breaks up. In conclusion, it is only possible to separate R_4 from the rest, because all other combinations would end up in more than two connected subsets and, therefore, false $ccps$.

From this example we can draw our **fourth** observation: If a complex hyperedge (v, w) is essential for the connectedness of the hypergraph, i.e., it is a complex articulation hyperedge, then it is impossible to partition the graph by separating one or two of its complex hypernodes v or w. In other words: There exists no minimal cut involving an edge (s, t) with $s \subset v \wedge t \subset v$ within a hypernode v that is part of an articulation hyperedge (v, w).

In order to benefit from our last observation, we propose the concept of a compound vertex (Definition 3.2.10). The basic idea is to group those vertices that compose a non-separable hypernode into a new index-introducing compound vertex. Particularly, we remove those vertices from the vertex (sub)set $S \subseteq V$ that have been grouped and introduce the compound vertex as a new v by adding it to S (actually to some S', as we will see). In case that non-separable hypernodes are overlapping, we group all overlapping vertex sets together. Those steps are performed through COMPOSECOMPOUNDVERTICES (Section 3.5.4). The result of this step is shown in Figure 3.20(c), where R_8 is the index-introducing compound vertex representing R_0, R_1, R_2, R_3 of Figure 3.20(a-b).

3.5.2. Structure of the Generic Partitioning Framework

With MINCUTCONSERVATIVEHYP, we have presented the first partitioning algorithm that can efficiently handle complex hypergraphs. Analyzing its frequent code paths, we have identified the computation of the subsumed neighborhood as a frequent and relatively expensive hot spot. Because MINCUTCONSERVATIVEHYP has to handle complex hyperedges, the neighborhood of a vertex or vertex set can not be precomputed any more. Furthermore, for every computation a subsumption test has to be executed with a complexity of $O(|E_{complex}|^2)$, where $E_{complex} = \{(v, w) \mid v, w \in E \wedge (|v| > 1 \vee |w| > 1)\}$ is the set of complex hyperedges. For the design of our generic partitioning framework the elimination of subsumed neighborhood computations was paramount. By applying a function s (Section 3.5.1) that maps complex hyperedges to simple edges, we were able to achieve that. Nevertheless, since complex hyperedges may or may not lie within a given (sub) hypergraph $H_{|S}$, the precomputed neighborhoods have to be adjusted accordingly.

Global Data Structures

Through the nature of top-down join enumeration, every call to TDPGHYPSUB (Figure 3.3) needs to hand over a vertex set to which we refer as $S_{current}$ for now. $S_{current}$ is a proper subset of the vertex set used in the parent invocation of TDPGHYPSUB. For the time being, we refer to the vertex set of the parent invocation as S_{parent} with $S_{current} \subset S_{parent}$. Thus, the precomputed neighbors of any element $x \in S_{current}$ can only be a subset (not necessarily a proper subset) of the precomputed neighbors in the parent invocation of TDPGHYPSUB for the same x. So an adjustment of precomputed neighbors can only mean the elimination and not addition of vertices within the neighborhood. Since we may not modify precomputed adjacency information of the parent invocation, we copy its adjacency information in order to be able to modify and use its copy. We therefore propose the usage of a stack, where we push with every call to the partitioning algorithm PARTITION$_X$ (the central method of our framework explained in the next subsection) a new entry onto the stack that is a copy of the old top entry. The declaration of the stack named $Info_{stack}$ as a global variable and the structure of its element named $StackEntry$ are given in Figure 3.25 and 3.23. Figure 3.24 shows the definition of the structure $HyperEdge$. Besides the hypernodes v and w it stores a representative $v_{rep} \subseteq v$ and $w_{rep} \subseteq w$ for each hypernode. We gain v_{rep} and w_{rep} as the result of the complex hyperedge (v, w) to simple edge (v_{rep}, w_{rep}) mapping as part of applying s (Section 3.5.1).

Pseudocode of PARTITION$_X$

With PARTITION$_X$ shown in Figure 3.21, we give the framework's central method that handles the calls to all other main methods. We differentiate between two cases: (1) the top-level case where the handed over $H_{|S}$ is equal to the query graph $H = (V, E)$ (Lines 3 to 5) and (2) all other invocations of PARTITION$_X$ where $H_{|S}$ is a proper subgraph of $H = (V, E)$ (Lines 6 to 8).

We identify case (1) by checking if the $Info_{stack}$ that is part of the global variables (Figure 3.25) is initialized yet. During the handling of case (1), we first initialize $Info_{stack}$ by a call to INITIALIZEINFOSTACK (Figure 3.26) in Line 3 of PARTITION$_X$. In Line 4, we apply the composition of $g^{-1} \circ s$ by invoking COMPUTEADJACENCYINFO with the whole hypergraph $H = (V, E)$ as the argument. The result is a connected undirected graph represented through the vertex set S and the precomputed neighborhood arrays N_s and N_h. The latter two are declared as global variables, shown in Figure 3.25. For performance reasons, we differentiate between the two. The elements of the array N_s have been computed by considering simple hyperedges only. The values for N_h originate from complex hyperedge to simple edge mappings. Line 5 transforms certain hypernodes into compound vertices in order to (a) regain some of the restrictiveness of the transformed hyperedges and to (b) speed up processing, since fewer vertices are involved.

The handling of case (2) takes place in Lines 6 to 8. By invoking MANAGEINFO STACK(S) (Line 6), a new $StackEntry$ is pushed onto the $Info_{stack}$ as a copy of the previous topmost entry. Through a call to CLEANSEHYPERNEIGHBOURS (Line 7), we adjust the adjacency information that needs modification because complex hyperedges have been cut off. By cut-off edges we refer to those complex hyperedges that have been part of the parent's (sub) hypergraph $H_{|S_{parent}}$ but are not fully contained in the current sub-hypergraph $H_{|S_{current}}$ with $S_{parent} \supset S_{current}$. RECOMPOSECOMPOUNDVERTICES is invoked from Line 8 to ensure the accuracy of compound vertices that have been adopted from the parent's invocation. This can mean that compound vertices are dissolved completely or their represented vertices are reassigned to new compound vertices in case of overlapping complex articulation hypernodes.

Line 9 determines whether the relatively expensive connection test assessing connectivity based on the original hypergraph is needed. The partitioning algorithm called in Line 10 only sees a simple graph with intermixed original and compound vertex nodes (index-reusing compound vertices, as we will see). Importantly, it does not need any knowledge about the vertices represented by the compound vertices. Finally, we loop through the emitted partitions of the simple graph (Line 11). We decode the emitted partitions (Section 3.5.4) by substituting the compound vertices with the original vertices (Line 12, 13) and apply the connection test (Line 15) if needed (Line 14). Note that if a connection test is necessary (Section 3.5.5), the last step is very important in order to filter out false ccps. Missing to filter out false ccps results in the generation of (sub)plans that rely on cross products and might be invalid [20]. Let $E_{complex} = \{(v, w) \mid v, w \in E \wedge (|v| > 1 \vee |w| > 1)\}$ be the set of complex hyperedges, then the complexity of the preprocessing step is in $O(|E_{complex}| * \frac{|V|^2}{2})$. The complexity of the enumeration algorithm in Line 10 remains unchanged. The complexity of the two additional connectivity tests is in $O(|V| + \frac{|E_{complex}|^2}{2})$ per emitted

```
PARTITION_X(H_|S)
    ▷ Input: a connected (sub) hypergraph H_|S
    ▷ Output: P_ccp
1   S' ← ∅
2   if TOP(Info_stack) = NIL                              ▷ V = S holds
3       INITIALIZEINFOSTACK                               ▷ Figure 3.26
4       COMPUTEADJACENCYINFO(H_|S)                        ▷ Section 3.5.3
5       S' ← COMPOSECOMPOUNDVERTICES(H_|S)                ▷ Section 3.5.4
6   else MANAGEINFOSTACK(S)                               ▷ Section 3.5.6
7       CLEANSEHYPERNEIGHBOURS(H_|S)                      ▷ Section 3.5.6
8       S' ← RECOMPOSECOMPOUNDVERTICES(H_|S)              ▷ Section 3.5.6
9   con ← CONNECTIONTESTREQUIRED(S')                      ▷ Section 3.5.5
10  P^sym_partitions ← PARTITION_{graph-aware}(G_|S')     ▷ Chapter 2
11  for all (l', r') ∈ P^sym_partitions
12      l ← DECODE(l')                                    ▷ Section 3.5.4
13      r ← DECODE(r')                                    ▷ Section 3.5.4
14      if con = TRUE
15          if ISCONNECTEDHYP(H_|l) ∧ ISCONNECTEDHYP(H_|r)  ▷ Section 3.5.5
16              P_ccp ← P_ccp ∪ {(l,r)} ∪ {(r,l)}
17          else P_ccp ← P_ccp ∪ {(l,r)} ∪ {(r,l)}
```

Figure 3.21.: Pseudocode for PARTITION$_X$

ccp (false *ccp*s included). Note that in many cases, the two tests can be avoided (see Section 3.5.5).

Not shown here but important: Since the struct *StackEntry* is pushed onto $Info_{stack}$ with every call to PARTITION$_X$ (Lines 3 and 6), it needs to be popped from $Info_{stack}$ before TDPGHYPSUB returns. The invocation of POP($Info_{stack}$) should be added after the loop of Lines 2 to 5 of TDPGHYPSUB (Figure 3.3).

A Call Graph

Figure 3.22 contains the call graph for the top-level case of PARTITION$_X$ where $S = V$ holds and V is the vertex set of the query graph. Because Figure 3.22 shows the top-level case, there is only one invocation of TDPGHYPSUB without further recursive self invocations. The call graph gives an overview of the methods used in our partitioning framework during the computation of $P_{ccp}(V)$. Sections 3.5.3, 3.5.4 and 3.5.5 will explain the invoked methods in detail. The case of all other innovations of PARTITION$_X$ where $S \subset V$ holds is discussed in Section 3.5.6.

3.5.3. Generating the Adjacency Information

All graph-aware partitioning algorithms like MINCUTLAZY [5] (Appendix A.1), MINCUTAGAT (Section 2.3), MINCUTCONSERVATIVE (Section 2.4) or MINCUT-BRANCH (Section 2.5) utilize the neighborhood information to extend connected sets. Thus, our generic partitioning framework has to provide this information to the particular partitioning algorithm PARTITION$_{graph-aware}$ it is instantiated with. We make this information available through the global variables shown in Figure 3.25 with ref-

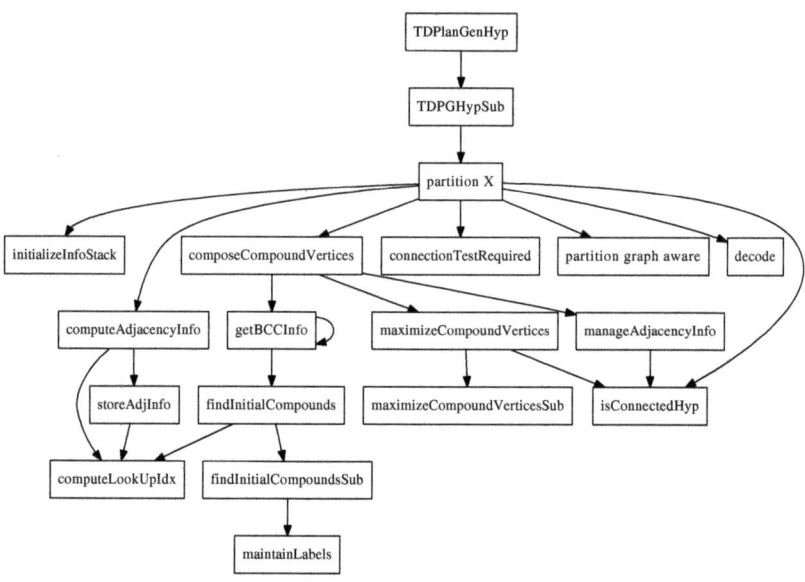

Figure 3.22.: Call graph for the top-level case of PARTITION$_X$

erence to Figures 3.23 and 3.24. Essentially, PARTITION$_{graph-aware}$ has to rely on the precomputed neighborhood array N_m of struct $StackEntry$ (Figure 3.23). The other variables mainly exist for performance and maintenance reasons and are explained later on. The initial setup is done by COMPUTEADJACENCYINFO given in Figure 3.29. Before going into the details of the pseudocode, we need to explain how the adjacency information can be stored.

Precomputed Neighborhoods

To capture the adjacency information of simple edges is relatively easy and straight forward. This is done by an associative array N_s that stores for a given vertex x the vertices adjacent to x, as defined in Figure 3.25. In practice, N_s is implemented as an array of bitvectors, as Section 3.5.7 will point out. Here the lookup for a given x works slightly different. First, we determine the index i of the given vertex x (Definition 3.2.2). Since x itself will be represented as a bitvector where only one bit is set, we simply have to determine the index of that particular bit. This can be done by the $bit\_scan\_forward$ assembler instruction. In a second step, we use i as an index into the array N_s. With access to the corresponding bitvector, we can determine the bits that are set. Each bit then corresponds to an index that represents a vertex in V. To compute the simple neighborhood $\mathcal{N}_{simple}(C)$ (Definition 3.2.14), we simply iterate over the bits that are set in the bitvector representing C. We use the corresponding index of each bit that is set to access the corresponding bitvector in N_s. The result of $\mathcal{N}_{simple}(C)$ then is the union of accessed bitvectors except the bits set in the bitvector of C. Thus, the adjacency information of a simple hyperedges can be easily stored and accessed in such an array of bitvectors.

For storing the adjacency information of complex hyperedges, we have to choose a different approach. There are three reasons for this. (1) First of all, we cannot determine a unique index of a given complex hypernode v the same way as before, because in the corresponding bitvector of v is more than one bit set. One might argue to choose the bitvector's integer value instead. But then the array of bitvectors will have a size of $2^{|V|}$, which is not practical for large Vs. As an alternative implementation, we could use a map. But then the lookup is slightly more costly, $O(log|V|)$ (e.g. in case of a red-black tree) instead of $O(1)$. Let us assume we have solved this problem. That brings us to our second reason. (2) For a given complex hypernode, there might exist more than one adjacent hypernode. Thus, an array or map of bitvectors is not sufficient anymore. We need to have a set of bitvectors instead. Hence, we can cope with the first two reasons by paying some performance penalties. Nevertheless, there is a third reason. (3) This approach is not suitable for computing the complex neighborhood $\mathcal{N}(S, C, \emptyset)$ (Definition 3.2.15). For the simple neighborhood, we only had to iterate over every vertex of C. But now we would have to consider every possible subset of C and would need to check our array or map if we found a set of bitvectors for that particular subset of C. Thus, we can conclude that the lookup of a precomputed complex neighborhood is infeasible.

Hence, we store the complex hyperedges. We can compute a hyperedge filter E_F that points only to those hyperedges that reference only vertices contained in the current vertex set S. To compute $\mathcal{N}(S, C, \emptyset)$, we have to consider all those hyperedges that are qualified by the filter. Thus, we have a complexity of $O(|E_{complex}|)$, where $E_{complex} = \{(v, w) \mid v, w \in E \land (|v| > 1 \lor |w| > 1)\}$ is the set of complex hyperedges. Since the neighborhood is computed many times, this will have a negative impact on the performance of the partitioning algorithm. The good news is that we will not need to compute $\mathcal{N}(S, C, \emptyset)$. Moreover, since we map the complex hyperedges to simple hyperedges, we can rely on the precomputed simple neighborhood. As we will see, the adjacency information of our simple hyperedges that we have generated by the complex to simple hyperedge mapping is stored in the array N_h instead of in N_s.

The Pseudocode in Detail

At the beginning of COMPUTEADJACENCYINFO (Figure 3.29), we precompute the simple neighborhood N_s (Figure 3.25) by iterating over all simple edges (Line 3 to 5). The complex hyperedges of a given hypergraph are stored in an array called $HyperEdges$ (Figure 3.25) of type $HyperEdge$ (Figure 3.24). The size of $HyperEdges$ is $|E_{complex}|$. Therefore, we loop over $E_{complex}$ in Line 8 of COMPUTEADJACENCYINFO and invoke STORECOMPLEXHYPEREDGE (Figure 3.30) in Line 9. STORECOMPLEXHYPEREDGE stores the two hypernodes v and w of the current complex hyperedge (v, w). The values for v_{rep} and w_{rep} are assigned later by a call to STOREADJACENCYINFO (Figure 3.32). Both values are used to store the result of the complex hyperedge (v, w) to simple edge (v_{rep}, w_{rep}) mapping. Thus, $v_{rep} \subseteq v$ and $w_{rep} \subseteq w$ holds.

To understand Lines 8 to 41, recall the third observation of Section 3.5.1. We solve the problem illustrated there by first pretending to substitute every complex hyperedge

(v, w) with all possible combinations ($= |v| * |w|$) of simple edges (loop of Line 11 to 20). For every created overlapping simple edge, we increase $card$ (Line 14). For every combination of indices i of $x_i \in v$ and j of $y_j \in w$ (Definition 3.2.2), we compute the position of the corresponding entry within the array $Ovlp$ (Line 1) by a call to COMPUTELOOKUPIDX (Line 13). The formula used in Line 1 of COMPUTELOOKUPIDX (Figure 3.27) guarantees space efficiency (SIZEOF($Ovlp$) = $\frac{|V|*(|V|-1)}{2}$). In Line 19 and 20 of COMPUTEADJACENCYINFO, we keep track of the simple edge and its array entry that is generated most frequently. After the generation of simple edges (they are not materialized yet), we check if we have found overlapping hyperedges (Line 22). If so, we materialize the simple edge that was generated most frequently (Line 30). At this point, we remove all other combinations of simple edges (Line 26 to 29) for the set of overlapping edges stored in $Ovlp[idx].E^{ref}$ (Line 23). Lines 33 to 36 spot the next largest set of overlapping hyperedges, and the process is started again. Those complex hyperedges that do not overlap are substituted with one simple edge in Lines 37 and 41 through a call to STOREADJACENCYINFO (Figure 3.32). We decided to store the substituted complex hyperedges not within the simple neighborhood N_s, but within N_h, where $_h$ stands for hyperneighborhood, although it is not an exact translation (Definition 3.2.15).

Storing the Adjacency Information

The purpose of STOREADJACENCYINFO is to update N_h, but also $HEdgeLkp$ and $HyperEdges$. Figure 3.25 declares $HEdgeLkp$ as an array of hyperedge references and $HyperEdges$ as an array of all complex hyperedges. Our generic partitioning framework needs both variables in order to reconstruct the complex hyperedge (v, w) for a given simple edge ($\{x\}, \{y\}$). From the handed over x_i and y_i we know that a simple hyperedge ($\{x_i\}, \{y_j\}$) is represented. Thereby, ($\{x_i\}, \{y_j\}$) is the result of the complex hyperedge to simple edge mapping where (v, w) is the corresponding complex hyperedge so that $x_i \in v \land y_i \in w$ holds. By calling COMPUTELOOKUPIDX(x_i, y_j), we can compute an index into $HEdgeLkp$ that returns a hyperedge reference in form of an index into $HyperEdges$.

In Line 3 of STOREADJACENCYINFO, we compute the index lkp. We use lkp to update $HEdgeLkp$ in Line 4. The generated simple hyperedge ($\{x_i\}, \{y_j\}$) is materialized in the particular $HyperEdges$ entry of the corresponding complex hyperedges E^{ref} in Lines 6 and 7.

3.5.4. Composing Compound Vertices

This section discusses how the information of non-separable hypernodes is encoded into the simple graph to make it more restrictive by preventing as many false $ccps$ as possible (fourth observation Section 3.5.1).

Merging Compound Vertices

In the following, we focus on the details of finding non-separable hypernodes and merging them into compound vertices. The process is started by invoking COMPOSECOMPOUNDVERTICES, as shown in Figure 3.33. In Lines 1 to 9 of COMPOSECOMPOUNDVERTICES, the variables for the recognition of biconnected components (Def-

```
1  define StackEntry as struct
2      E_F^{ref} set<hyperedge references>          ▷ corresponding to current S
3      E_C^{ref} set<hyperedge references>          ▷ hyperedge ref. partly cut off
4      S' vertex set                                 ▷ S' ⊇ S_{org}
5      S_{org} vertex set                            ▷ remaining original vertices
6      S_{compounds}^{disconnected}                  ▷ disconnected compounds
7      S_A a vertex set                              ▷ index-introducing compounds
8      N_m associative array of vertex sets          ▷ merged neighbors: N_s ∪ N_h
9      Compound_{map} a map<vertex set → vertex set> ▷ {R_i} → compound vertex
10     Compound_{map}^{-1} a map<vertex set → vertex set> ▷ compound vtx → {R_i,...R_j}
```

Figure 3.23.: Struct $StackEntry$

```
1  define HyperEdge as struct
2      v vertex set
3      w vertex set
4      v_{rep} vertex set      ▷ v_{rep} ⊆ v ∧ |v_{rep}| ≤ 1 holds
5      w_{rep} vertex set      ▷ w_{rep} ⊆ w ∧ |w_{rep}| ≤ 1 holds
```

Figure 3.24.: Struct $HyperEdge$

```
1  declare N_s associative array of vertex sets
2  declare N_h associative array of vertex sets
3  declare HEdgeLkp array of hyper edge references
4  declare HyperEdges an array< HyperEdge >                   ▷ Figure 3.24
5  declare Label_{map} a map<vertex set → vertex set>         ▷ {R_i,...R_j} → compound
6  declare Label_{map}^{-1} a map<vertex set → vertex set>    ▷ compound → {R_i,...R_j}
7  declare IdxIntroV_{map} a map<vertex set → vertex set>     ▷ {R_i} → index-introducing
8  declare Info_{stack} a stack<StackEntry>                   ▷ Figure 3.23
9  declare E_A^{ref} a set<hyperedge references>              ▷ all articulation hyperedges
```

Figure 3.25.: Global Variables

INITIALIZEINFOSTACK

```
1  PUSH(Info_{stack}, new StackEntry)
```

Figure 3.26.: Pseudocode for INITIALIZEINFOSTACK

COMPUTELOOKUPIDX(x_i, y_j)

▷ **Input:** vertex labels i, j (Definition 3.2.2) with $x_i \in S \wedge y_j \in S$
```
1  return  MAX(i,j)*(MAX(i,j)-1)/2 + MIN(i,j)
```

Figure 3.27.: Pseudocode for COMPUTELOOKUPIDX

inition 2.1.18) are initialized. Line 11 invokes the recognition of the non-separable hypernodes. With a call to MAXIMIZECOMPOUNDVERTICES in Line 12, we try to

```
1   define Overlap as struct
2       E^{ref}
3       card
4       x vertex set
5       y vertex set
```

Figure 3.28.: Struct *Overlap* used by COMPUTEADJACENCYINFO

enlarge disconnected hypernodes. Section 3.5.5 will explain in detail how MAXIMIZE-COMPOUNDVERTICES works.

Once the call to GETBCCINFO and the subsequent call to MAXIMIZECOMPOUND-VERTICES are returned, the following holds: TOP($Info_{stack}$).S' will contain only original vertices that are not part of any non-separable hypernode. The rest of the vertices $v \in S \setminus$ TOP($Info_{stack}$).S' will be mapped to index-introducing compound vertices. We store the mapping in the global variable $IdxIntroV_{map}$. Note that a given v can be mapped to more than one index-introducing compound vertex. With the information stored in $IdxIntroV_{map}$, we merge overlapping articulation hypernodes to a new compound vertex that represents the union of hypernodes (Line 14 to 32).

Therefore, we loop in Line 15 through S'', which contains all original vertices that are represented by at least one compound vertex. We declare h in order to store the union of overlapping hypernodes and initialize it in Line 16. With Z and I, we keep track of the compound vertices that represent the overlapping hypernodes. I maintains those we already have investigated and Z those we still have to consider. Z is initialized (Line 19) with the compound vertices that represent v (which was arbitrary chosen from S'' in Line 17). Within the loop in Lines 21 to 28, we investigate all compound vertices contained in Z by incrementally removing vertices in Line 23 and possibly adding vertices in Line 27. Line 25 applies a reverse lookup (through $Label_{map}^{-1}$) of the index-introducing compound vertex u that was chosen out of Z (Line 22). We add to h the result of the lookup, which are the vertices represented by u. For every vertex x (Line 26) contained in one of the hypernodes in question, we consult $IdxIntroV_{map}$ (Line 27) to enlarge Z with compound vertices that correspond to x minus those already investigated (and kept in I). That way, all compound vertices in question have to be added at one point to Z, either in Line 19 or Line 27. By incrementally taking one element at a time out of Z and adding the vertices it encompasses to the new hypernode h, we ensure that h gets maximally enlarged. Line 28 removes all vertices contained in h from S'', and the process continues until the last h of overlapping non-separable hypernodes is found.

In Line 29, we transform the overlapping index-introducing compound vertices into a new index-reusing compound vertex with the index i. Thereby, we assign i with the smallest index (Definition 3.2.2) among the indices used by the vertices contained in h. Undoubtedly, reusing an index complicates things. As an alternative, we could just reassign one of the overlapping index-introducing compound vertices in order to represent the vertices contained in h. Or as proposed in [10] we could even assign a completely new index-introducing compound vertex. But the approach of adding index-introducing compound vertices to a vertex set S' that is feed to PARTITION$_{graph-aware}$ has one disadvantage that can cause performance penalties. The vertex sets used here

COMPUTEADJACENCYINFO($H_{|S}$)
    ▷ **Input:** vertex (sub)set $S \subseteq V$
1 **declare** $Ovlp$ an array $< Overlap >$ ▷ defined in Figure 3.28
2 **declare** $E_{hyp}^{ref} \leftarrow \emptyset$ as a set of hyperedge references
3 **for all** $(\{x\}, \{y\}) \in E$ ▷ all simple hyperedges of $H_{|S}$
4      $N_s[x] \leftarrow N_s[x] \cup \{y\}$
5      $N_s[y] \leftarrow N_s[y] \cup \{x\}$
6 $max \leftarrow 0$
7 $idx \leftarrow 0$
8 **for all** $(v, w) \in E \mid |v| > 1 \vee |w| > 1$ ▷ all complex hyperedges of $H_{|S}$
9      $ref \leftarrow$ STORECOMPLEXHYPEREDGE(v, w)
10     $E_{hyp}^{ref} \leftarrow E_{hyp}^{ref} \cup \{ref\}$
11   **for all** $x_i \in v$
12   **for all** $y_j \in w$
13          $lkp \leftarrow$ COMPUTELOOKUPIDX(x_i, y_j)
14          $Ovlp[lkp].card \leftarrow Ovlp[lkp].card + 1$
15          $Ovlp[lkp].E^{ref} \leftarrow Ovlp[lkp].E^{ref} \cup \{ref\}$
16          $Ovlp[lkp].x \leftarrow x_i$
17          $Ovlp[lkp].y \leftarrow y_j$
18   **if** $Ovlp[lkp].card > max$
19              $max \leftarrow Ovlp[lkp].card$
20              $idx \leftarrow lkp$
21 TOP$(Info_{stack}).E_F^{ref} \leftarrow E_{hyp}^{ref}$
22 **while** $max > 1$ ▷ for overlapping hyperedges
23   **for all** $ref \in Ovlp[idx].E^{ref} \cap E_{hyp}^{ref}$
24        $(v, w) \leftarrow$ DEREFERENCE(ref) ▷ Figure 3.31
25        $E_{hyp}^{ref} \leftarrow E_{hyp}^{ref} \setminus \{ref\}$
26   **for all** $x_i \in v$
27   **for all** $y_j \in w$
28                $lkp \leftarrow$ COMPUTELOOKUPIDX(x_i, y_j)
29                $Ovlp[lkp].card \leftarrow Ovlp[lkp].card - 1$
30   STOREADJACENCYINFO$(Ovlp[idx].x, Ovlp[idx].y, Ovlp[idx].E^{ref})$
31     $max \leftarrow 0$
32     $idx \leftarrow 0$
33   **for all** $i : 0 \leq i <$ SIZEOF$(Ovlp)$ ▷ find next max $Ovlp[i].card$
34   **if** $Ovlp[i].card > max$
35            $max \leftarrow Ovlp[i].card$
36            $idx \leftarrow i$
37 **for all** $ref \in E_{hyp}^{ref}$ ▷ all non-overlapping hyperedges
38     $(v, w) \leftarrow$ DEREFERENCE(ref) ▷ Figure 3.31
39     $x \leftarrow$ arbitrary element of v ▷ e.g. with the smallest index
40     $y \leftarrow$ arbitrary element of w ▷ e.g. with the smallest index
41   STOREADJACENCYINFO$(x, y, \{ref\})$

Figure 3.29.: Pseudocode for COMPUTEADJACENCYINFO

are represented by bitvectors. Generating index-introducing compound vertices implies occupying more bits. If we reach a point where the number of bits occupied is larger than the word size, we have to work with word-size-exceeding bitvectors

STORECOMPLEXHYPEREDGE(v, w)
    ▷ **Input:** vertex sets v and w representing two hypernodes
    ▷ **Output:** reference to the entry in $HyperEdges$ (Figure 3.25)
1   $ref \leftarrow$ find next available entry in $HyperEdges$
2   $HyperEdges[ref].v \leftarrow v$
3   $HyperEdges[ref].w \leftarrow w$
4   $HyperEdges[ref].v_{rep} \leftarrow \emptyset$
5   $HyperEdges[ref].w_{rep} \leftarrow \emptyset$
6   mark $HyperEdges[ref]$ as occupied
7   **return** ref

Figure 3.30.: Pseudocode for STORECOMPLEXHYPEREDGE

DEREFERENCE(ref)
    ▷ **Input:** ref a hyperedge reference
    ▷ **Output:** a hyperedge (v, w)
1   $v \leftarrow HyperEdges[ref].v$
2   $w \leftarrow HyperEdges[ref].w$
3   **return** (v, w)

Figure 3.31.: Pseudocode for DEREFERENCE

STOREADJACENCYINFO(x_i, y_j, E^{ref})
    ▷ **Input:** vertex x_i, y_j with $x_i \in S \wedge y_j \in S$, a set of hyperedge references E^{ref}
1   $N_h[x_i] \leftarrow N_h[x_i] \cup \{y_j\}$
2   $N_h[y_j] \leftarrow N_h[y_j] \cup \{x_i\}$
3   $lkp \leftarrow$ COMPUTELOOKUPIDX(x_i, y_j)
4   $HEdgeLkp[lkp] \leftarrow HEdgeLkp[lkp] \cup E^{ref}$
5   **for all** $ref \in E^{ref}$
6      $HyperEdges[ref].v_{rep} \leftarrow \{x_i\}$
7      $HyperEdges[ref].w_{rep} \leftarrow \{y_j\}$

Figure 3.32.: Pseudocode for STOREADJACENCYINFO

that slow down bitvector operations noticeably. Therefore, we restrict ourselves not to occupy more bits than necessary. Thus, we limit ourself to $|V|$, where V is the vertex set of the query graph. Note that this is not entirely true, since the members $CompoundMap_{map}$ and $CompoundMap_{map}^{-1}$ of $StackEntry$ and the global variables $Label_{map}$, $Label_{map}^{-1}$ and $IdxIntroV_{map}$ still reference index-introducing compound vertices, but those variables are not accessed by PARTITION$_{graph-aware}$. In fact, only a few performance uncritical methods of our generic partitioning framework need to deal with these variables.

To differentiate between original vertices contained in the vertex set V of our query graph and index-reusing compound vertices, we maintain the member S_{org} in the struct $StackEntry$ that contains only non-compound vertices that are not represented by any compound vertex at the same time. In Line 30, the new vertex set TOP($Info_{stack}$).S' (as returned later on in Line 34) is enlarged with the index-reusing compound vertex that represents the new h. Lines 31 and 32 make the index-reusing compound vertex known to the vertices it represents. Finally, we call MANAGEADJACENCYINFO in order to set up the merged neighborhood TOP($Info_{stack}$).N_m.

COMPOSECOMPOUNDVERTICES($H_{|S}$)
  ▷ **Input:** connected (sub)graph $H_{|S}$
  ▷ **Output:** S' a set of vertex sets
1 **declare** stack of edges E_{stack}
2 **for** each vertex $x \in S$
3 $color[x] \leftarrow$ WHITE
4 $low[x] \leftarrow |S| + 1$
5 $\pi[x] \leftarrow$ NIL
6 $parent[x] \leftarrow$ NIL
7 $desc[x] \leftarrow \{x\}$
8 $count \leftarrow 0$
9 $t \leftarrow$ arbitrary $x \in S$
10 TOP($Info_{stack}$).$S' \leftarrow S$
11 GETBCCINFO(t)
12 MAXIMIZECOMPOUNDVERTICES(S)
13 TOP($Info_{stack}$).$S_{org} \leftarrow$ TOP($Info_{stack}$).S'
14 $S'' \leftarrow S \setminus$ TOP($Info_{stack}$).S' ▷ vertices represented by index-introducing c.
15 **while** $S'' \neq \emptyset$
16 $h \leftarrow \emptyset$ ▷ h stores the new hypernode
17 $v \leftarrow \{y\} : y \in S''$
18 $S'' \leftarrow S'' \setminus v$
19 $Z \leftarrow IdxIntroV_{map}[v]$
20 $I \leftarrow \emptyset$
21 **while** $Z \neq \emptyset$
22   $u \leftarrow \{z\} : z \in Z$
23   $Z \leftarrow Z \setminus u$
24   $I \leftarrow I \cup u$
25   $h \leftarrow h \cup Label_{map}^{-1}[u]$
26   **for all** $x \in h$
27    $Z \leftarrow Z \cup (IdxIntroV_{map}[\{x\}] \setminus I)$
28    $S'' \leftarrow S'' \setminus h$
29 $compound \leftarrow \{\text{MIN}_{index}(h)\}$ ▷ vertex with smallest index of h
30 TOP($Info_{stack}$).$S' \leftarrow$ TOP($Info_{stack}$).$S' \cup compound$
31 **for all** $x \in h$
32   TOP($Info_{stack}$).$Compound_{map}[\{x\}] \leftarrow compound$
33 MANAGEADJACENCYINFO($H_{|S}$)
34 **return** TOP($Info_{stack}$).S'

Figure 3.33.: Pseudocode for COMPOSECOMPOUNDVERTICES

The pseudocode for MANAGEADJACENCYINFO is given in Figure 3.34. It is a modification of [10]. Here, we follow a new approach, where we merge N_s and N_h into TOP($Info_{stack}$).N_m (Line 2 of MANAGEADJACENCYINFO). This has the advantage that PARTITION$_{graph-aware}$ only has to work with one precomputed neighborhood instead of consulting two at the same time, which improves performance. Within the first loop of Lines 1 to 5, we ensure that if x is adjacent to a vertex y that is represented by a compound vertex, the neighborhood of x also contains that index-reusing compound vertex TOP($Info_{stack}$).$Compound_{map}[\{y\}]$. Note that if $y \in$ TOP($Info_{stack}$).S_{org} holds, TOP($Info_{stack}$).$Compound_{map}[\{y\}]$ will be empty.

MANAGEADJACENCYINFO($H_{|S}$)
1 **for all** $x \in S$
2   TOP($Info_{stack}$).$N_m[x] \leftarrow$ TOP($Info_{stack}$).$N_m[x] \cup N_s[x] \cup N_h[x]$
3   **for all** $y \in (N_s[x] \cup N_h[x])$
4   TOP($Info_{stack}$).$N_m[x] \leftarrow$ TOP($Info_{stack}$).$N_m[x] \cup$
                  TOP($Info_{stack}$).$Compound_{map}[\{y\}]$
5   TOP($Info_{stack}$).$N_m[x] \leftarrow$ TOP($Info_{stack}$).$N_m[x] \setminus \{x\}$
6 **for all** $x \in$ TOP($Info_{stack}$).$S' \setminus$ TOP($Info_{stack}$).S_{org}
7      $h \leftarrow$ TOP($Info_{stack}$).$Compound_{map}^{-1}[\{x\}]$
8   **if** ISCONNECTEDHYP($H_{|h}$) $\neq$ TRUE
9   TOP($Info_{stack}$).$S_{compounds}^{disconnected} \leftarrow$ TOP($Info_{stack}$).$S_{compounds}^{disconnected} \cup \{x\}$
10   **for all** $y \in (h \setminus \{x\})$
11   TOP($Info_{stack}$).$N_m[x] \leftarrow$ TOP($Info_{stack}$).$N_m[x] \cup$
                  TOP($Info_{stack}$).$N_m[y]$

Figure 3.34.: Pseudocode for MANAGEADJACENCYINFO

Through the second loop (Lines 6 to 11) the neighborhood of the index-reusing compound vertices x are precomputed. This means that the current values for TOP($Info_{stack}$).$N_m[x]$ have to be completed, since so far, they only contain the adjacent vertices of the old x. This is done by adding the missing adjacency information of the other vertices also represented by the compound vertex x (Lines 10 to 11). Line 9 maintains TOP($Info_{stack}$).$S_{compounds}^{disconnected}$ that contains all index-reusing compound vertices that represent disconnected hypernodes. We keep track of this information to decide later on (Line 9 of PARTITION$_X$) if we need to perform connection tests with the information of the original hypergraph $H_{|S}$.

Discovering Non-Separable Hypernodes

As has been said, GETBCCINFO is responsible for discovering the non-separable hypernodes. This is done by determining the complex articulation hyperedges. During the transformation of a complex hypergraph H into a simple hypergraph $s(H)$, the complex articulation hyperedges are mapped to simple hyperedges. Now, if the complex hyperedge's substitute is recognized as a biconnected component (Definition 2.1.18) in the simple graph, this indicates that the complex hyperedge must be an articulation hyperedge. Actually, it is possible that there are overlapping hyperedges mapped to the same simple edge, but we will take care of this case. Thus, in order to determine non-separable hypernodes, we have to discover the biconnected components of the simple graph. Therefore, we used the algorithmic skeleton of [1, 9].

As mentioned, the variables for the recognition of biconnected components are initialized in Lines 1 to 9 of COMPOSECOMPOUNDVERTICES. We presume that the details of depth-first search and pre-order numbering are known and omit any further explanation [4].

The stack of graph edges E_{stack} is used to distinguish between the tree edges and back edges that are not captured. Tree edges are those that lead to all the accessed vertices during the discovery of vertices. Back edges are the rest of the graph edges that would close the cycles to already visited vertices. We denote the set of tree edges with E_t and the set of back edges with E_b. It holds that $E = E_t \cup E_b$ with $E_b \cap E_t = \emptyset$.

For the recognition of cycles, we need an additional associative array *low*. It holds the following:

$$low[x] = \text{MIN}(\{df[x]\} \cup \{df[y] \mid y \in D(x)\}),$$

where *df* is the pre-order number and $D(x)$ is defined as:

$$D(x) = \{y \mid \exists z(z,y) \in E_b, y \stackrel{*}{\to} x \stackrel{*}{\to} z\}.$$

In other words, the set $D(x)$ includes all vertices y with a back edge $(z,y) \in E_b$, and x is a descendant of y and z a descendant of x in the directed spanning tree $S(V, E_t)$. Note that the vertex x is a descendant of y if $df[y] < df[x]$ holds. Hence, z is also a descendant of y, and it holds that $df[y] < df[x] < df[z]$. The calculation of $low[x]$ can be embedded into the depth-first search procedure if the formula is rewritten in terms of values of $low[s]$ at the direct children $s \in C(x)$ of x in $S(V, E_t)$ and of the preorder numbers of the vertices connected to x via back edges.

$$low[x] = \text{MIN}(\{df[x]\} \cup \{low[s] \mid s \in C(x)\} \cup \{df[y] \mid y \in D(x)\})$$

The set $C(x)$ is defined as:

$$C(x) = \{s \mid s \in \mathcal{N}(x) \land df[x] < df[s]\}.$$

Due to the recursive iteration, the final value of $low[x]$ is not known before the list of vertices adjacent to x is fully processed. Note that in the definition of C, we use $\mathcal{N}(x)$ to determine the adjacent vertices to x. In Line 5 of GETBCCINFO, we compute $\mathcal{N}(x)$ by merging $N_s[x] \cup N_h[x]$. If a vertex x is an articulation vertex and the entry point of a biconnected component $G^{BCC} = (V_i, E_i)$ where $x, s \in V_i$ holds, it is recognized by $low[s] \geq df[x]$. This is also true for those start vertices t (Line 9 of COMPOSECOMPOUNDVERTICES) that are not also an articulation vertex.

In Line 4 of GETBCCINFO, the value of $low[x]$ is initialized. Since during processing $low[x] \leq df[x]$ holds, its preorder number is chosen. As the first part of the previous rewritten formula, the value of $low[x]$ is adjusted to the minimum value between $low[y]$ from the son y of x and itself in Line 25. The second part of the definition is implemented in Line 28. The check of Line 26 ensures that $(x,y) \in E_b$ is really a back edge and not just a tree edge.

The condition in Line 10 of GETBCCINFO indicates, if evaluated to TRUE, that a biconnected component was found. More precisely: It means that either x is the start node t (assigned in Line 9 and handed over in Line 11 of Figure 3.33), or an articulation vertex was found that is the only link to another biconnected component. In Line 11, we declare *desc* to store the descendants of x, i.e., all vertices z where every possible path $z \to^* t$ would involve x. Those descendants are gathered in Lines 14 and 17 and finally stored with (possibly) other descendants of x (x can be the parent vertex for several biconnected components) in Line 24.

Lines 12 to 19 will pop all edges ($\{e_1\}, \{e_2\}$) belonging to this biconnected component from the stack of edges E_{stack}. Thereby, we update *desc* and set the parent for every vertex (Line 15, 18) in the biconnected component. As has been mentioned, in case $x = t$ holds it is possible that x is not an articulation vertex, but only a member

GETBCCINFO(x)
    ▷ **Input:** vertex $x \in S$
1   $color[x] \leftarrow$ GRAY
2   $count \leftarrow count + 1$
3   $df[x] \leftarrow count$
4   $low[x] \leftarrow df[x]$
5   **for all** $y \in (N_s[x] \cup N_h[x])$
6   **if** $color[y] =$ WHITE
7   PUSH$(E_{stack}, (\{x\}, \{y\}))$
8         $\pi[y] \leftarrow x$
9   GETBCCINFO(y)
10   **if** $low[y] \geq df[x]$
11          $desc \leftarrow \emptyset$
12   **repeat** $(\{e_1\}, \{e_2\}) \leftarrow$ POP(E_{stack})
13   **if** $e_1 \neq x$
14               $desc \leftarrow desc \cup desc[e_1]$
15               $parent[e_1] \leftarrow x$
16   **if** $e_2 \neq x$
17               $desc \leftarrow desc \cup desc[e_2]$
18               $parent[e_2] \leftarrow x$
19   **until** $(\{e_1\}, \{e_2\}) = (\{x\}, \{y\})$
20   **if** $low[x] = low[y]$ ▷ is t articulation vertex?
21             $parent[x] \leftarrow x$
22   **if** $low[x] \neq low[y] \wedge y \in N_h[x] \wedge desc \cap N_s[x] = \emptyset$
23   FINDINITIALCOMPOUNDS(x,y)
24          $desc[x] \leftarrow desc[x] \cup desc$
25       $low[x] \leftarrow$ MIN$(low[x], low[y])$
26   **else if** $y \neq \pi[x]$
27   PUSH$(E_{stack}, (\{x\}, \{y\}))$
28         $low[x] \leftarrow$ MIN$(low[x], df[y])$
29 $color[x] \leftarrow$ BLACK

Figure 3.35.: Pseudocode for GETBCCINFO

of the current biconnected component. In order to differentiate between the two cases later on, we set x's parent to itself (Line 21) if x is not an articulation vertex (Line 20).

Line 22 checks for several conditions: (1) if x is an articulation vertex $low[x] \neq low[y]$ and not just t, (2) if $(\{x\}, \{y\})$ substitutes a hyperedge and (3) if in the original hypergraph x is not connected to any other node $z \in desc$ by a simple edge. Only if all three conditions are met, FINDINITIALCOMPOUNDS is invoked in Line 23.

The pseudocode of FINDINITIALCOMPOUNDS is given in Figure 3.36. Entering FINDINITIALCOMPOUNDS, we know that there must exist at least one complex hyperedge (v, w) in the original graph with $x \in v \wedge y \in w$. With the help of the lookup index computed from the labels i, j in Line 1 (Figure 3.27), we get the hyperedge references of the original hypergraph via the global array $HEdgeLkp$ (which was set up by STOREADJACENCYINFO). At this point, it is possible that more than one reference is returned. In this case, the referenced complex hyperedges must overlap. Although not necessary, but for reasons of simplicity, we demand that just one reference exists (Line 3) before FINDINITIALCOMPOUNDSSUB for the hypernodes v and w is called.

FINDINITIALCOMPOUNDS(x_i, y_j)

    ▷ **Input:** vertices $x_i, y_i \in V$
1   $lkp \leftarrow$ COMPUTELOOKUPIDX(x_i, y_j)
2   **if** $|HEdgeLkp[lkp]| = 1$
3      $(v, w) \leftarrow HEdgeLkp[lkp]$
4   FINDINITIALCOMPOUNDSSUB(v)
5   FINDINITIALCOMPOUNDSSUB(w)
6      $E_A^{ref} \leftarrow E_A^{ref} \cup$ REFERENCES($\{(v,w)\}$)

FINDINITIALCOMPOUNDSSUB(v)

1   **if** $|v| > 1$
2      $label \leftarrow$ MAINTAINLABELS(v)   ▷ assigning index-introducing compound v.
3   TOP($Info_{stack}$).$S' \leftarrow$ TOP($Info_{stack}$).$S' \setminus v$
4   TOP($Info_{stack}$).$S_A \leftarrow$ TOP($Info_{stack}$).$S_A \cup label$
5   **for all** $x \in v$
6         $IdxIntroV_{map}[\{x\}] \leftarrow IdxIntroV_{map}[\{x\}] \cup label$

Figure 3.36.: Pseudocode for FINDINITIALCOMPOUNDS

MAINTAINLABELS(v)

    ▷ **Input:** vertex set $v \in S$
    ▷ **Output:** vertex set containing index-introducing vertex
1   **if** KEYDOESNOTEXIST($Label_{map}, v$)
2      $k \leftarrow$ SIZE($Label_{map}$) $+ |V|$ ▷ V is the vertex set of the query graph
3      $z_k \leftarrow$ new index-introducing compound vertex labeled k
4      $Label_{map}[v] \leftarrow \{z_k\}$
5      $Label_{map}^{-1}[\{z_k\}] \leftarrow v$
6   **return** $\{z_k\}$
7   **else**
8   **return** $Label_{map}[v]$

Figure 3.37.: Pseudocode for MAINTAINLABELS

FINDINITIALCOMPOUNDSSUB ensures that the handed over hypernode v is really complex (Line 1). If so, we assign an index-introducing compound vertex that represents the vertices contained in v by a call to MAINTAINLABELS (Figure 3.37). Furthermore, for every vertex $x \in v$ we (1) remove x from the vertex set TOP($Info_{stack}$).S' and (2) x as part of the hypernode v is mapped to its corresponding index-introducing compound vertex $IdxIntroV_{map}[v]$.

Decoding Compound Vertices

As Section 3.5.1 explains, we need to substitute the index-reusing compound vertices in every emitted partition of the partitioning algorithm. This is done by DECODE, as given in Figure 3.38. In Line 1, we initialize *decoded* with the original vertices that are not represented by any compound vertex. After that, we loop over the index-reusing compound vertices (Line 2) contained in C' and substitute them with the group of vertices they represent (Line 3).

DECODE(C')
   ▷ **Input:** vertex set C'
1   $decoded \leftarrow C' \cap \text{TOP}(Info_{stack}).S_{org}$
2   **for all** $x \in C' \setminus \text{TOP}(Info_{stack}).S_{org}$ ▷ only index-reusing compound vertices
3      $decoded \leftarrow decoded \cup \text{TOP}(Info_{stack}).Compound_{map}^{-1}[\{x\}]$
4   **return** $decoded$

Figure 3.38.: Pseudocode for DECODE

Compound Vertices - An Example

Let us get back to our motivation example for compound vertices of Section 3.5.1. From the graph shown in Figure 3.20(a), we gained the simple graph of Figure 3.20(b) by calling COMPUTEADJACENCYINFO. But as it turned out, this was not restrictive enough, since three of the four generated partitions were false *ccp*s (symmetric counter pairs ignored). By invoking GETBCCINFO, we gain the following information: $Label_{map}^{-1} = \{(\{R_5\} \to \{R_2, R_3\}), (\{R_6\} \to \{R_0, R_1\}), (\{R_7\} \to \{R_0, R_1, R_2\})\}$ and $IdxIntroV_{map} = \{(\{R_0\} \to \{R_6, R_7\}), (\{R_1\} \to \{R_6, R_7\}), (\{R_2\} \to \{R_5, R_7\}), (\{R_3\} \to \{R_5\})\}$ and $\text{TOP}(Info_{stack}).S' = \{R_4\}$.

Once we reach Line 29 of COMPOSECOMPOUNDVERTICES, $h = \{R_0, R_1, R_2, R_3\}$ holds. We introduce R_0 as a new index-reusing compound vertex representing h. After Line 30 of COMPOSECOMPOUNDVERTICES, $compound = \{R_0\} \wedge \text{TOP}(Info_{stack}).S' = \{R_0, R_4\}$ holds. The resulting simple graph is shown in Figure 3.20(c). Note that instead of the index-reusing compound vertex R_0, an index-introducing compound vertex R_0 is shown. This was done in order not to complicate things while motivating our central ideas in Section 3.5.1. Any graph-aware partitioning algorithm will produce only one partition: $(\{R_0\}, \{R_4\})$ (or its symmetric partition $(\{R_4\}, \{R_0\})$). And finally, a call to DECODE($\{R_0\}$) returns $\{R_0, R_1, R_2, R_3\}$ and DECODE($\{R_4\}$) returns $\{R_4\}$. Since both $\{R_4\}$ and the decoded set $\{R_0, R_1, R_2, R_3\}$ are connected, the partition is proved to be a *ccp* and is returned together with its symmetric counter pair (Lines 16 or 17 of PARTITION$_X$) without generating any false *ccp*s.

3.5.5. Economizing on Connection Tests

Let us briefly recall that non-inner joins are not freely reorderable because certain join reorderings result in different non-equivalent plans that return different query results when executed. Furthermore, it is well known that valid operator orderings can be encoded by transforming simple edges into hyperedges [2, 20, 21, 27]. Complex hypergraphs that are a result of those transformations can be mainly categorized as complex cycle-free hypergraphs (Section 3.2.1). We strongly believe that among all complex query graphs that can be found in real-world scenarios, the majority belongs to this category. The only common exception will be graphs that contain complex hyperedges originating from complex predicates.

CONNECTIONTESTREQUIRED(S')

▷ **Input:** set S' that may contain compound vertices
▷ **Output:** returns TRUE if connection test can be avoided
1 **return** TOP($Info_{stack}$).$S_{compounds}^{disconnected} \cap S' = \emptyset \wedge E_A^{ref} \supset$ TOP($Info_{stack}$).E_F^{ref}

Figure 3.39.: Pseudocode for CONNECTIONTESTREQUIRED

Avoiding Connection Tests

For complex cycle-free hypergraphs, there are certain scenarios where we do not need a connection test. Since we have to run at least one connection test for every emitted join partition, saving the effort in doing so would increase efficiency significantly. In general, two conditions have to be met in order to be able to avoid the connection tests: (1) All complex hyperedges need to be articulation hyperedges. (2) All complex hypernodes need to be connected.

We check for these two conditions by a call to CONNECTIONTESTREQUIRED in Line 9 of PARTITION$_X$. The pseudocode for CONNECTIONTESTREQUIRED is given in Figure 3.39. Condition (1) is checked by ensuring that $E_A^{ref} \supset$ TOP($Info_{stack}$).E_F^{ref} holds. Thereby, E_A^{ref} is a set of hyperedge references that point to all articulation hyperedges, and TOP($Info_{stack}$).E_F^{ref} points to all complex hyperedges that reference only vertices of the (sub) graph. Hyperedge references are stored in the form of integers that are an index to the corresponding entry in the hyperedge array. We store hyperedge references as a bitvector. To check for Condition (2), we need to compare the set of index-reusing compound vertices that are disconnected TOP($Info_{stack}$).$S_{compounds}^{disconnected}$ with S'. Hereby, TOP($Info_{stack}$).$S_{compounds}^{disconnected}$ is computed in Lines 8 and 9 of MANAGEADJACENCYINFO.

Even if a complex hypernode is disconnected, we might be able to connect it by merging it with adjacent vertices. But we cannot risk to restrict the graph by enlarging the complex hypernode too much. Otherwise, we might prevent the computation of valid *ccps*. Thus, we have to determine under which circumstances it is safe to enlarge a hypernode. Note that enlarging a node has a positive side effect: The number of vertices in TOP($Info_{stack}$).S' is decreased because more vertices are represented by the same compound vertex. That in turn increases the graph-aware partitioning algorithms performance notably, since a graph with fewer vertices and fewer edges is considered.

Before we determine how to enlarge a hypernode, let us take a look at Figure 3.40(a). Here, R_3 is only connected to the rest of the graph through R_2, R_4. But the latter hypernode is not connected. The only way to connect R_2 with R_4 is through R_1 and R_0, R_5. Thus, there exists only one valid *ccp*: ($\{R_0, R_1, R_2, R_4, R_5\}, \{R_3\}$) (and its symmetric counter pair). In fact, if we do not include R_0, R_1, R_5, we have to partition the graph into at least three connected subgraphs.

Figure 3.40(b) shows the transformed graph of Figure 3.40(a) after applying COMPUTEADJACENCYINFO. We can observe that R_1 and R_0 lie on every possible path $R_2 \to^* R_4$. We can generalize our observation: If there exists a non-separable hypernode that is not connected, it can be enlarged with all vertices that lie on every possible path (in the mapped simple graph) between the connected subsets of the disconnected hypernode. Since the vertices that are candidates for the enlargement have to lie

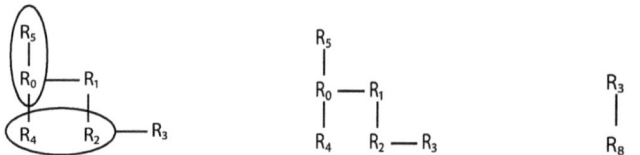

Figure 3.40.: (a) Hypergraph, (b) simple graph and (c) final graph

on every path, all vertices that qualify for the enlargement in the end are articulation vertices by definition.

Enlarging Disconnected Hypernodes

Non-connected hypernodes are enlarged by MAXIMIZECOMPOUNDVERTICES, as given in Figure 3.41. Since this method relies on the knowledge of the biconnected components of the graph, we invoke it after calling GETBCCINFO, but before merging the overlapping hypernodes in COMPOSECOMPOUNDVERTICES.

Therefore, we loop through the set of compound vertices S_A (Line 1 of MAXIMIZECOMPOUNDVERTICES), which was computed by FINDINITIALCOMPOUNDSSUB in Line 4. Next, we check whether the corresponding hypernode h (Line 2) is connected (Line 3). The loop of Lines 7 to 16 is responsible to enlarge the hypernode h. Therefore, we use two sets Z and I, whereby Z holds the vertices of the initial h (Line 5) and I keeps track of the already investigated vertices of the initial h. Once all members of Z are investigated, the stop condition of the loop is met.

The idea is as follows: We take an element of Z and assign it to y. There are two possibilities: y is either already part of h or an ancestor of an element of h. In the latter case, it must be an articulation vertex and/or the start vertex t (Line 9 of Figure 3.33). If it is an articulation vertex, we can add it to h (Line 10), since all paths between $desc[y] \cap h$ and other members of the hypernode $h \setminus desc[y]$ must contain y. We choose the next y to be its parent (Line 12). Note that the descendants of y are either already processed or part of different biconnected components. In the latter case, they will be processed later on if they intersect with Z, or they are of no interest. If they are not of interest, this is because they will not be part of every path connecting the different subsets of h.

Before we continue with the next y, we have to check in Line 9 if (1) y has not been processed yet, i.e., $y \notin Z$ or (2) the descendants of y cover the whole hypernode h. In the latter case, we do not need to go any further (following the parents), because we would process other biconnected components that are not of interest. We can discard the members of those components since they cannot be part of every path between the disconnected members of the non-connected hypernode h.

Since we might have interrupted the loop (Line 9) because $h \not\subseteq desc[y]$ holds, we still have to add y to h (Line 14). But there is the chance that $y = t$ holds where t is the start vertex. Now there are two possibilities: either y is also an articulation vertex or it is not (see Section 3.5.4). The differentiation between the two cases is encoded through Line 21 of Figure 3.35. Therefore, we have to ensure that $parent[y] = \text{NIL}$ holds first, otherwise y might not be contained in every possible path between the disconnected parts of h.

MAXIMIZECOMPOUNDVERTICES(S)
   ▷ **Input:** vertex set S
1 **for all** $x \subset \text{TOP}(Info_{stack}).S_A$ ▷ all index-introducing compound v.
2    $h \leftarrow Label_{map}^{-1}[\{x\}]$
3   **if** ISCONNECTEDHYP(h) = TRUE
4   **continue**
5    $Z \leftarrow h$
6    $I \leftarrow \emptyset$
7   **while** $Z \neq \emptyset$
8      $y \leftarrow z \in Z$
9   **while** $h \not\subseteq desc[y] \wedge y \notin I$
10        $h \leftarrow h \cup \{y\}$
11        $I \leftarrow I \cup \{y\}$
12        $y \leftarrow parent[y]$
13   **if** $parent[y] = $ NIL
14          $h \leftarrow h \cup \{y\}$
15      $Z \leftarrow Z \setminus \{y\}$
16      $I \leftarrow I \cup \{y\}$
17   **if** $h \neq Label_{map}^{-1}[\{x\}]$
18   MAXIMIZECOMPOUNDVERTICESSUB($\{x\}, h$)

MAXIMIZECOMPOUNDVERTICESSUB(v, h)
1 **if** KEYDOESNOTEXIST($Label_{map}, h$) $\neq$ TRUE
2    $label \leftarrow Label_{map}[h]$
3   TOP($Info_{stack}$).$S_A \leftarrow$ (TOP($Info_{stack}$).$S_A \setminus v$) $\cup\, label$
4   TOP($Info_{stack}$).$S' \leftarrow$ (TOP($Info_{stack}$).S') $\setminus h$
5   **for all** $x \in h$
6      $IdxIntroV_{map}[\{x\}] \leftarrow (IdxIntroV_{map}[\{x\}] \setminus v) \cup label$
7 **else** CHANGEKEY($Label_{map}, Label_{map}^{-1}[v] \rightarrow h$)
8    $Label_{map}^{-1}[v] \leftarrow h$
9   TOP($Info_{stack}$).$S' \leftarrow$ TOP($Info_{stack}$).$S' \setminus h$
10   **for all** $x \in h \setminus Label_{map}^{-1}[v]$
11      $IdxIntroV_{map}[\{x\}] \leftarrow IdxIntroV_{map}[\{x\}] \cup v$
12 update all hyperedges (v, w) where $v \subseteq h \vee w \subseteq h$ holds

Figure 3.41.: Pseudocode for MAXIMIZECOMPOUNDVERTICES

Finally, the condition of 17 checks if h was enlarged. If so, we have to apply the changes by invoking MAXIMIZECOMPOUNDVERTICESSUB. Now there are two possibilities for the new h: (1) either there is no compound vertex assigned or (2) there is one assigned because the new h is also the endpoint of a different articulation hyperedge. In Lines 1 to 6 and 7 to 11, we change the assignments of the $IdxIntroV_{map}$ and the vertex set TOP($Info_{stack}$).S' according to both cases. In Line 12, we update the corresponding hyperedge.

Let us get back to our example of Figure 3.40 with the disconnected hypernode $\{R_2, R_4\}$. Before invoking MAXIMIZECOMPOUNDVERTICES, the following holds: $Label_{map}^{-1} = \{(\{R_6\} \rightarrow \{R_2, R_4\}), (\{R_7\} \rightarrow \{R_0, R_5\})\}$ and $IdxIntroV_{map} = \{(\{R_0\} \rightarrow \{R_7\}), (\{R_2\} \rightarrow \{R_6\}), (\{R_4\} \rightarrow \{R_6\}), (\{R_5\} \rightarrow \{R_7\})\}$. Once MAXIMIZECOMPOUNDVERTICES returns, $Label_{map}^{-1} = \{(\{R_6\} \rightarrow \{R_0, R_1, R_2, R_4\}), (\{R_7\} \rightarrow \{R_0, R_5\})\}$ holds. Furthermore, the entry for R_0 in

$IdxIntroV_{map}$ was changed to $\{R_6, R_7\}$ and $(\{R_1\} \to \{R_6\})$ was inserted. Note that the entry for R_5 remains the same. Once the call to COMPOSECOMPOUNDVERTICES returns, we have merged the index-introducing compound vertices to a single index-reusing compound vertex R_0. The resulting simple graph is shown in Figure 3.40(c) with $\text{TOP}(Info_{stack}).S' = \{R_0, R_3\}$. Note that instead of the index-reusing compound vertex R_0, an index-introducing compound vertex R_8 is shown. Similarly to Section 3.5.4, this was done in order not to complicate things while motivating our central ideas of Section 3.5.1. Further note that now all two conditions for avoiding the connection tests are met.

Storing Set Connectivity Information

We propose to store the information whether a vertex set C is connected or not into the memotable. Besides TRUE and FALSE, we need UNKNOWN. Now every time ISCONNECTEDHYP($H_{|C}$) is called, we check whether an entry in the memotable for the given vertex set C exists. If not, we create one and invoke the connection test since its current value is UNKNOWN to set it to TRUE or FALSE. In all other cases, we just return its value, which saves us additional connection tests. Note that since our mappings of hypergraphs into simple graphs are relatively restrictive, there will be only a few entries in the memotable with the value FALSE.

3.5.6. Efficient Subgraph Handling

Due to the nature of top-down join enumeration, a partitioning algorithm is called many times, each time with a different subgraph $H_{|S}$. So far, we have only discussed the top-level case as explained in Section 3.5.1, where $H_{|S} = H_{|V} = H$ holds. But invoking COMPUTEADJACENCYINFO and COMPOSECOMPOUNDVERTICES from PARTITION$_X$ for every proper subgraph of H input is to expensive. Instead, we reuse the information already computed by COMPUTEADJACENCYINFO and COMPOSECOMPOUNDVERTICES as stored in the global variables (Figures 3.25 and 3.23). But unfortunately, the adjacency information kept in N_m (Figure 3.23) might need adjustments to comply with the current subset of vertices stored in S. Otherwise, we might miss to compute valid *ccps* for the current S. If we applied COMPUTEADJACENCYINFO alone (without the application of COMPOSECOMPOUNDVERTICES), this would not be necessary. This is because COMPUTEADJACENCYINFO implements the composition of $g^{-1} \circ s$ only. In other words, a graph simplification $s(H)$ with a possible loss of restrictiveness and a subsequent application of g^{-1} allows for the computation of false *ccps* but does not prevent the emission of valid *ccps*. But by invoking COMPOSECOMPOUNDVERTICES, we substitute single vertices stored in S by introducing index-reusing compound vertices.

The general idea of COMPOSECOMPOUNDVERTICES (Section 3.5.4, motivated by the fourth observation of Section 3.5.1) is the transformation of non-separable hypernodes to compound vertices. Thus, we gain a different simple graph to which we refer as G for now. In most scenarios G has fewer edges and fewer vertices than $g^{-1}(s(H_{|S}))$. The output S' of COMPOSECOMPOUNDVERTICES (Line 5 of PARTITION$_X$) is the vertex set of G. Since S' contains only vertices of S and index-reusing compound vertices, the indices used in S' must be a (not necessarily proper)

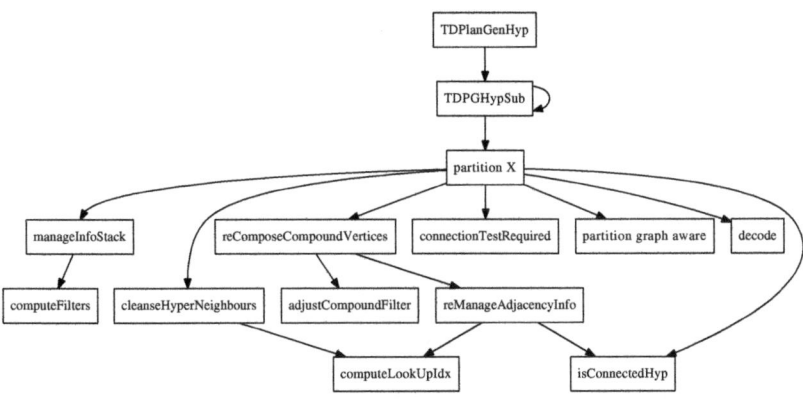

Figure 3.42.: Call graph for the top-level case of PARTITION$_X$

subset of the indices used in S. For the rare case of $S' = S$, $G = g^{-1}(s(H_{|S}))$ will hold. In all other cases, we need to modify N_m at some point during the top-down traversal of TDPLANGENHYP. We have reached such an instance when a complex articulation hyperedge (v, w) becomes cut off because it is contained in the minimal cut of the parent partitioning. If such a hyperedge (v, w) is cut off, then one of its hypernodes (say w) is not contained in the new S anymore. Now if the other hypernode v with $v \subseteq S$ is a complex hypernode so that $|v| > 1$ holds, v must have been non-separable for the parent S. For the current S, complex hypernodes of other complex articulation hyperedges (that reference only vertices of the current S) might still reference a superset of v. But if that is not the case, v is not non-separable anymore and, hence, the corresponding compound vertex needs to be dissolved or recomputed (if it is a merger of different overlapping non-separable hypernodes). In any case, this requires a modification of N_m. To put this into different words: The application of COMPOSECOMPOUNDVERTICES guarantees that the same $P_{ccp}(S)$ for that specific S can be computed (false ccps already removed) but not the same P_{ccp} (Section 3.2.1).

As Section 3.5.2 has pointed out, PARTITION$_X$ differentiates between two cases: Case (1), to which we refer as top-level case where $S = V$ holds, and Case (2), which covers all other cases where $S \subset V$ holds. Figure 3.42 shows the call graph for Case (2). Thus TDPGHYPSUB must have been called at least two times which is indicated by the arrow that starts from and points to the box of TDPGHYPSUB. In this section, we cover Case (2). Hence, we explain all depicted methods that are directly or indirectly called by PARTITION$_X$, except CONNECTIONTESTREQUIRED (Section 3.5.5), PARTITION$_{graph-aware}$ (Chapter 2), DECODE (Section 3.5.4), COMPUTELOOKUPIDX (Section 3.5.3) and ISCONNECTEDHYP (Section 3.3.3).

Managing the $Info_{stack}$

For maintenance reasons, besides N_m other variables have to be modified as well. As already mentioned in Section 3.5.2, we group those volatile variables in the structure $StackEntry$ (Figure 3.23). For every subsequent call to PARTITION$_X$, we push a copy of the old topmost $StackEntry$ onto $Info_{stack}$ in order to be able to modify

MANAGEINFOSTACK(S)
    ▷ **Input:** connected set S not containing any compound vertices
1   $E_F^{ref} \leftarrow \text{TOP}(Info_{stack}).E_F^{ref}$
2   $\text{PUSH}(Info_{stack}, \text{TOP}(Info_{stack}))$
3   COMPUTEFILTERS(S, E_F^{ref})

Figure 3.43.: Pseudocode for MANAGEINFOSTACK

COMPUTEFILTERS($S, E_{F_{parent}}^{ref}$)
    ▷ **Input:** connected set S, set of old hyperedge references $E_{F_{parent}}^{ref}$
1   $\text{TOP}(Info_{stack}).E_F^{ref} \leftarrow \emptyset$
2   $\text{TOP}(Info_{stack}).E_C^{ref} \leftarrow \emptyset$
3   **for all** $ref \in E_{F_{parent}}^{ref}$
4      $(v, w) \leftarrow \text{DEREFERENCE}(ref)$ ▷ Figure 3.31
5   **if** $v \subset S \wedge w \subset S$
6         $\text{TOP}(Info_{stack}).E_F^{ref} \leftarrow \text{TOP}(Info_{stack}).E_F^{ref} \cup \{ref\}$
7   **elseif** $(v \subset S \wedge w \not\subset S) \vee (v \not\subset S \wedge w \subset S)$
8         $\text{TOP}(Info_{stack}).E_C^{ref} \leftarrow \text{TOP}(Info_{stack}).E_C^{ref} \cup \{ref\}$
9   **if** $ref \in E_A^{ref}$
10   **if** $v \not\subset S$
11              $\text{TOP}(Info_{stack}).S_A \leftarrow \text{TOP}(Info_{stack}).S_A \setminus v$
12   **else** $\text{TOP}(Info_{stack}).S_A \leftarrow \text{TOP}(Info_{stack}).S_A \setminus w$

Figure 3.44.: Pseudocode for COMPUTEFILTERS

it. This is done by a call to MANAGEINFOSTACK (Line 6 of PARTITION$_X$) with the pseudocode given in Figure 3.43.

Besides pushing a copy of the current *StackEntry* on top of $Info_{stack}$ (Line 2), MANAGEINFOSTACK invokes COMPUTEFILTERS. The pseudocode for COMPUTE-FILTERS is given in Figure 3.44. We call it to speed up processing by maintaining two sets of complex hyperedge references: (1) the current set of complex hyperedge references E_F^{ref} and (2) the set of complex cut-off hyperedge references E_C^{ref}. This way, E_C^{ref} will be a subset of the parent E_F^{ref}, which is passed in as $E_{F_{parent}}^{ref}$. Furthermore, the set of index-introducing compound vertices S_A is cleansed. Therefore, the index-introducing compound vertices that represent vertices not contained in the current S anymore are removed. This can only happen if a complex articulation hyperedge is cut off (Line 9 of COMPUTEFILTERS).

Once the current call to TDPGHYPSUB returns, we pop the topmost *StackEntry* again (Section 3.5.2).

After MANAGEINFOSTACK is called, PARTITION$_X$ invokes CLEANSEHYPER-NEIGHBOURS in Line 7 and RECOMPOSECOMPOUNDVERTICES subsequently in Line 8. We will explain CLEANSEHYPERNEIGHBOURS next.

Cleansing of Hyperneighbors

The pseudocode for CLEANSEHYPERNEIGHBOURS is given in Figure 3.45. Its sole purpose is to remove adjacency information that was derived from adjacent complex hyperedges that were cut off during the top-down traversal of TDPGHYPSUB. If outdated adjacency information is not removed, PARTITION$_{graph-aware}$ will produce additional false ccps, which will result in a notably performance penalty. But what is even more important, our connection test avoidance technique will not function properly any more. This means we might avoid connection tests, because according to the criteria implemented in CONNECTIONTESTREQUIRED (Figure 3.39), they are not required for some scenarios. But through outdated adjacency information, PARTITION$_{graph-aware}$ is likely to produce false ccps that will not get caught because of those omitted tests.

As previously mentioned, we discover the complex hyperedges that were cut off through COMPUTEFILTERS and store them into TOP($Info_{stack}$).E_C^{ref}. In case a complex articulation hyperedge was cut off, $|\text{TOP}(Info_{stack}).E_C^{ref}| = 1$ will hold. Otherwise, TOP($Info_{stack}$).E_C^{ref} can contain zero to many references. So, what we have to do is to check for every reference in TOP($Info_{stack}$).E_C^{ref} how it has contributed to the computation of N_m.

There are three different sources considered when N_m is populated: (1) N_s, that holds the simple neighborhood, (2) N_h, that is computed from the result of complex hyperdge to simple edge mappings and (3) the application of the TOP($Info_{stack}$).$Compound_{map}^{-1}$ mapping for the index-reusing compound vertex elements of N_m. Since any graph-aware partitioning algorithm PARTITION$_{graph-aware}$ intersects its neighborhood computation with the vertex set S of the (sub) graph $G_{|S}$ it was called with, source (1) needs no adjustment. But we have to ensure that the information originating from source (2) and (3) is still accurate for the current S.

The associative array N_m stores the adjacency information of a given complex hyperedge (v, w) with the help of two representatives v_{rep}, w_{rep} with $v_{rep} \subseteq v \wedge |v_{rep}| = 1 \wedge w_{rep} \subseteq w \wedge |w_{rep}| = 1$ (Figure 3.24). To check if v is connected to w, we have to check among all members $z \in v$ if TOP($Info_{stack}$).$N_m[z]$ is not disjoint with w. Alternatively, since the information in N_m needs to be symmetric, we could also check if for any $z \in w$, TOP($Info_{stack}$).$N_m[z]$ intersects with v. Let ref be the index of the corresponding $HyperEdges[ref]$ entry that represents the hyperedge (v, w). Now assume w with $w \not\subseteq S$ was cut off, because of $ref \in \text{TOP}(Info_{stack}).E_C^{ref}$ and $v \subseteq S$ holds. Further, let x be the vertex of the one-element set v_{rep}, which is the representative of v and y the vertex of the one-element set w_{rep}, which is the representative of w for (v, w). Then we need to adjust N_m. This is done by removing y from TOP($Info_{stack}$).$N_m[x]$ and x from TOP($Info_{stack}$).$N_m[y]$. Actually, the latter is not really necessary, since TOP($Info_{stack}$).$N_m[y]$ will not be accessed by PARTITION$_{graph-aware}$, because $y \notin S$ holds. Furthermore, if all members z with $z \in w$ are cut off so that $z \notin S$ holds, we can even skip the adjustment for that particular (v, w). The reason for that is the same as for source (1): PARTITION$_{graph-aware}$ intersects its neighborhood computation with the vertex set S so that the vertex y representing w will not be in the result set. This is especially true when (v, w) is a complex articulation hyperedge that was cut off.

CLEANSEHYPERNEIGHBOURS($H_{|S}$)

1 **if** TOP($Info_{stack}$).$E_C^{ref} \subseteq E_A^{ref}$
2   **return**
3 $Z \leftarrow$ TOP($Info_{stack}$).E_C^{ref}
4 **while** $Z \neq \emptyset$
5      $ref \leftarrow z \in Z$
6      $Z \leftarrow Z \setminus \{ref\}$
7      $(v, w) \leftarrow$ DEREFERENCE(ref)
8      $x \leftarrow$ ELEMENTOF($HyperEdges[ref].v_{rep}$)
9      $y \leftarrow$ ELEMENTOF($HyperEdges[ref].w_{rep}$)
10     $lkp \leftarrow$ COMPUTELOOKUPIDX(x, y)
11   **if** $x \subset S \wedge y \subset S \wedge (v \not\subset S \vee w \not\subset S) \wedge$
             $HEdgeLkp[lkp] \cap$ TOP($Info_{stack}$).$E_F^{ref} = \emptyset$
12         $Z \leftarrow Z \setminus HEdgeLkp[lkp]$
13         $c_v \leftarrow$ ELEMENTOF(TOP($Info_{stack}$).$Compound_{map}[x]$)
14         $c_w \leftarrow$ ELEMENTOF(TOP($Info_{stack}$).$Compound_{map}[y]$)
15   **if** $\{c_v\} \cap \{x\} = \emptyset \wedge \{c_w\} \cap \{y\} = \emptyset$
16   TOP($Info_{stack}$).$N_m[x] \leftarrow$ TOP($Info_{stack}$).$N_m[x] \setminus \{y\}$
17   TOP($Info_{stack}$).$N_m[y] \leftarrow$ TOP($Info_{stack}$).$N_m[y] \setminus \{x\}$
18   **if** $c_v \neq$ NIL $\vee c_w \neq$ NIL
19             $h_v \leftarrow x$
20   **if** $c_v \neq$ NIL
21                 $h_v =$ TOP($Info_{stack}$).$Compound_{map}[\{c_v\}]$
22   **if** $c_w \neq$ NIL
23                     $h_v \leftarrow h_v \cap$ TOP($Info_{stack}$).$N_m[c_w]$
24             $h_w \leftarrow y$
25   **if** $c_w \neq$ NIL
26                 $h_w \leftarrow$ TOP($Info_{stack}$).$Compound_{map}[\{c_w\}]$
27   **if** $c_v \neq$ NIL
28                     $h_w \leftarrow h_w \cap$ TOP($Info_{stack}$).$N_m[c_v]$
29             $E_{Tmp}^{ref} \leftarrow \emptyset$
30   **for all** $l \in h_v$
31   **if** $N_s[l] \cap h_w \neq \emptyset$
32                     $E_{Tmp}^{ref} \leftarrow \emptyset$
33   **break**
34   **for all** $r \in h_w$
35                     $lkp \leftarrow$ COMPUTELOOKUPIDX(l, r)
36                     $E_{Tmp}^{ref} \leftarrow E_{Tmp}^{ref} \cup HEdgeLkp[lkp]$
37   **if** $E_{Tmp}^{ref} \cap$ TOP($Info_{stack}$).$E_F^{ref} = \emptyset \wedge E_{Tmp}^{ref} \neq \emptyset$
38                 $diff \leftarrow \{y\} \cup \{c_w\}$
39   TOP($Info_{stack}$).$N_m[x] \leftarrow$ TOP($Info_{stack}$).$N_m[x] \setminus diff$
40   **if** $c_v \neq$ NIL
41   TOP($Info_{stack}$).$N_m[c_v] \leftarrow$ TOP($Info_{stack}$).$N_m[c_v] \setminus diff$
42                 $diff \leftarrow \{x\} \cup \{c_v\}$
43   TOP($Info_{stack}$).$N_m[y] \leftarrow$ TOP($Info_{stack}$).$N_m[y] \setminus diff$
44   **if** $c_w \neq$ NIL
45   TOP($Info_{stack}$).$N_m[c_w] \leftarrow$ TOP($Info_{stack}$).$N_m[c_w] \setminus diff$

Figure 3.45.: Pseudocode for CLEANSEHYPERNEIGHBOURS

Now let us take a look at the pseudocode of CLEANSEHYPERNEIGHBOURS. In Line 1, we start by checking if there was a complex articulation hyperedge cut off. If so, nothing needs to be done for now, and we can return the call (Line 2). Otherwise, we loop over all complex hyperedge references (Lines 4 to 45). In Line 5, we choose one arbitrary hyperedge reference ref. Thereby, ref will be an index into the array $HyperEdges$ (Figure 3.25). We remove ref from the set Z in Line 6. In Lines 8 and 9, we look up the representatives of v and w (Figure 3.24). The representatives have been selected by COMPUTEADJACENCYINFO and have been attached to the corresponding hyperedge by STOREADJACENCYINFO (Figure 3.32).

With the first part of the expression in Line 11, we check for the previously discussed scenario where one hypernode was not completely cut off and its representative is still contained in S. To explain the condition's second part, we need to take a look at how COMPUTEADJACENCYINFO maps complex hyperedges to simple edges. In order to be as restrictive as possible, we try to map two or more overlapping hyperedges to one simple edge (third observation of Section 3.5.1). Now we check with $HEdgeLkp[lkp] \cap \text{TOP}(Info_{stack}).E_F^{ref} = \emptyset$ if all of those complex hyperedges with the same mapping have really been cut off, otherwise we cannot change N_m for those elements.

In Line 12, we remove the rest of the overlapping hyperedges mapped to the same simple edge from Z in order to reduce the iterations of the loop of Lines 4 to 45. Depending on some additional conditions that we explain later, N_m is adjusted either in Lines 16 and 17 or 39 and 43.

So far, we only have discussed the cleansing of two of the three possible sources for the computation of N_m: N_s and N_h. The cleansing of source (3) related adjacency information is more complex because index-reusing compound vertices are involved that coexist in N_m together with the vertices they represent. Therefore, we also need to check if the index-reusing compound vertex c_v that represents a representative x of v is still linked to the index-reusing compound vertex c_w of y. Further, either one of x or y might not be represented by a compound vertex. Depending on the scenario, up to six adjustments might be necessary, which we apply in Lines 38 to 45. In the following, we explain the necessary checks to determine if those adjustments are justified.

In Lines 13 and 14, the index-reusing compound vertices of x and y are discovered. If they exist, c_v and c_w will hold the corresponding compound vertex. If no such vertex exists, the value will be NIL. We apply the adjustment for source (2) in Lines 16 and 17 under the following conditions: (1) There is no complex articulation hyperedge among the cut-off edges (Lines 1 and 2). (2) Both v and w or either one are partly cut off (Line 11). (3) The representatives x and y are still contained in S (Line 11). (4) If x or y are represented by an index-reusing compound vertex c_v or c_w, respectively, then they must be of different value (Line 15). If this is not the case, we have to check further conditions and might still apply the identical adjustments in Lines 39 and 43.

The following example shows why the check in Line 15 is necessary: Let us take a look at Figure 3.46(a), where a complex hypergraph with five relations is depicted. A call to COMPUTEADJACENCYINFO transforms the complex hypergraph into the simple graph of Figure 3.46(b). A call to COMPOSECOMPOUNDVERTICES produces the intermediated index-introducing compound vertex R_5 in order to represent the non-separable hypernode R_0, R_4. During the process, COMPOSECOMPOUNDVERTICES transforms R_5 into the index-reusing compound relation R_0 and

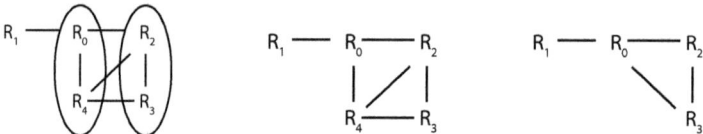

Figure 3.46.: (a) Hypergraph, (b) simplified graph (COMPUTEADJACENCYINFO) and (c) final graph with R_0 as compound vertex

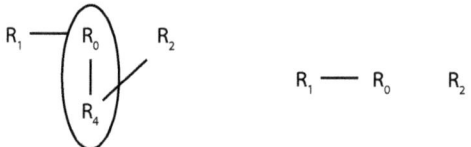

Figure 3.47.: (a) Sub-hypergraph of Figure 3.46 (b) a disconnected graph with R_0 as compound vertex

returns $S' = \{R_0, R_1, R_2, R_3\}$. The result is shown in Figure 3.46(c), where R_0 represents R_0 and R_4. PARTITION$_{graph-aware}$ will produce four *ccps*. One of these will be $(\{R_0, R_1, R_2\}, \{R_3\})$, which gets decoded as $(\{R_0, R_1, R_2, R_4\}, \{R_3\})$ and $(\{R_3\}, \{R_0, R_1, R_2, R_4\})$. Therefore, TDPGHYPSUB will invoke PARTITION$_X$ with the subgraph $H_{|\{R_0, R_1, R_2, R_4\}}$ depicted in Figure 3.47(a). Now CLEANSEHYPER-NEIGHBOURS is called, where TOP$(Info_{stack}).E_C^{ref}$ contains one reference to the cut-off complex hyperedge $(v, w) = (\{R_0\}, \{R_2, R_3\})$. Thereby, x is set to R_0 and y to R_2. Line 13 assigns c_v with R_0 and Line 14 c_w with NIL. The check of Line 15 would fail since $\{c_v\} \cap \{x\} \neq \emptyset$. But without the test, we would delete R_2 from $N_m[R_0]$ and R_0 from $N_m[R_2]$. Hence, CLEANSEHYPERNEIGHBOURS would produce the disconnected simple graph of Figure 3.47, which would be no valid input for PARTITION$_{graph-aware}$.

Once the control flow passes the check of Line 18, the following conditions are met: The conditions (1), (2), (3) still hold. Condition (4) is optional. (5) Both x and y or either one are represented by an index-reusing compound vertex. (6) Because of (1), (2), (3) and (5), both the hypernodes v and w or either one is only partly represented by an index-reusing compound vertex. In other words, there exists at least one non-separable hypernode that overlaps with v or w. (7) Because of (5) and (6), if v overlaps with such a non-separable hypernode, then x must be contained by that hypernode. The same holds for y.

It is important to note that besides a scenario (a) where (1), (2), (3) and (4) hold or a scenario (b) where (1), (2), (3), (5), (6) and (7) hold, adjustments neither have to nor can be applied. Note that the set of all possible scenarios (a) and the set of all possible scenarios (b) is not disjoint. Further note that the conditions for scenario (b) are necessary but not sufficient. We explain what else has to be considered. Let us assume both c_v and c_w are not NIL. Hence, there exist two node sets h_v and h_w that are represented by c_v and c_w, respectively. Because of condition (5), $x \in h_v \wedge y \in h_w$ holds. We know that h_v was connected to h_w before (v, w) was cut off. But before we disconnect h_v from h_w by adjusting N_m in Lines 38 to 45, we have to make sure that there is no other link. This could be either a simple or a complex hyperedge of the original hypergraph.

For the investigation of simple edge links, we utilize N_s. Therefore, we loop through all vertices l in h_v (Line 30) and check if if $N_s[l] \cap h_w \neq \emptyset$ holds (Line 31). If that is the case, we can continue with the next cut-off edge (Line 7). To determine if there exists another complex hyperedge-link is slightly more costly. This is because we need to consult for every pair $(l \in h_v, r \in h_w)$ (Lines 30 and 34) the $HEdgeLkp$-array (Lines 35 and 36) to check if a complex hyperedge (s,t) with $s \in S \wedge l \in s \wedge t \in S \wedge r \in t$ exists. Once we have ensured (Line 37) that no such link exists, we apply the adjustments in Lines 38 to 45.

Apart from the case where both c_v and c_w are not NIL, there are also cases where only either one of c_v or c_w is not NIL. For those we also have to ensure that no other link between either x and vertices in h_w or y and vertices in h_v respectively exists before we can apply the adjustments. We take care of these different cases by assigning h_v or h_w dynamically, depending on the situation. So h_v or h_w might hold a whole set of vertices represented by c_v or c_w (Lines 21 and 26) or a single vertex x or y (Lines 19 and 24). In the following, we refer to the additional condition of scenario (b) as condition (8).

In order to increase efficiency by decreasing the number of iterations of the loops in Lines 30 and 34, we try to reduce h_v and h_w in Lines 23 and 28 to only those vertices where links point to.

Now the only thing left to be discussed is whether we really have to differentiate between scenarios (a) and (b), i.e., are there scenarios where only conditions (1), (2), (3) and (4) hold, but not condition (5), (6), (7) and (8). Therefore, consider the hypergraph of Figure 3.48(a). The result of the call to COMPUTEADJACENCYINFO is given in Figure 3.48(b). Through the invocation of COMPOSECOMPOUNDVERTICES with the subsequent call to GETBCCINFO, two index-introducing compound vertices R_6 and R_7 are produced that represent the non-separable hypernodes $\{R_1, R_5\}$ and $\{R_0, R_5\}$. COMPOSECOMPOUNDVERTICES merges them to $\{R_0, R_1, R_5\}$ and maps them to the index-reusing compound vertex R_0. The result of this step is shown in Figure 3.48(c), where $S' = \{R_0, R_2, R_3, R_4\}$ holds. PARTITION$_{graph-aware}$ will produce three ccps. One of them will be $(\{R_0, R_3, R_4\}, \{R_2\})$, which gets decoded as $(\{R_0, R_1, R_3, R_4, R_5\}, \{R_2\})$ and $(\{R_2\}, \{R_0, R_1, R_3, R_4, R_5\})$. Thus, TDPGHYP-SUB will invoke PARTITION$_X$ with the subgraph $H_{|\{R_0, R_1, R_3, R_4, R_5\}}$ depicted in Figure 3.49(a). Since this is not the top-level case, PARTITION$_X$ calls CLEANSEHYPERNEIGHBOURS, where TOP$(Info_{stack}).E_C^{ref}$ contains one reference to the cut-off complex hyperedge $(v,w) = (\{R_1, R_2\}, \{R_3\})$. Thereby, x gets set to R_1 and y to R_3. Line 13 assigns c_v with R_0 and Line 14 c_w with NIL. The check of Line 15 will not fail, since $\{c_v\} \cap \{x\} = \emptyset$ holds. Hence $(v,w) = (\{R_1, R_2\}, \{R_3\})$ is identified as scenario (a). Thus, Lines 16 and 17 would delete the link between R_1 and R_3. Now let us see if it is also classified as scenario (b). In fact, all conditions (1), (2), (3), (5), (6), (7) hold, except for condition (8). Thereby, $h_v = \{R_0, R_1, R_5\}$ and $h_w = \{R_3\}$ hold, but because of Line 31 $N_s[R_0] = \{R_3\}$ is checked and, therefore, Lines 38 to 45 are not executed. Without the adjustment of Lines 16 and 17 and after applying RECOMPOSECOMPOUNDVERTICES, the input graph for PARTITION$_{graph-aware}$ looks like the graph of Figure 3.49(b). Here, R_0 represents $\{R_0, R_5\}$ only. The reassignment is done by RECOMPOSECOMPOUNDVERTICES, as will be explained in

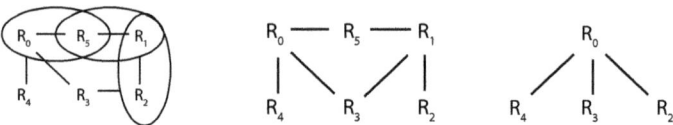

Figure 3.48.: (a) Hypergraph, (b) simplified graph (COMPUTEADJACENCYINFO) and (c) final graph with R_0 as compound vertex

Figure 3.49.: (a) Sub-hypergraph of Figure 3.48 (b) simple graph with R_0 as compound vertex

short. Since the edge (R_1, R_3) is not correct because $(\{R_1, R_2\}, \{R_3\})$ was cut off, PARTITION$_{graph-aware}$ will produce with $(\{R_0, R_4\}, \{R_1, R_3\})$ a false ccp, which can be avoided through the implementation of Lines 16 and 17. $(\{R_0, R_4\}, \{R_1, R_3\})$ would be decoded to $(\{R_0, R_4, R_5\}, \{R_1, R_3\})$ and $(\{R_1, R_3\}, \{R_0, R_4, R_5\})$. Since the conditions for avoiding the connection tests are met, both partitions would be emitted. Thus, an incorrect result would be produced.

Recomposing Compound Vertices

The application of COMPOSECOMPOUNDVERTICES substitutes single vertices that are elements of a non-separable hypernode by index-reusing compound vertices. This only happens when complex articulation hyperedges are present. The transformation of non-separable hypernodes to compound vertices is important for the efficiency of the partitioning process, since the computation of many false ccps is prevented. At some point during the top-down traversal of TDPGHYPSUB, complex articulation hyperedges are cut off and non-separable hypernodes represented by index-reusing compound vertices are not non-separable anymore. Hence, the index-reusing compound vertices that represent the complex hypernode of such a cut-off complex articulation hyperedge need to be recomputed or, as in many cases, completely dissolved. This is the task of RECOMPOSECOMPOUNDVERTICES. The pseudocode is given in Figure 3.50. The main difference to COMPOSECOMPOUNDVERTICES is that no calls to GETBCCINFO and MAXIMIZECOMPOUNDVERTICES are made. Instead, the information is mainly stored in $Label_{map}^{-1}$, $IdxIntroV_{map}$, TOP$(Info_{stack}).Compound_{map}$ and TOP$(Info_{stack}).Compound_{map}^{-1}$ is reused, which increases efficiency. We start by checking if the cut-off edge was complex. If so, we ensure whether it was also an articulation hyperedge. This is done in Line 1 of RECOMPOSECOMPOUNDVERTICES. Otherwise, the call is returned immediately. In Lines 3 and 4, we dereference and assign the one articulation hyperedge that was cut off to (v, w). We determine the hypernode u of (v, w) that is still in S in Lines 5 to 8. Then we check if u can be removed from TOP$(Info_{stack}).S_A$ by a call to ADJUSTCOMPOUNDFILTER (Figure 3.51) in Line 9.

The task of ADJUSTCOMPOUNDFILTER is to determine if u is also the hypernode of another complex articulation hyperedge (Line 5 of ADJUSTCOMPOUNDFILTER). Therefore, all complex articulation hyperedges that reference only vertices in the current S need to be considered (Line 3). If no other non-separable hypernode that matches u was found, u can be removed (Line 9 ADJUSTCOMPOUNDFILTER). Note that the other hypernode of (v,w) that is not u was already removed from $\text{TOP}(Info_{stack}).S_A$ either in Line 11 or 12 of COMPUTEFILTERS.

We rely on the accuracy of $\text{TOP}(Info_{stack}).S_A$ in Lines 19 and 28 of RECOMPOSECOMPOUNDVERTICES. With $compound_o$, we reference the old index-reusing hypernode that represented u and possibly other overlapping non-separable hypernodes (Line 10 of RECOMPOSECOMPOUNDVERTICES). The vertex set corresponding to $compound_o$ is assigned to $hypernode_o$ (Line 11).

Let us denote with h_u the vertex set that is represented by u. Then we know that $u \subseteq h_u \subseteq hypernode_o$ must hold. Further, assume for now that by calling ADJUSTCOMPOUNDFILTER u was removed from $\text{TOP}(Info_{stack}).S_A$. Then we know that h_u is non-separable anymore. Now if $h_u = hypernode_o$ holds, we have to dissolve the index-reusing hypernode $compound_o$. Otherwise, if $h_u \subset hypernode_o$ holds, then $hypernode_o$ is a merger of non-separable hypernodes. In that case, we have to determine how and if the other non-separable hypernodes overlap. New index-reusing compound vertices may need to be introduced.

This is done by the loop of Lines 15 to 38. The approach is quite similar to the one implemented in COMPOSECOMPOUNDVERTICES. We explain only the differences and refer to Section 3.5.4 for the details. Instead of looping over all single vertices that are represented by any index-introducing compound vertex (Line 15 of COMPOSECOMPOUNDVERTICES), only the vertices of $hypernode_o$ need to be considered (Line 15 of RECOMPOSECOMPOUNDVERTICES). For all other vertices, nothing will change. If a $y \in hypernode_o$ with $y \in h_u$ is not also a member of any other non-separable hypernode, it cannot be represented by an index-reusing compound vertex any more. Hence, the initial vertex set h is set to $h = v = \{y\}$ (Line 17). So if no non-separable hypernode containing y exists, the vertex set Z will be empty (Line 19) and the loop of Lines 22 to 29 will not be entered. Then, Line 36 will remove the index-reusing compound vertex mapping for y and Line 37 will add y back to $\text{TOP}(Info_{stack}).S_{org}$. The latter is important for a proper functioning of DECODE. In case there is another non-separable hypernode that still contains y, this is handled in the same way as in COMPOSECOMPOUNDVERTICES. The only difference is that we have to intersect the $IdxIntroV_{map}$ lookup with $\text{TOP}(Info_{stack}).S_A$ in Lines 19 and 28. This is important because not all members of $IdxIntroV_{map}[v = \{y\}]$ or $IdxIntroV_{map}[\{x\}]$ are necessary non-separable hypernodes within the current S.

Line 39 ensures that $\text{TOP}(Info_{stack}).S_{compounds}^{disconnected}$ does not contain the old index-reusing compound vertex. We need $\text{TOP}(Info_{stack}).S_{compounds}^{disconnected}$ for the determination if connection tests can be avoided in CONNECTIONTESTREQUIRED. Finally, the changes made by RECOMPOSECOMPOUNDVERTICES have to be encoded into $\text{TOP}(Info_{stack}).N_m$. Therefore, REMANAGEADJACENCYINFO is called in Line 41.

We give the pseudocode for REMANAGEADJACENCYINFO in Figure 3.52. In Lines 4 to 9, we recompute the neighborhood for the vertex c_o by consulting N_s in Lines 4 to 5 and N_h in Lines 6 to 9. This is important since the original value of

RECOMPOSECOMPOUNDVERTICES($H_{|S}$)
    ▷ **Input:** connected (sub)graph $H_{|S}$
    ▷ **Output:** S' a set of vertex sets
1 **if** $E_A^{ref} \cap \text{TOP}(Info_{stack}).E_C^{ref} = \emptyset \vee \text{TOP}(Info_{stack}).E_C^{ref} = \emptyset$
2   **return** $\text{TOP}(Info_{stack}).S'$
3 $ref \leftarrow \text{ELEMENTOF}(\text{TOP}(Info_{stack}).E_C^{ref})$
4 $(v, w) \leftarrow \text{DEREFERENCE}(ref)$ ▷ Figure 3.31
5 $u \leftarrow \emptyset$
6 **if** $v \subseteq S$
7    $u \leftarrow v$
8 **else** $u \leftarrow w$
9 ADJUSTCOMPOUNDFILTER(u)
10 $compound_o \leftarrow \text{TOP}(Info_{stack}).Compound_{map}[u]$
11 $hypernode_o \leftarrow \text{TOP}(Info_{stack}).Compound_{map}^{-1}[compound_o]$
12 $\text{TOP}(Info_{stack}).S' \leftarrow \text{TOP}(Info_{stack}).S' \setminus compound_o$
13 $S'' \leftarrow hypernode_o$ ▷ contains only vertices represented by index-introducing v.
14 $added \leftarrow \emptyset$
15 **while** $S'' \neq \emptyset$
16    $v \leftarrow \{y\} : y \in S''$
17    $h \leftarrow v$ ▷ h stores the new hypernode
18    $S'' \leftarrow S'' \setminus v$
19    $Z \leftarrow IdxIntroV_{map}[v] \cap \text{TOP}(Info_{stack}).S_A$
20    $I \leftarrow \emptyset$
21    $X \leftarrow v$
22   **while** $Z \neq \emptyset$
23      $u \leftarrow \{z\} : z \in Z$
24      $Z \leftarrow Z \setminus u$
25      $I \leftarrow I \cup u$
26      $h \leftarrow h \cup Label_{map}^{-1}[u]$
27   **for all** $x \in (h \setminus X)$
28        $Z \leftarrow Z \cup ((IdxIntroV_{map}[\{x\}] \cap \text{TOP}(Info_{stack}).S_A) \setminus I)$
29      $X \leftarrow X \cup h$
30    $S'' \leftarrow S'' \setminus h$
31    $toadd \leftarrow \{\text{MIN}_{index}(h)\}$ ▷ vertex with smallest index of h
32   **if** $|h| > 1$
33      $\text{TOP}(Info_{stack}).Compound_{map}^{-1}[toadd] \leftarrow h$
34   **for all** $x \in h$
35        $\text{TOP}(Info_{stack}).Compound_{map}[\{x\}] \leftarrow toadd$
36   **else** $\text{TOP}(Info_{stack}).Compound_{map}[h] \leftarrow \emptyset$
37    $\text{TOP}(Info_{stack}).S_{org} \leftarrow \text{TOP}(Info_{stack}).S_{org} \cup toadd$
38    $added \leftarrow added \cup toadd$
39 $\text{TOP}(Info_{stack}).S_{compounds}^{disconnected} \leftarrow \text{TOP}(Info_{stack}).S_{compounds}^{disconnected} \setminus added$
40 $\text{TOP}(Info_{stack}).S' \leftarrow \text{TOP}(Info_{stack}).S' \cup added$
41 REMANAGEADJACENCYINFO($H_{|S}, compound_o, hypernode_o, added$)
42 **return** $\text{TOP}(Info_{stack}).S'$

Figure 3.50.: Pseudocode for RECOMPOSECOMPOUNDVERTICES

$\text{TOP}(Info_{stack}).N_m[c_o]$ was overwritten with the merged adjacency information of the whole vertex set $hypernode_o$. But before we can reset $\text{TOP}(Info_{stack}).N_m[c_o]$, we need to store its current value into Z. We will rely on this information in Lines

ADJUSTCOMPOUNDFILTER(u)

▷ **Input:** index-introducing compound vertex u
1 **if** $|u| > 1$
2      $referenced \leftarrow$ FALSE
3   **for all** $ref \in ($TOP$(Info_{stack}).E_F^{ref} \cap E_A^{ref})$
4          $(v, w) \leftarrow$ DEREFERENCE(ref)
5   **if** $v = u \vee w = u$
6              $referenced \leftarrow$ TRUE
7   **break**
8   **if** $referenced \neq$ TRUE
9   TOP$(Info_{stack}).S_A \leftarrow$ TOP$(Info_{stack}).S_A \setminus u$

Figure 3.51.: Pseudocode for ADJUSTCOMPOUNDFILTER

11 and 23. This is because the adjacency information needs only adjustments between the elements of Z and the elements of $hypernode_o$. The other values for the other elements of S will remain unchanged.

Since N_h was computed in order to reflect the adjacency between hypernodes through complex hyperedges, we need to check if this information is still accurate for the current S. Therefore, we check for every pair (x, c_o) (Lines 7 and 8) if there is at least one hyperedge that only references vertices in S.

In Line 10, we determine between two cases: Case (1) is that some vertices of $hypernode_o$ are still represented by an index-introducing compound vertex. In that case, there have been overlapping non-separable hypernodes. Otherwise, the index-reusing compound vertex was completely dissolved, to which we refer as case (2). We process case (1) in Lines 11 to 22 and case (2) in Lines 23 to 24.

During the handling of case (1), we iterate over all members x of Z (Line 11). First, we update the neighborhood of x as stored in TOP$(Info_{stack}).N_m[x]$ in Lines 11 to 14. For every x we remove c_o from its neighbors TOP$(Info_{stack}).N_m[x]$ (Line 12). Then we iterate over every member y of x' neighbors that is a member of $hypernode_o$ at the same time so that $y \in$ TOP$(Info_{stack}).N_m[x] \wedge y \in hypernode_o$ holds. We enlarge TOP$(Info_{stack}).N_m[x]$ now with the new index-reusing compound vertex of y (Line 14). If y is not represented by a compound vertex, then TOP$(Info_{stack}).Compound_{map}^{-1}[y] = \emptyset$ will hold (Line 36 of RECOMPOSECOMPOUNDVERTICES).

After the updates on TOP$(Info_{stack}).N_m[x \in Z]$, the neighborhood of the vertices $x \in added$ recently added to TOP$(Info_{stack}).S'$ is recomputed (Lines 16 to 20). Since this part is identical to the Lines 8 to 11 of MANAGEADJACENCYINFO, we omit further explanation. In Lines 21 and 22, we make the new compound vertices known to their corresponding neighbors.

The handling of case (2) is much simpler. Since the index-reusing compound vertex c_o was dissolved, we only have to remove the reference to c_o from c_o's old neighbors $x \in Z$. But since $c_o \in$ TOP$(Info_{stack}).S_{org}$ holds, we need to keep the adjacency information stored in $N_s[c_o] \cup N_h[c_o]$. Therefore, we have to consult the recently recomputed TOP$(Info_{stack}).N_m[c_o]$. If TOP$(Info_{stack}).N_m[c_o]$ is disjoint to $\{x\}$ with $x \in Z$ (Line 23), then c_o needs to be deleted from TOP$(Info_{stack}).N_m[x]$ (Line 24).

REMANAGEADJACENCYINFO($H_{|S}$, $compound_o$, $hypernode_o$, $added$)
1 $c_o \leftarrow$ ELEMENTOF($compound_o$)
2 $Z \leftarrow$ TOP($Info_{stack}$).$N_m[c_o]$
3 TOP($Info_{stack}$).$N_m[c_o] \leftarrow \emptyset$
4 **for all** $x \in (N_s[c_o] \cap S)$
5 TOP($Info_{stack}$).$N_m[c_o] \leftarrow$ TOP($Info_{stack}$).$N_m[c_o] \cup$
   $\{x\} \cup$ TOP($Info_{stack}$).$Compound_{map}[\{x\}]$
6 **for all** $x \in (N_h[c_o] \cap S)$
7 $lkp \leftarrow$ COMPUTELOOKUPIDX(x, c_o)
8 **if** $HEdgeLkp[lkp] \cap$ TOP($Info_{stack}$).$E_F^{ref} \neq \emptyset$
9   TOP($Info_{stack}$).$N_m[c_o] \leftarrow$ TOP($Info_{stack}$).$N_m[c_o] \cup$
    $\{x\} \cup$ TOP($Info_{stack}$).$Compound_{map}[\{x\}]$
10 **if** $added \not\subseteq$ TOP($Info_{stack}$).S_{org}
11 **for all** $x \in Z$
12   TOP($Info_{stack}$).$N_m[x] \leftarrow$ TOP($Info_{stack}$).$N_m[x] \setminus compound_o$
13   **for all** $y \in$ TOP($Info_{stack}$).$N_m[x] \cap hypernode_o$
14   TOP($Info_{stack}$).$N_m[x] \leftarrow$ TOP($Info_{stack}$).$N_m[x] \cup$
     TOP($Info_{stack}$).$Compound_{map}^{-1}[y]$
15 **for all** $x \in added$
16   $h \leftarrow$ TOP($Info_{stack}$).$Compound_{map}^{-1}[\{x\}]$
17   **if** ISCONNECTEDHYP($H_{|h}$) $\neq$ TRUE
18   TOP($Info_{stack}$).$S_{compounds}^{disconnected} \leftarrow$ TOP($Info_{stack}$).$S_{compounds}^{disconnected} \cup \{x\}$
19   **for all** $y \in h$
20   TOP($Info_{stack}$).$N_m[x] \leftarrow$ TOP($Info_{stack}$).$N_m[x] \cup$
     TOP($Info_{stack}$).$N_m[y]$
21   **for all** $y \in$ TOP($Info_{stack}$).$N_m[x]$
22   TOP($Info_{stack}$).$N_m[y] \leftarrow$ TOP($Info_{stack}$).$N_m[y] \cup \{x\}$
23 **else for all** $x \in$ (TOP($Info_{stack}$).$N_m[c_o] \setminus Z$)
24 TOP($Info_{stack}$).$N_m[x] \leftarrow$ TOP($Info_{stack}$).$N_m[x] \setminus compound_o$

Figure 3.52.: Pseudocode for REMANAGEADJACENCYINFO

3.5.7. Implementation Details

The efficiency of our framework depends heavily on the type of data structures used. To represent sets, we use bitvectors. As bitvector, we use the $uint32\_t$ or $uint64\_t$ type. Thus, a set of vertices is represented by bits in the bitvector. Our global variables of Figure 3.25 and 3.23 are based on bitvectors. The arrays N_s, N_h and N_m, for example, are arrays of bitvectors with $|V|$ elements. Similarly, we implemented $Label_{map}^{-1}$, $IdxIntroV_{map}$ and $Compound_{map}$. We compute the entry or index into the array by using the $bit\_scan\_forward$ assembler instruction. This gives us the least significant bit index for a given bitvector. The result of this operation is the index of the array. Only for $Label_{map}$ we have to use a real map implementation.

Our frameworks maps complex hyperedges to simple edges. Assume (v, w) is a complex hyperedge and $(\{x\}, \{y\})$ the corresponding simple edge with $x \in v \wedge y \in w$. In our implementation, we declared a structure called $HyperEdge$ (Figure 3.24) containing four bitvectors: v, w, v_{rep}, w_{rep} to hold the information of (v, w) and $(\{x\}, \{y\})$, where v_{rep} is representing v and w_{rep} is representing w such that $v_{rep} = \{x\} \wedge w_{rep} = \{y\}$ holds. All complex hyperedges are stored in an array called

HyperEdges (Figure 3.25) of type *HyperEdge* (Figure 3.24). An hyperedge reference is then the index of that array position. Again, we use bitvectors to represent E_A^{ref}, E_F^{ref} and E_C^{ref}. We applied the same idea for $HEdgeLkp$. Since $HEdgeLkp$ is an array of complex hyperedge references, we implemented it as an array of bitvectors.

For our discussion, we differentiated between index-introducing and index-reusing compound vertices. Therefore, we assigned k with $\text{SIZE}(Label_{map}) + |V|$ in Line 2 of MAINTAINLABELS in order to ensure that the new compound vertices z_k are really index-introducing, i.e., that $z_k \notin V$ holds. In our implementation, we do not add the additional $|V|$ since a strict differentiation between index-introducing and index-reusing compound vertices is not really necessary.

3.6. Evaluation

This section is structured as follows: We start by explaining our setup in Sections 3.6.1 and 3.6.2. Section 3.6.3 gives an organizational overview. Finally, we present our results in Sections 3.6.4 to 3.6.7. Our empirical evaluation is threefold:

- First, in Sections 3.6.4 and 3.6.5 we give a performance analysis of our algorithms for randomly generated queries. Thereby, we differentiate between (1) queries that contain complex predicates and inner joins only and (2) those that contain inner joins but also non-inner joins without considering complex predicates.

- Second, we give a short analysis of the overhead produced by our generic partitioning framework in Section 3.6.6. Therefore, we use the same randomly generated standard queries as in Section 2.6.2.

- Whereas the first two parts of the evaluation consider synthetic workloads, the third part investigates the performance when the TPC-H [34] and the TPC-DS [33] queries are considered. Furthermore, we include results for the query graphs gained from the SQLite test suite [29]. We present those results in Section 3.6.7.

3.6.1. Implementation

For all plan generators, no matter whether they work top-down or bottom-up, a shared optimizer infrastructure was established. It contains the common functions to instantiate, fill, and look up the memotable, initialize and use plan classes, estimate cardinalities, calculate costs, and compare plans. Thus, the different plan generators differ only in those parts of the code responsible for enumerating *ccps*.

For the cost estimation of joins, we decided to use the formulas developed by Haas et al. [17]. They have the advantage of being very precise.

3.6.2. Workload

There are two situations giving rise to complex hyperedges: (1) the TES as produced by CD-A [20] indicating non-reorderability of non-inner joins and (2) complex predicates referencing more than two relations.

In Sections 3.6.4 and 3.6.5, we distinguish between these two cases. Thus, we have implemented two kinds of query graph generators. The first graph generator is based on a random operator tree generator that attaches all different inner and non-inner join operators. Here, we make only one assumption. More than half of all attached join operators should be inner join operators. We then compute acyclic complex hypergraphs from these generated operator trees with the conflict detector CD-A, as proposed in [20]. To gain cyclic graphs, we determine all subgraphs of a given hypergraph that are connected by inner join edges only. Within those subgraphs, we randomly generate more inner join edges. We call the generated graphs non-inner join query graphs, although the majority of edges are still inner join edges. We refer to those graphs as non-inner/simple.

The second graph generator generates random acyclic and cyclic graphs, containing simple edges only. Thereby, the edges are randomly added by selecting two relation's indices using uniformly distributed random numbers. After having generated a simple graph, the generator starts transforming simple edges to complex hyperedges at random. Therefore, it randomly chooses between 3 parameters: (1) and (2) the size of the hypernodes connected through the new hyperedge and (3) if the simple edge that is transformed is part of a cycle or not, i.e., is the only connection between two connected subgraphs or not. An edge is only transformed if the resulting complex hyperedge is not subsumed by any other edge. Essentially, this generator generates hypergraphs with complex hyperedges that model complex join predicates involving more than two relations. Therefore, we call the generated graphs complex predicate query graphs and refer to them as inner/complex.

To generate cardinalities and selectivities, we follow the approach of [12] as described in Section 4.4.2. Note that since we do not apply branch-and-bound pruning techniques, the assigned cardinalities and selectivities were not important for our studies.

In Section 3.6.7, we compare the runtime performance of our plan generators with different benchmarks. Therefore, we computed the query graphs for all queries of the TPC-H [34] and the TPC-DS [33] benchmarks. As basis for the query graph computation, we used the explain output of the IBM DB2 10.1 LUW database management system [18]. For every query we took the operator tree from the explain output and reduced it to a join tree. Thereby, every base relation of the join tree introduced a new vertex into the query graph. We assigned every vertex with the cardinality of the base relation if no local predicate could be applied. Otherwise, we took the optimizer's cardinality estimate when all corresponding local predicates had been applied. The hyperedges were extracted from the predicates that were attached to the join operators. In case a materialized intermediate result in the form of a temporary relation TMP was referenced, we located the TMP operator in the join tree. Instead of a simple hyperedge, we introduce a complex hyperedge. For the part referencing the TMP operator, we introduced a complex hypernode that contained all base relations underneath that TMP operator. Hence, if two TMP operators were referenced in the join predicate, the corresponding hyperedges had two complex hypernodes at the end. For several TPC-DS queries the DB2 optimizer applied subplan sharing. Since the root node of every subplan is a TMP operator, we did not convert every join predicate referencing that TMP into a complex hyperedge. Instead, we introduced only a complex hypernode for every first predicate that we encountered referencing such a shared subplan via a TMP. For all other references to the same TMP, we introduced a new vertex in the query graph. We assigned the vertex with a cardinality corresponding to the same TMP. If (local) predicates could be applied on that TMP, we took the cardinality after the predicate application. In order to simplify things, we ignored groupings and $UNION$ operations. Although not valid, we transformed every $UNION$ into an inner join with a selectivity of one. We modeled the corresponding edge as a complex hyperedge. Thereby, all base relations as a whole on each side of the $UNION$ formed a complex hypernode.

As third benchmark, we took the SQLite test suite [29]. The query graphs for the SQLite test suite were provided through the courtesy of Thomas Neumann and obtained from the HyPer optimizer [32].

3.6.3. Organizational Overview

In our empirical analysis, we compare the performance of six top-down join enumerators:

- TDBASICHYP as the instantiated TDPLANGENHYP (Section 3.3.1) variant with naive partitioning PARTITION$_{naiveHyp}$ (Section 3.3.2)

- TDMCLHYP$_{naive}$ as the instantiated TDPLANGENHYP variant with MINCUTLAZY [5] (Appendix A.2). Thereby, we apply a graph mapping of complex hyperedges to simple hyperedges where every complex hypernode is represented by the vertex with the smallest index. We reuse Lines 37 to 40 of COMPUTEADJACENCYINFO. We filter out false *ccp*s with ISCONNECTEDHYP (Section 3.3.3).

- TDMCBHYP$_{naive}$ as the instantiated TDPLANGENHYP variant with MINCUTBRANCH (Section A.2). We apply COMPUTEADJACENCYINFO (Section 3.5.3) and filter out false *ccp*s with ISCONNECTEDHYP (Section 3.3.3).

- TDMCCHYP as the instantiated TDPLANGENHYP (Section 3.3.1) variant with MINCUTCONSERVATIVEHYP (Section 3.4).

- TDMCBHYP as TDPLANGENHYP instantiated with PARTITION$_X$ (Section 3.5) and MINCUTBRANCH as partitioning algorithm (Section 2.5).

- TDMCCFWHYP as TDPLANGENHYP instantiated with PARTITION$_X$ (Section 3.5) and MINCUTCONSERVATIVE as partitioning algorithm (Section 2.4).

Table 3.6.3 gives a summarized overview of the six different algorithms. In order to put all top-down plan generators into perspective, we include the results of Moerkotte and Neumann's DPHYP [21] as the state of the art in bottom-up join enumeration via dynamic programming.

We present our results in terms of the quotient of the algorithm's execution time and the execution time of DPHYP. We refer to this quotient as the *normed time*. Table 3.4 shows the average, minimum, and maximum normed time over the whole workload for non-inner/simple and inner/complex queries.

Since the normed time for DPHYP is always 1, we rather give its elapsed time in seconds. Figure 3.53 displays the runtime results for acyclic/inner/complex and

Name	Partitioning Strategy	Remarks
TDBASICHYP	PARTITION$_{naiveHyp}$	Sec. 3.3.2
TDMCLHYP$_{naive}$	COMPUTEADJACENCYINFO+MINCUTLAZY	Sec. 3.5.3, A.2
TDMCBHYP$_{naive}$	COMPUTEADJACENCYINFO+MINCUTBRANCH	Sec. 3.5.3, A.2
TDMCCHYP	MINCUTCONSERVATIVEHYP	Sec. 3.4
TDMCBHYP	PARTITION$_X$+MINCUTBRANCH	Sec. 3.5.2, 2.5
TDMCCFWHYP	PARTITION$_X$+MINCUTCONSERVATIVE	Sec. 3.5.2, 2.4

Table 3.3.: Names of different plan generation algorithms and the corresponding partitioning strategies.

Figure 3.54 for acyclic/non-inner/simple queries. We give the number of vertices on the abscissa and the execution time in log scale on the ordinate. We draw lines to connect the averaged execution times.

For randomly generated cyclic queries, the algorithms' performance results deviate significantly for the same number of vertices. Thus, we cannot show the results for different numbers of vertices at the same time. Figures 3.55 and 3.56 present the results for 10 and 15 vertices for cyclic/inner/complex queries. The results for 10 and 15 vertices for cyclic/non-inner/simple queries are shown in Figures 3.57 and 3.58.

For the experiments with the randomly generated queries (Section 3.6.4 and 3.6.5), we include only those query graphs in our evaluation that all plan generators could process in less than 100 seconds. In the third part of our experiments, where we evaluated the runtime performance with the benchmark queries, we measured the compile time only for those query graphs with equal or less than 32 vertices. Here, we applied no time constraint.

The workload of the randomly generated queries consists of more than 50000 query graphs. We generated graphs up to 20 vertices of non-inner/simple queries and graphs up to 22 vertices of inner/complex queries. Thereby, among the cyclic queries the number of edges per number of vertices is evenly distributed. In fact, when generating the cyclic queries, we took care that the minimal number of edges was equal to the number of vertices and that the maximal number of edges was at least twice the number of vertices. Every graph had to have at least one complex hyperedge.

Our experiments of Sections 3.6.4 to 3.6.6 were conducted on an Intel Pentium D with 3.4 GHz, 2 Mbyte second level cache and 3 Gbyte of RAM running openSUSE 12.1. The performance evaluation of Section 3.6.7 was conducted on an i7 Intel Quad Core with 3.4 (1.6) GHz, 8 Mbyte second level cache and 4 Gbyte of RAM running openSUSE 12.1. On both machines, we used the Intel C++ compiler with the compiler option O3.

3.6.4. Evaluation of Random Acyclic Query Graphs

The results for acyclic/inner/complex and acyclic/non-inner/simple are shown in Figure 3.53, Figure 3.54 and on the left side of Table 3.4.

When comparing the performance results between acyclic/non-inner/simple and acyclic/inner/complex queries, each algorithm retains its unique trend. Nevertheless, on average plans for non-inner/simple queries had a lower compile time. As it turns

Algorithm	min	max	avg	min	max	avg
	acyclic/non-inner/simple			cyclic/non-inner/simple		
DPHyp	0.0001 s	0.0591 s	0.0007 s	0.0001 s	1.2355 s	0.0076 s
TDBasicHyp	1.1667 ×	14047 ×	981 ×	0.9428 ×	15227 ×	928 ×
TDMcLHyp$_{naive}$	0.3147 ×	12.78 ×	2.4984 ×	0.2851 ×	14.46 ×	2.1679 ×
TDMcBHyp$_{naive}$	0.2727 ×	12.52 ×	2.0636 ×	0.2308 ×	14.06 ×	1.7020 ×
TDMcCHyp	0.1888 ×	4.0108 ×	1.2180 ×	0.1189 ×	3.5678 ×	1.1529 ×
TDMcBHyp	0.1049 ×	2.6388 ×	0.9752 ×	0.0925 ×	2.1425 ×	0.8760 ×
TDMcCFwHyp	0.1049 ×	2.5003 ×	1.0020 ×	0.0964 ×	2.0638 ×	0.8920 ×
Algorithm	min	max	avg	min	max	avg
	acyclic/inner/complex			cyclic/inner/complex		
DPHyp	0.0001 s	0.4384 s	0.0096 s	0.0003 ×	44.31 s	2.1758 s
TDBasicHyp	2.3023 ×	32292 ×	986 ×	1.0340 ×	52102 ×	20.11 ×
TDMcLHyp$_{naive}$	0.7091 ×	5.1429 ×	1.5532 ×	1.2000 ×	7.3271 ×	1.6273 ×
TDMcBHyp$_{naive}$	0.5636 ×	4.8001 ×	1.2767 ×	0.8092 ×	2.4777 ×	1.1721 ×
TDMcCHyp	0.6545 ×	3.2344 ×	1.3783 ×	0.8295 ×	2.0265 ×	1.3510 ×
TDMcBHyp	0.4364 ×	2.4328 ×	1.0159 ×	0.7573 ×	1.5730 ×	1.0266 ×
TDMcCFwHyp	0.4727 ×	1.8794 ×	1.0486 ×	0.7600 ×	1.6072 ×	1.0361 ×

Table 3.4.: Performance results for random queries

out, the average size of a hypernode associated to an average hyperedge is distinctly higher for non-inner/simple join queries. Hence, the number of *ccps* for acyclic/non-inner/simple queries has to be lower, which makes them easier to compile, since fewer plans have to be considered.

Further, we observe the following for acyclic query graphs. The performance of TDBasicHyp with an average normed runtime of 980 and a worst case normed runtime of 32300 is unacceptable. TDMcLHyp$_{naive}$ shows the second highest normed runtimes, but performs much better than TDBasicHyp. Nevertheless, its runtime behavior is not robust, as a worst case normed runtime of 12.8 indicates. In fact, if queries with an increasing number of vertices are considered, the differences to TDMcCHyp, TDMcCFwHyp, TDMcBHyp and DPHyp are increasing.

We can study the effect of using compound vertices (Section 3.5.4), an improved connection test handling (Section 3.5.5) and further optimizations (Section 3.5.6) by comparing TDMcBHyp with TDMcBHyp$_{naive}$. For acyclic/non-inner/simple queries, there is an average runtime difference of about an factor of two. Looking at acyclic/inner/complex queries, the differences between TDMcBHyp and TDMcBHyp$_{naive}$ are not that high.

Among all top-down join enumeration algorithms, TDMcBHyp performs best on average, although the differences to TDMcCFwHyp are negligible. Comparing the performances between TDMcBHyp and DPHyp, we see that TDMcBHyp dominates for acyclic/non-inner/simple queries but not for acyclic/inner/complex queries.

Looking at the max/min normed runtimes, we see that TDMcBHyp can be slower by a factor of at most 2.6, but also by a factor of up to $0.1^{-1} = 10$ faster than DPHyp.

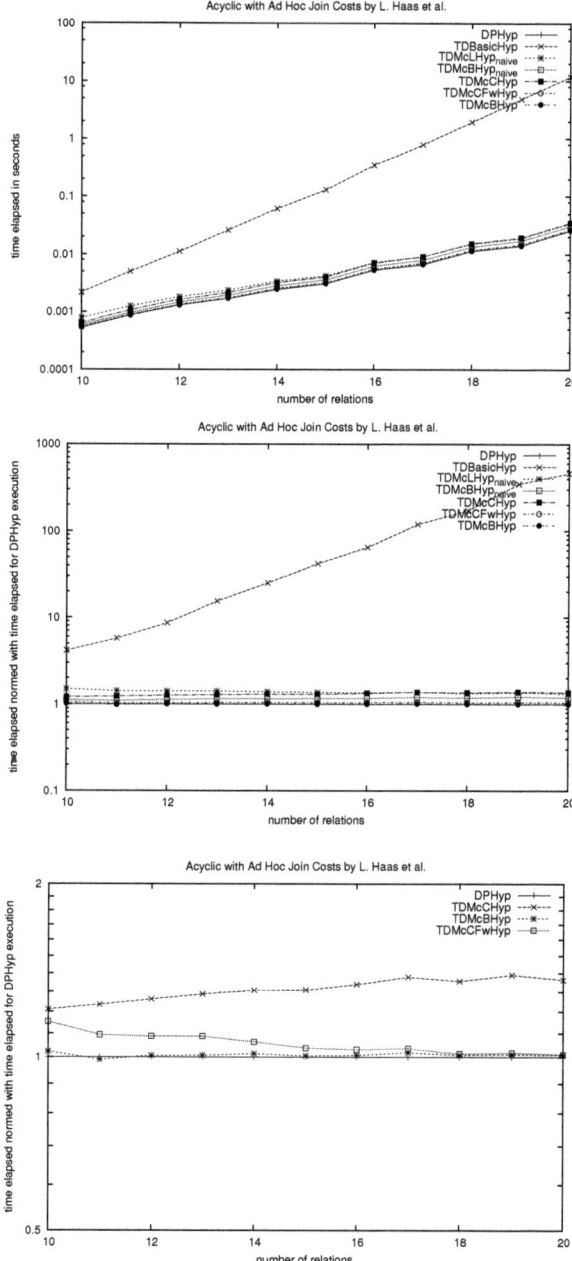

Figure 3.53.: Acyclic/inner/complex

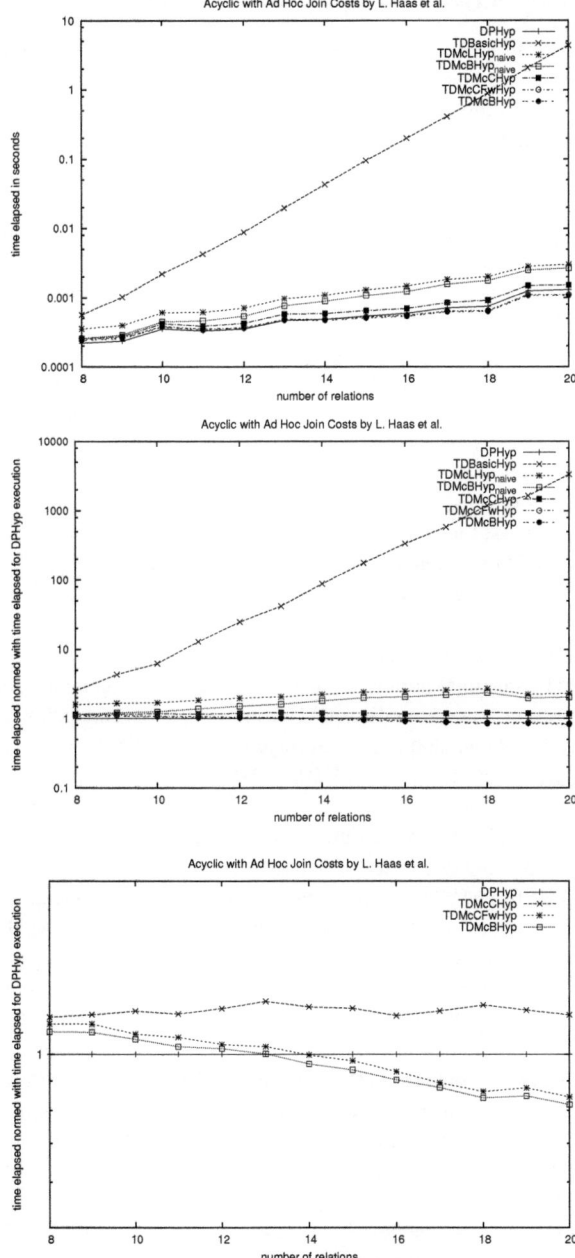

Figure 3.54.: Acyclic/non-inner/simple

3.6.5. Evaluation of Random Cyclic Query Graphs

Let us look at the performance for random cyclic queries. Again, we distinguish between the case where complex hyperedges exist only due to conflicts of non-inner joins (cyclic/non-inner/simple) and the case where they result from complex predicates (cyclic/inner/complex).

Here, for any fixed number of relations, the variations in runtime are enormous. More specifically, they heavily depend on the number of edges. This is obvious, as we imagine to add edges to a chain until we get a clique. Hence, we fixed the number of relations to some medium number 10 (and 15) and varied the number of edges from 10 to 24 (15 to 40) in case of cyclic/non-inner/simple and up to 40 (80) in case of cyclic/inner/complex queries.

Considering Figures 3.55, 3.56, 3.57 and 3.58, we observe that (except for TDBASICHYP) the runtimes of all algorithms increase heavily with the number of edges. This is due to the increased search space size. TDBASICHYP only shows a slight increase in runtime if more edges are present. This can easily be explained by observing that adding edges leads to a higher connectivity within the graph and thus to more ccps. With a higher number of ccps, the connection tests of PARTITION$_{naive}$ have fewer failures. Furthermore, the test for connectedness becomes cheaper on average: Since more connecting edges might exist, interconnected subsets are faster to merge. Hence, with an increasing number of edges for a fixed number of vertices, TDBASICHYP becomes more competitive.

Looking at the right side of Table 3.4, we observe that with an average normed runtime of 928 and a maximal normed runtime of 15227 for cyclic/non-inner/simple queries, TDBASICHYP must be discarded from further consideration. Again, TDMCLHYP$_{naive}$ has the second highest average normed runtimes and is dominated by all other plan generators except for TDBASICHYP. The performance of TDMC-CHYP is in the medium span. For cyclic/non-inner/simple queries, it performs better than TDMCBHYP$_{naive}$, but for cyclic/inner/complex the opposite is true.

Once again, there is roughly a factor of two runtime differences between TDMCB-HYP$_{naive}$ and TDMCBHYP when non-inner/simple queries are considered. Thus, the usage of compound vertices and the proposed improved connection test handling pays off. For cyclic/inner/complex queries, the differences between the two algorithms are much smaller. This is as expected, since those type of queries are usually not complex-cycle free. Hence, fewer compound vertices are introduced and fewer connection tests can be avoided.

Again, TDMCBHYP dominates TDMCCFWHYP. Since both algorithms use the same generic partitioning framework, the differences are only due the application of different graph-partitioning strategies. As MINCUTBRANCH and MINCUTCONSERVATIVE are almost equally competitive, the normed runtime of TDMCCFWHYP is only slightly higher.

For cyclic/non-inner/simple queries, even DPHYP is dominated by TDMCBHYP. As the minimal normed runtime of 0.09 indicates, TDMCBHYP has a clear advantage over DPHYP in certain scenarios because TDMCBHYP uses compound vertices and, therefore, enlarges an already connected set by a whole adjacent hypernode at once. DPHYP, on the other hand, incrementally enlarges a connected set by one member of the adjacent hypernode at a time. There can be as many invocations of DPHYP's

Algorithm	min	max	avg	min	max	avg
	Chain $(8 \leq |V| \leq 30)$			Star $(8 \leq |V| \leq 26)$		
DPHYP	$0.0005\,s$	$0.0316\,s$	$0.0097\,s$	$0.0029\,s$	$76.1274\,s$	$8.7825\,s$
TDMCB	$0.6600 \times$	$1.3332 \times$	$0.9768 \times$	$0.9091 \times$	$1.1000 \times$	$1.0044 \times$
TDMCBHYP	$0.6666 \times$	$1.5410 \times$	$0.9781 \times$	$0.9118 \times$	$1.1333 \times$	$1.0056 \times$

Algorithm	min	max	avg	min	max	avg
	Cycle $(8 \leq |V| \leq 30)$			Clique $(8 \leq |V| \leq 19)$		
DPHYP	$0.0013\,s$	$0.0880\,s$	$0.0367\,s$	$0.0236\,s$	$64.3322\,s$	$11.6768\,s$
TDMCB	$0.4606 \times$	$1.0790 \times$	$0.9626 \times$	$0.9629 \times$	$1.0696 \times$	$1.0246 \times$
TDMCBHYP	$0.4647 \times$	$1.1081 \times$	$0.9666 \times$	$0.9648 \times$	$1.0788 \times$	$1.0281 \times$

Table 3.5.: Chain, Star, Cycle and Clique queries: minimum, maximum and average of the normed runtimes

sub-methods without any emission of ccps as there are proper connected subsets of the adjacent hypernode. However, the number of connected subsets is limited to the number of sets that contain the same representative vertex of the neighborhood (see [21] for more details). In the worst case, this number corresponds to $2^{|n|-1} - 2$, with $|n|$ being the size of the hypernode. As the average normed runtime of 0.88 indicates, these cases are rare. Nevertheless, with a maximal normed runtime of 2.14, TDMCB-HYP seems to be more robust in terms of sensitivity to the current vertex labeling of the input graph.

3.6.6. Overhead Detection

In order to determine the overhead induced by our framework we evaluated TDMCB-HYP on the standard cases of simple query graphs: chains, stars, cycles, and cliques. We included TDMCB (Section 2.5), that is not capable of handling complex hypergraphs. We run these four different query graph classes for different numbers of relations (n). The results are shown in Table 3.5. Note that the runtimes of TDMCB and TDMCBHYP are almost identical, indicating that there is no measurable overhead.

3.6.7. Performance Evaluation with Different Benchmarks

We investigate three benchmarks. For the TPC-H [34] and TPC-DS [33] benchmarks, we used the generated plans of the IBM DB2 LUW database management system [18] to extract the query graphs. The query graphs for the SQLite test suite [29] were extracted from the HyPer optimizer [32].

Thus, we could benefit from optimization techniques such as unnesting and subplan sharing. We used complex hyperedges to prevent reordering conflicts. The runtimes reported here do not include the preparation time for computing the query graphs.

Tables 3.7, 3.8 and 3.9 give the summarized results for the three benchmarks. Thereby, the first column gives the overall runtime for processing the workload with a given plan generator. We refer to that value as H/DS/SQLite-total time. In the second column the overall normed runtime is given. The H/DS/SQLite-total time for a given algorithm is divided by DPHYP's H/DS/SQLite-total time. We refer to that value as

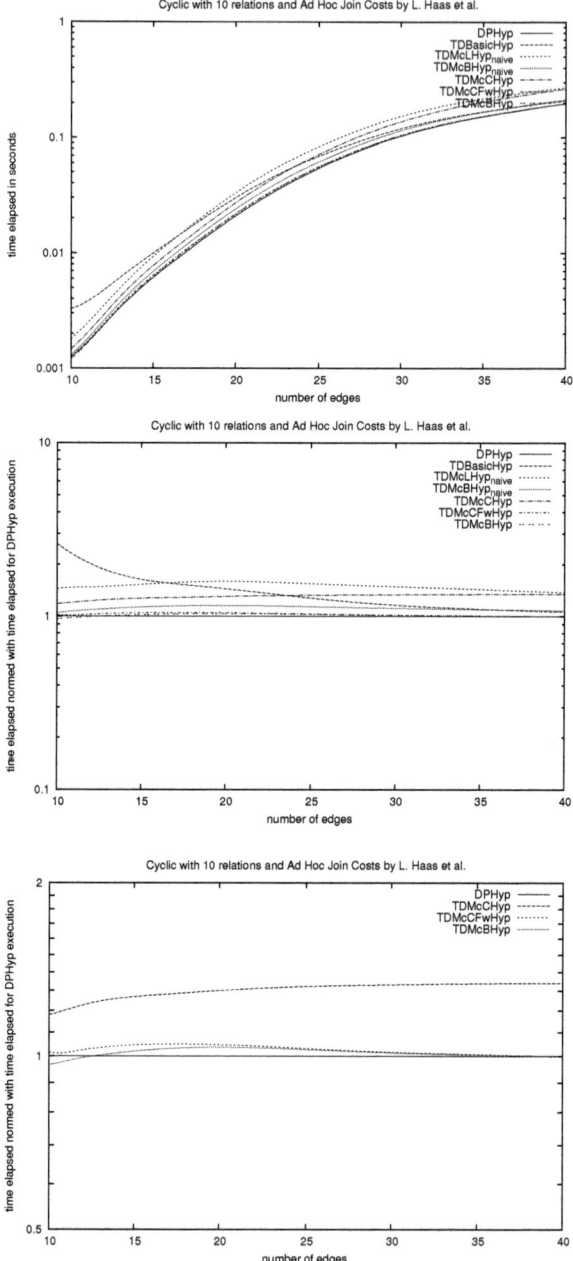

Figure 3.55.: Cyclic/inner/complex with 10 relations

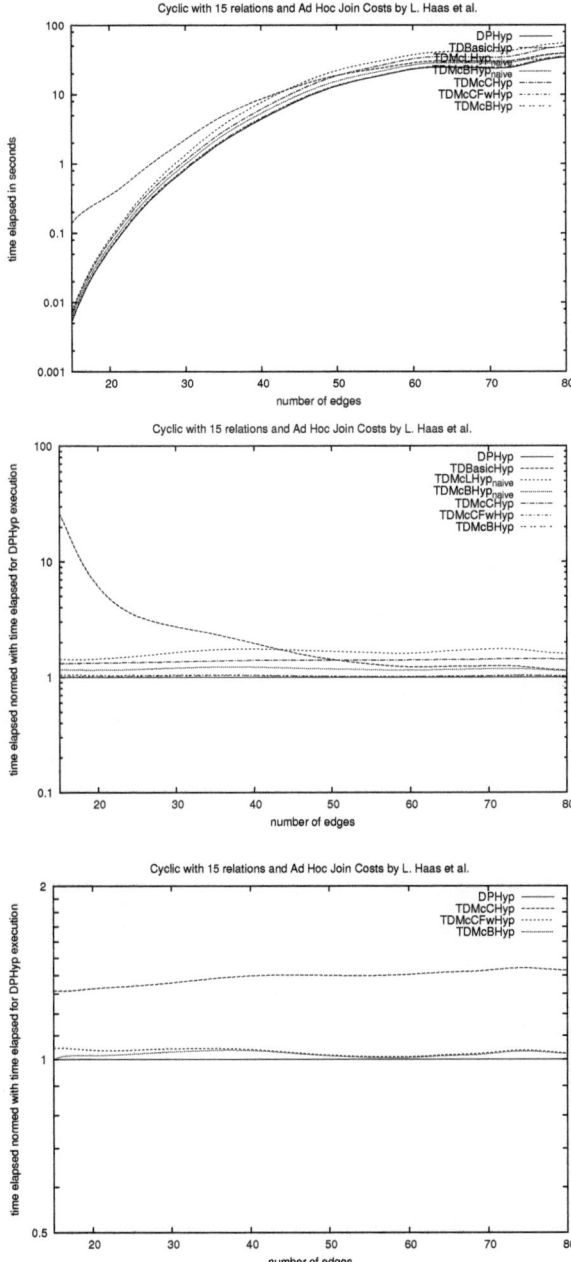

Figure 3.56.: Cyclic/inner/complex with 15 relations

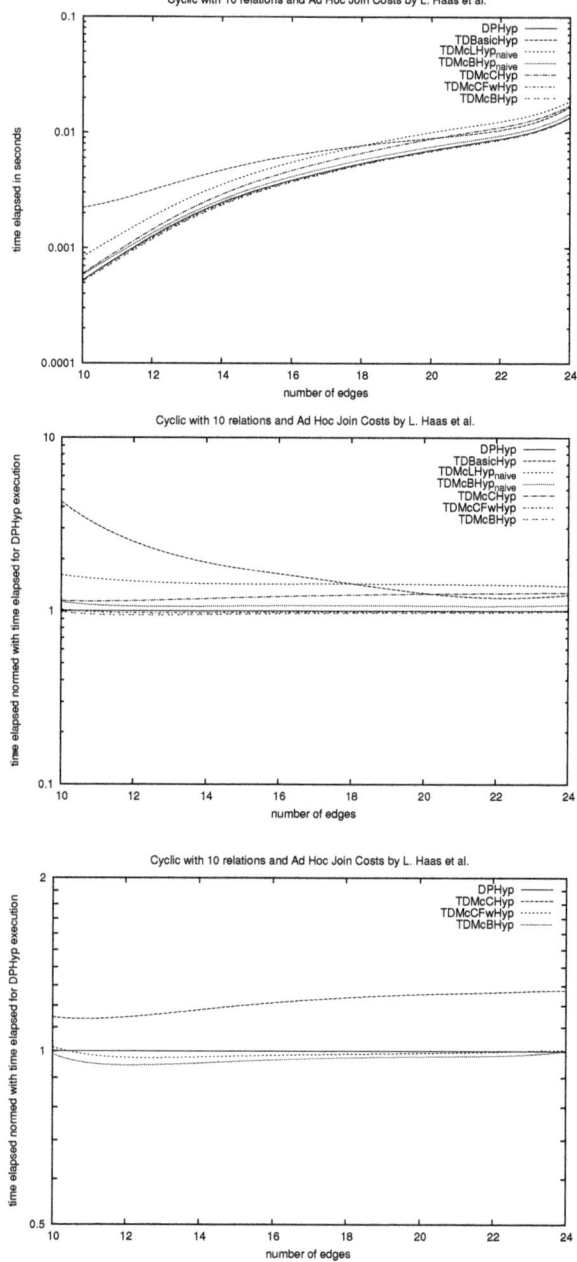

Figure 3.57.: Cyclic/non-inner/simple with 10 relations

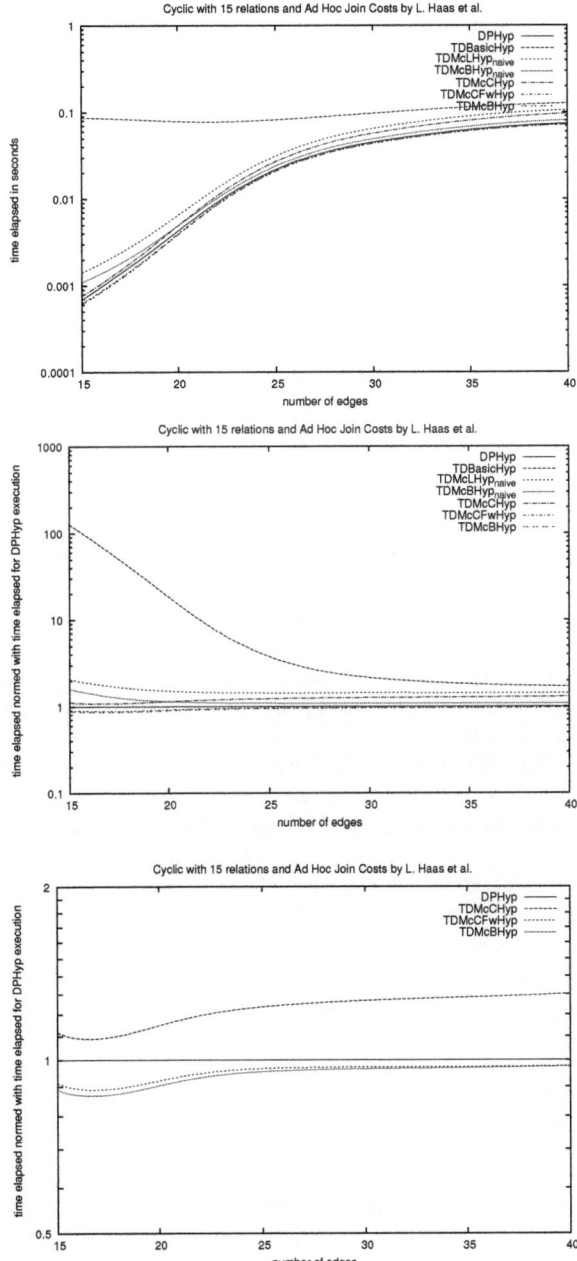

Figure 3.58.: Cyclic/non-inner/simple with 15 relations

Algorithm	Q2	Q5	Q7	Q8	Q9	Q20	Q21
TDBasicHyp	1.18 ×	1.24 ×	1.25 ×	1.44 ×	1.01 ×	1.16 ×	1.56 ×
TDMcLHyp$_{naive}$	1.35 ×	1.47 ×	1.35 ×	1.15 ×	1.21 ×	1.36 ×	1.45 ×
TDMcBHyp$_{naive}$	1.13 ×	1.10 ×	1.09 ×	0.95 ×	0.94 ×	1.08 ×	1.11 ×
TDMcCHyp	1.16 ×	1.25 ×	1.19 ×	1.05 ×	1.08 ×	1.20 ×	1.23 ×
TDMcCFwHyp	1.11 ×	1.08 ×	1.04 ×	0.89 ×	0.89 ×	1.12 ×	1.13 ×
TDMcBHyp	1.15 ×	1.05 ×	1.01 ×	0.88 ×	0.88 ×	1.03 ×	1.10 ×

Table 3.6.: Normed runtimes for TPC-H Queries with more than 4 tables referenced

overall normed runtime. For the value in the third column, we take the normed runtime for every query and compute the average of all normed runtimes of the whole workload. To be more precise, for that value we compute the sum of all query-specific normed runtimes and divide the sum by the number of query graphs the workload consists of. We call this value averaged normed runtime.

TPC-H

We considered all TPC-H queries except for those that did not contain any join (Q1 and Q6). For Q14 and Q17, we gained the same query graph. Thus, we ignored the query graph for Q17 and considered only the graph for Q14.

For those queries referencing more than 4 tables, we give the normed runtime results in Table 3.6. Hereby Q2, Q20 reference 5 relations, Q5, Q7, Q9, Q21 6 relations, and Q8 8 relations. Queries Q2 and Q20 have 4 join edges, Q21 has 5 edges, Q5, Q7 and Q9 have 6 edges and Q8 has 7 edges.

For the 19 TPC-H queries we investigated, we give the summarized results in Table 3.7. We can observe that H-total time is very low. This is as expected, since the queries reference 8 relations at the most. Thus, the performance differences between the algorithms are very low. Nevertheless, when looking at the overall normed runtime, TDMcCFwHyp and TDMcBHyp dominate all other algorithms. Considering the averaged normed runtimes, the results are different. Thus, we have investigated the reason for the differences between the overall normed runtime and the average normed runtime. As it turns out, TDMcCFwHyp and TDMcBHyp exhibit a better normed runtime for queries with a higher number of relations than for queries referencing only a few number of relations. Since queries with a higher number of relations usually take longer to compile, the performance results of these queries have a larger influence on the overall normed runtime.

TPC-DS

In Table 3.8 we give the summarized results for the TPC-DS benchmark. With an overall normed runtime of 185, TDBasicHyp is distinctly outperformed by all other algorithms. This is due to the fact that some TPC-DS queries reference a higher number of relations. The runtime performance differences between all other algorithms are not that large. Looking at the overall normed runtime values, we can deduce that TDMcBHyp dominates all other algorithms including DPHyp. DPHyp performs second best and is closely followed by TDMcCFwHyp, which performs third best.

Algorithm	$\sum$	overall normed	average normed
DPHYP	0.00069 s	1.0000 ×	1.0000 ×
TDBASICHYP	0.00086 s	1.2468 ×	1.0812 ×
TDMCLHYP$_{naive}$	0.00089 s	1.2946 ×	1.3311 ×
TDMCBHYP$_{naive}$	0.00070 s	1.0260 ×	1.0417 ×
TDMCCHYP	0.00078 s	1.1372 ×	1.1210 ×
TDMCCFWHYP	0.00069 s	0.9989 ×	1.0871 ×
TDMCBHYP	0.00067 s	0.9822 ×	1.1066 ×

Table 3.7.: Overall sum of elapsed time, overall normed runtime and average normed runtime for TPC-H Queries

Algorithm	$\sum$	overall normed	average normed
DPHYP	0.40269 s	1.0000 ×	1.0000 ×
TDBASICHYP	72.77494 s	180.7233 ×	3081.9210 ×
TDMCLHYP$_{naive}$	0.53662 s	1.3326 ×	1.5160 ×
TDMCBHYP$_{naive}$	0.46422 s	1.1528 ×	1.2675 ×
TDMCCHYP	0.52345 s	1.2999 ×	1.1670 ×
TDMCCFWHYP	0.42106 s	1.0456 ×	1.0826 ×
TDMCBHYP	0.39770 s	0.9876 ×	1.0586 ×

Table 3.8.: Overall sum of elapsed time, overall normed runtime and average normed runtime for TPC-DS Queries

Algorithm	$\sum$	overall normed	average normed
DPHYP	981.00958 s	1.0000 ×	1.0000 ×
TDMCCHYP	1620.57226 s	1.6519 ×	1.4347 ×
TDMCCFWHYP	1286.18479 s	1.3111 ×	1.1925 ×
TDMCBHYP	1228.61938 s	1.2524 ×	1.1495 ×

Table 3.9.: Overall sum of elapsed time, overall normed runtime and average normed runtime for 337 queries of the SQLite test suite

SQLite Test Suite

For an evaluation with the SQLite test suite queries, we have considered only a subset of the algorithms. Table 3.9 gives the results. From the SQLite-total time, we can see that the queries take in average much longer to compile than the TPC-H and TPC-DS queries. In fact, the queries considered here reference up to 32 relations. We can observe that DPHYP outperforms all other algorithms by at least 25%. TDMCB-HYP performs second best and dominates TDMCCFWHYP, although the differences are not that high. Section 4 will show that by utilizing the branch-and-bound pruning capabilities, TDMCBHYP and TDMCCFWHYP can overcome the performance disadvantage of 25% − 30%. In fact, by considering the same workload we show that when TDMCBHYP and TDMCCFWHYP are paired with our novel and advanced branch-and-bound pruning strategies, DPHYP is outperformed by a factor of two.

4. Branch-and-Bound Pruning

4.1. Motivation

An advantage of top-down join enumeration is that it can leverage the benefits of branch-and-bound pruning that are not available to bottom-up processing. The sole reason for this lies in the processing order of top-down join enumeration that is demand-driven. This means that a join tree for a subset of relations S is built only upon request, as outlined in Section 2.2.1. If such a request for S is made, there are two possibilities: (1) Either the optimal join tree is already computed because a call with the same S has been made before. Or (2) the tree needs to be computed by considering all possible ccps (S_1, S_2) for S with further recursive self invocations for S_1 and S_2. Because of the demand-driven nature, the search space can be curtailed by applying branch-and-bound pruning strategies. The beauty of these pruning strategies is that they are risk-free: They can speed up processing by several orders of magnitude, while at the same time they preserve the optimality of the final join tree.

DeHaan and Tompa categorized the branch-and-bound based pruning strategies into *accumulated-cost-bounding* ACB and *predicted-cost-bounding* PCB [5]. These two pruning methods can be combined into an effective pruning mechanism (APCB) [5].

Let us explicitly state two obvious observations. (1) Different top-down join enumeration algorithms lead to different enumeration orders. (2) Different enumeration orders (can) lead to a different pruning behavior. This leads to the question of the robustness of a pruning strategy, where we call a pruning strategy robust if it behaves equally well in different top-down enumeration strategies.

We show how APCB can be improved (a) in terms of effectiveness, (b) in terms of robustness and (c), most importantly, by avoiding the worst-case behavior otherwise observed. We achieve this by integrating seven new techniques into APCB.

Applying this improved version of APCB will accelerate plan generation for our generated workload by an average factor of 10 and decrease the worst-case behavior by a factor of $25 - 225$ when compared with APCB. And as we will see, our new pruning method is more robust than APCB because its pruning efficiency is less dependent on the enumeration strategy used. By considering the TPC-H [34], TPC-DS [33] and SQLite test suite [29] queries, we were able to support our claims. In particular, we show how our improvements speed up plan generation by 100% when compared with DPHyp [21] as the state-of-the-art in bottom-up plan generation.

This chapter is organized as follows. In Section 4.2, we describe ACB, PCB and APCB. Section 4.3 explains our technical advances [12]. An evaluation is presented in Section 4.4.

BUILDTREE($\circ, S, Tree_1, Tree_2, b$)
    ▷ **Input:** (join) operator $\circ$, vertex set S, two optimal subjoin trees, cost budget b
1   $cT \leftarrow$ CREATETREE($Tree_1, Tree_2$)
2   **if** $cost(cT) \leq b$
3   **if** $BestTree[S] =$ NULL $\vee\ cost(BestTree[S]) > cost(cT)$
4         $BestTree[S] \leftarrow cT$
5   **if** $\circ$ is commutative
6      $cT \leftarrow$ CREATETREE($Tree_2, Tree_1$)
7   **if** $cost(cT) \leq b$
8   **if** $BestTree[S] =$ NULL $\vee\ cost(BestTree[S]) > cost(cT)$
9            $BestTree[S] \leftarrow cT$

Figure 4.1.: Pseudocode for BUILDTREE

4.2. Accumulated-Cost Bounding and Predicted-Cost Bounding

We start by making a necessary modification to BUILDTREE. After that we explain accumulated-cost and predicted-cost bounding [5], and describe how they can be combined.

4.2.1. Building a Join Tree

As has been said in Section 3.3.1, BUILDTREE is used to construct a join tree by combining two optimal subjoin trees and comparing its costs with $BestTree[S]$, which holds the cheapest join tree found so far. We give the pseudocode in Figure 4.1. For an explanation of the basic functionality, we refer to Section 3.3.1. New is the cost budget b that is handed over as input parameter. An actual budget is only passed within the context of our improvements to branch-and-bound pruning (Section 4.3), otherwise the budget will be assigned with ∞. The checks in Line 2 and 7 ensure that only join trees with lower costs than the cost budget allows for are registered with $BestTree[S]$. Hence, the invocation of BUILDTREE does not guarantee any more that $BestTree[S] \neq$ NULL holds.

4.2.2. Accumulated-Cost Bounding

As implemented in Volcano [16], Cascades [15], and Columbia [28], this bounding technique passes a cost budget to the top-down join enumeration procedure. We give the pseudocode for accumulated-cost bounding integrated in our generic top-down join enumeration algorithm in Figure 4.2 with TDPG$_{ACB}$ by modifying [6]. During the recursive descent, each instance of TDPG$_{ACB}$ subtracts costs from the handed-over budget as soon as they become known. The descent is aborted once the budget drops below zero. Every call that returns with a join tree has produced an optimal join tree. If no join tree is returned, the handed-over budget was not sufficient. Line 2 iterates over the *ccp*s for S. The first step in the loop is to determine the cost for combining the two subjoin trees. These costs can be subtracted from the budget b (Line 6) and

```
TDPG_ACB(G|S, b)
        ▷ Input: connected sub graph G|S, cost budget b
        ▷ Output: an optimal join tree for G|S
1    if BestTree[S] = NULL ∧ lB[S] ≤ b
2        for all (S1, S2) ∈ P_ccp(S)
3            for ∘ ∈ O
4                if APPLICABLE(∘, S1, S2)
5                    c⋈ ← cost of operator ∘
6                    b' ← MIN(b, cost(BestTree[S])) − c⋈
7                    lT ← TDPG_ACB(G|S1, b')
8                    if lT ≠ NULL
9                        b' ← b' − cost(lT)
10                       rT ← TDPG_ACB(G|S2, b')
11                       if rT ≠ NULL
12                           BUILDTREE(∘, S, lT, rT, b)
13   if BestTree[S] = NULL
14       lB[S] = b
15   return BestTree[S]
```

Figure 4.2.: Pseudocode for TDPG$_{ACB}$

handed over to the child invocation for S_1 (Line 7). If no tree for S_1 is returned, it becomes obvious that no join tree for the partition (S_1, S_2) can be constructed that is cheaper than MIN$(b, cost(BestTree[S]))$. Hence, there is no need to request a join tree for S_2. Otherwise, if a subjoin tree for S_1 has been found, the budget for S_2 is adjusted by decreasing b' with the cost for constructing the tree of S_1 (Line 9). Line 9 invokes the recursive descent for S_2 with a tighter bound than for S_1. Upon return of the call, a join tree for S can only be registered with $BestTree[S]$ if (1) a tree for S_2 was returned, (2) the combined tree is cheaper than the budget allows for and (3) it is cheaper than all other trees produced so far. Line 11 takes care of (1), and BUILDTREE (Section 4.2.1) handles (2) and (3). Every time a new and cheaper join tree for S has been registered with $BestTree[S]$, the budget b' for all other ccps for S can be adjusted (Line 6) instead of resetting it to the b that was handed over. If after the enumeration of all ccps for S (Line 2) no tree has been found that is cheaper than b, the lower bound $lB[S]$ is set to b. If a join for S is requested another time with a budget b'', the call can be returned immediately if the tree was already built and registered with $BestTree[S]$ or b'' is smaller than $lB[S]$ (Line 1). Note that if the lower bound for S is not set, $lB[S]$ returns 0. The initial budget for the top-level call to TDPG$_{ACB}$ is set to ∞.

4.2.3. Predicted-Cost Bounding

As has been shown, accumulated-cost bounding prunes the search space by passing budget information top-down. Predicted-cost bounding as a contribution of Columbia [28] follows the opposite approach by estimating the costs of the subjoin trees that lie below in the recursive search tree. The main idea is to find a lower bound in terms of

$\text{TDPG}_{PCB}(G_{|S})$
    ▷ **Input:** connected sub graph $G_{|S}$
    ▷ **Output:** an optimal join tree for $G_{|S}$
1 **if** $BestTree[S] = \text{NULL}$
2   **for all** $(S_1, S_2) \in P_{ccp}(S)$
3   **for** $\circ \in O$
4   **if** APPLICABLE($\circ,S_1,S_2$)
5   **if** LBE($\circ, S_1, S_2$) $\leq cost(BestTree[S])$
6   BUILDTREE($G_{|S}$, $\text{TDPG}_{PCB}(G_{|S_1})$,
                                  $\text{TDPG}_{PCB}(G_{|S_2}), \infty$)
7 **return** $BestTree[S]$

Figure 4.3.: Pseudocode for TDPG_{PCB}

join costs for a given ccp (S_1, S_2) before actually requesting the two corresponding optimal subjoin trees to be built through two different recursive descents. If now the estimate which is specific for that ccp is larger than the cost of a join tree already built for S, the cheapest join tree for S clearly cannot consist of a join between S_1 and S_2. Hence, the effort of subcalls with S_1 and S_2 can be spared.

In Figure 4.3, the pseudocode after [5] for top-down join enumeration enhanced with predicted-cost bounding is given with TDPG_{PCB}. It is identical to TDPGHYPSUB, except for Line 5, where the lower bound estimate LBE is compared to the costs of $BestTree[S]$, which serves as an upper bound. If there is no join tree for S known yet, $cost(BestTree[S])$ will return ∞.

The lower bound estimation procedure LBE depends upon the cost model used in the optimizer. For our experiments, we use the I/O cost model for ad hoc join costs, as proposed in [17].

4.2.4. Combining the Methods

A combination of both bounding methods is very beneficial, as [5] points out. This can be done by inserting the call of LBE between Lines 4 and 5 of TDPG_{ACB}. The inserted code has the following form:

4.5   **do if** LBE(S_1, S_2) $\leq$ MIN($b, cost(BestTree[S])$)

Again, if there is no join tree registered with $BestTree[S]$, $cost(BestTree[S])$ will return ∞. In this case, b is chosen as the comparison value, in all other cases $cost(BestTree[S])$ will be the smaller value of the two. We denote the combined method by TDPG_{APCB}.

4.2.5. An Example for Accumulated-Predicted-Cost Bounding

To exemplify how TDPG_{APCB} works, we revisit the example of Section 2.2.3. Therefore, we reuse the graph of Figure 2.6 and the corresponding selectivities and cardinalities of Figure 2.7. Again, we use C_{out} as cost function (Section 2.1.2). As partitioning strategy we use PARTITION$_{naive}$.

Entry	L	S	$lB[S]$	current ccp	b'	LBE
1	0	$\{R_0, R_1, R_2, R_3\}$	0	$(\{R_0\}, \{R_1, R_2, R_3\})$	∞	10
2	1	$\{R_1, R_2, R_3\}$	0	$(\{R_1\}, \{R_2, R_3\})$	∞	10
3	2	$\{R_2, R_3\}$	0	$(\{R_2\}, \{R_3\})$	∞	0
4	1	$\{R_1, R_2, R_3\}$	0	$(\{R_1, R_2\}, \{R_3\})$	20	100000
5	2	$\{R_1, R_2\}$	-	$(\{R_1\}, \{R_2\})$	-	-
6	1	$\{R_1, R_2, R_3\}$	0	$(\{R_1, R_3\}, \{R_2\})$	20	100
7	2	$\{R_1, R_3\}$	-	$(\{R_1\}, \{R_3\})$	-	-
8	0	$\{R_0, R_1, R_2, R_3\}$	0	$(\{R_0, R_1\}, \{R_2, R_3\})$	21	1020
9	1	$\{R_0, R_1\}$	-	$(\{R_0\}, \{R_1\})$	-	-
10	0	$\{R_0, R_1, R_2, R_3\}$	0	$(\{R_0, R_1, R_2\}, \{R_3\})$	21	10000
11	1	$\{R_0, R_1, R_2\}$	-	$(\{R_0\}, \{R_1, R_2\})$	-	-
12	1	$\{R_0, R_1, R_2\}$	-	$(\{R_0, R_1\}, \{R_2\})$	-	-
13	1	$\{R_0, R_1, R_2\}$	0	$(\{R_0, R_1, R_3\}, \{R_2\})$	21	10
14	2	$\{R_0, R_1, R_3\}$	-	$(\{R_0\}, \{R_1, R_3\})$	-90	-
15	2	$\{R_0, R_1, R_3\}$	-	$(\{R_0, R_1\}, \{R_3\})$	-90	-

Table 4.1.: Exemplified execution of TDPG$_{APCB}$ instantiated with PARTITION$_{naive}$ for the input graph of Figure 2.6

Table 4.1 shows the different states during execution. Here, the first column is the table entry that serves as reference. The second column displays the recursion level, with 0 indicating the root invocation. The input parameter S is shown in the third column, the corresponding lower bound (lB) for S in the fourth column, and the current ccp that is being processed is displayed by the fifth column. In the sixth and seventh column, we list the current budget b' and the result of the LBE call with the current ccp as input. The rows that are grayed out are prevented though branch-and-bound pruning. Since the corresponding values are not computed, we have taken them from Section 2.2.3.

We can observe that through the predicted cost-bounding component, we prevent the entries $5, 7, 9, 11$ and 12. The accumulated cost-bounding component prevents the entries 14 and 15 by returning the call for $S = \{R_0, R_1, R_3\}$ in Line 1 of TDPG$_{APCB}$ (Figure 4.2).

4.3. Technical Advances

This section describes our improvements to accumulated-predicted cost bounding. We name the new algorithm TDPG$_{APCBI}$ because it is based on TDPG$_{APCB}$. The pseudocode is given in Figure 4.4.

First of all — and not indicated in the pseudocode — we propose an *advancement of the* LBE *method* to [5], as described in [12]. Instead of basing its computation solely on an estimation, we include information which we already know. For this, we increase the return value of LBE by the costs of the optimal join trees for S_1 or S_2 or at least $lB[S_1]$ or $lB[S_2]$ respectively, if this information is already available. However, we can add $lB[S_1]$ to the estimate only if the costs for $BestTree[S_1]$ are not known yet, that is if $BestTree[S_1] = $ NULL holds. The same is true for S_2.

$\text{TDPG}_{PACBI}(G_{|S}, b)$
 ▷ **Input:** connected sub graph $G_{|S}$, cost budget b
 ▷ **Output:** an optimal join tree for $G_{|S}$
1 **if** $BestTree[S] \neq \text{NULL}$ and $cost(BestTree[S]) \leq b$
2 **return** $BestTree[S]$
3 **if** $lB[S] > b$
4 **return** NULL
5 **if** $attempts[S] > 0$
6 **if** $b < uB[S]$
7   $b \leftarrow uB[S]$
8 **else** $b \leftarrow \text{MAX}(b, lB[S] * 2^{attempts[S]})$
9 $attempts[S] \leftarrow attempts[S] + 1$
10 **if** $uB[S] < b \land uB[S] > 0$
11 $b \leftarrow uB[S]$
12 $nlB \leftarrow \infty$
13 **for all** $(S_1, S_2) \in P_{ccp}(S)$
14 **for** $\circ \in O$
15   **if** APPLICABLE($\circ, S_1, S_2$)
16   **if** $\text{LBE}(\circ, S_1, S_2) > \text{MIN}(b, cost(BestTree[S]))$
17     $nlB \leftarrow \text{MIN}(nlB, \text{LBE}(S_1, S_2))$
18   **continue**
19    $c_{\bowtie} \leftarrow$ minimal costs of operator $\bowtie$
20    $b' \leftarrow \text{MIN}(b, cost(BestTree[S]))$
21   **if** $BestTree[S_2] \neq \text{NULL}$
22     $cr \leftarrow cost(BestTree[S_2])$
23   **else** $cr \leftarrow lB[S_2]$
24    $b' \leftarrow b' - c_{\bowtie}$
25    $lT \leftarrow \text{TDPG}_{PACBI}(G_{|S_1}, b' - cr)$
26   **if** $lT \neq \text{NULL}$
27     $c_{lT} \leftarrow cost(lT)$
28     $b' \leftarrow b' - c_{lT}$
29     $rT \leftarrow \text{TDPG}_{PACBI}(G_{|S_2}, b')$
30   **if** $rT \neq \text{NULL}$
31   BUILDTREE($\circ, G_{|S}, lT, rT, b$)
32      $c_{rT} \leftarrow cost(rT)$
33      $nlB \leftarrow \text{MIN}(nlB, c_{lT} + c_{rT} + c_{\bowtie})$
34   **else** $nlB \leftarrow \text{MIN}(nlB, c_{lT} + lB[S_2] + c_{\bowtie})$
35   **else** $nlB \leftarrow \text{MIN}(nlB, lB[S_1] + cr + c_{\bowtie})$
36 **if** $BestTree[S] = \text{NULL}$
37 $lB[S] \leftarrow \text{MAX}(b, nlB)$
38 **return** $BestTree[S]$

Figure 4.4.: Pseudocode for TDPG_{ACBI}

Second, we make use of a *join heuristic* to decrease the initial budget [12]. For our implementation we have used GOO [7] which is in $O(|V|^3)$. But instead of using only the cost of the whole join tree produced by the heuristic as a total bound, we also include the cost of its produced subtrees. For this, we introduce with $uB[S]$ another bound that is populated by the cost of the join and subjoin trees produced by the heuristic. If now an upper bound for S exists ($uB[S] > 0$) and the passed-in budget b is greater, we decrease b and set it to $uB[S]$ (Line 11).

Third, we *improve the lower bounds*. Instead of setting lB to the current b when no join tree was found for b (compare to Line 14 of TDPG$_{ACB}$), we compare b to the minimum of all LBE results and take the maximum of the two [12]. This comes in handy when the predicted cost bounding component rejects all *ccp*s for S (Line 16 of TDPG$_{PACBI}$). For this, nlB is introduced in Line 12 and set to ∞. Its minimum is computed over all *ccp*s for S in Line 17, notably before predicted cost bounding rejects a *ccp* (Line 16). In Line 37, we set its value if no join tree within the budget b was found. Lines 33, 34 and 35 extend this idea further by also considering cases where the corresponding LBE results are smaller than b, but join tree construction still fails because b is not high enough. Note that in Line 33 the value of nlB may still be decreased, even when BUILDTREE constructs a join tree that is cheaper than b. But this is irrelevant, since $lB[S]$ is only set if no join tree could be constructed (Line 36).

Fourth, a *rising budget* is proposed in [12] as the solution for the worst case behavior of accumulated cost bounding observed in [5]. Accumulated cost bounding is efficient by preventing top-down join enumeration from building expensive subtrees that cannot be part of an optimal solution. But in several cases, it might increase optimization time significantly, compared to top-down join enumeration without it. This occurs when a join tree for S is requested several times, and each time the budget b that is passed in is slightly higher than before. If the slightly increased budgets are still too low to produce the cheapest join tree, the results are unnecessary computations of $P_{ccp}^{sym}(S)$ and the corresponding subtree requests that might even have the same cascading negative effect. As a solution to this problem, we count the number of times a request to TDPG$_{PACBI}$ with the same S has been made in Line 9 and store it in $attempts[S]$. If now a join tree for S is requested the second time and it has not already been constructed the first time, the budget is increased and set to $lB[S] * 2^{attempts[S]}$ if b is not higher already (Line 8). If we have an upper bound for S, we make an exception and set b to that upper bound $uB[S]$ right away (Line 7).

Fifth, TDPG$_{PACBI}$ *tightens the budget* which is passed in to the call for requesting the left subjoin tree comprising the relations of S_1 more intelligently [12]. For this, we include information about the costs of the right join tree comprising the relations of S_2 or at least its lower bound $lB[S_2]$. This is done through Lines 21 to 23 and 25. Note that if the lower bound for S is not set, $lB[S]$ returns 0.

Sixth, we change the order in which the partitioning algorithm selects its next neighbor (Section 2.1.1) [12], e.g., Line 6 of MINCUTCONSERVATIVE (Section 2.4) or Lines 7, 13 of MINCUTBRANCH (Section 2.5). In our implementation, the next neighbor is selected by the least significant bit of the bitvector that stores the rest of the neighborhood to be processed. Therefore, we propose a re-numbering of the nodes in the query graph. The preferred processing order of neighbors is taken from the join tree produced by our join heuristic. We renumber the vertices by a breadth-first traversal of the join tree. As our experiments have shown, the effect is that the join tree and its subtrees produced by the heuristics are mostly planned first and, thus, before other join trees during the top-down join enumeration.

Seventh, not shown in the pseudocode either, we use the LBE method to *initialize the lower bounds* $lB[S_1]$ and $lB[S_2]$, if not set already. Although LBE takes both S_1 and S_2 as an argument at the same time, lower bound estimates for S_1 and S_2 are usually computed separately, dependent on the costs functions used. We modify LBE such that it calls INITLOWERBOUND(S_i) for every uninitialized lower bound $lB[S_i]$ it encounters with $i = 1...2$. One possibility for implementing INITLOWERBOUND is as follows: We compute the value for $lB[S_i]$ as the sum of the costs for scanning the base relations contained in S_i as required by any join operation that has a base relation as input. Obviously, the seventh advancement needs to be tightly coupled with our first advancement. The advantage of setting lB comes mainly into play when the result of the LBE$(\circ, S_1, S_2)$ is smaller than MIN$(b, cost(BestTree[S]))$. Here, it increases the changes that the search for S_1 and S_2 can be curtailed. There are two reasons for this: (1) We might be able to stop the descent in Line 4 for S_1 and S_2 because of the condition in Line 3, since now $lB[S_i] \neq 0$ will hold. And (2) the budgets for S_1 or S_2 are further decreased by either $lB[S_2]$ in case of $BestTree[S_2]$ = NULL or $lB[S_1]$ in case of $BestTree[S_1]$ = NULL holds. Without the advancement, $lB[S_i]$ might still be 0.

4.4. Evaluation

This section summarizes our experimental findings. First, we describe our general setup in Sections 4.4.1 and 4.4.2. Then we give our evaluation, which is threefold:

- In Section 4.4.3, we analyze the pruning behavior for randomly generated queries without complex hyperedges, including the standard shapes: chain, star, cycle and clique queries.

- Section 4.4.4 investigates our pruning techniques for generated queries with complex hyperedges. We differentiate between (1) queries that contain complex predicates and inner joins only and (2) those that contain inner joins but also non-inner joins without considering complex predicates.

- Whereas the first two parts of the evaluation consider synthetic workloads, the third part investigates the pruning behavior when the TPC-H [34] and TPC-DS [33] queries are considered. Furthermore, we include results for the query graphs gained from the SQLite test suite [29]. Those results are presented in Section 4.4.5.

4.4.1. Implementation

For all plan generators, no matter whether they work top-down or bottom-up, a shared optimizer infrastructure was established. It contains the common functions to instantiate, fill, and look up the memotable, initialize and use plan classes, estimate cardinalities, calculate costs, and compare plans. Thus, the different plan generators differ only in those parts of the code responsible for enumerating *ccp*s and to utilize pruning (if applied).

For the cost estimation of joins, we decided to use the formulas developed by Haas et al. [17]. They have the advantage of being very precise. The lower bound estimation

Relation Size	Prob.
10-100	15%
100-1000	30%
1000-10000	25%
10000-100000	20%

Domain Size	Prob.
2-10	5%
10-100	50%
100-500	35%
500-1000	15%

Figure 4.5.: Relation and domain sizes for random join queries, as proposed by Steinbrunn et al.

method LBE (Section 4.2.3) bases its estimate on reading the intermediate relations that are the input for the next join. In order to assign an initial lower bound as proposed by our seventh advancement, we sum up the costs for scanning the base relations contained in S_1 or S_2, respectively, as required by any join operation that has a base relation as input.

4.4.2. Workload

We generated our workload with a generic query graph generator that proceeds in two steps: First, a list of vertices and edges is generated. And second, selectivities and cardinalities are attached to the edges and vertices of the graph.

Let us start with the first step: For the experiments conducted in Section 4.4.3, we proceed with the same technique as described in Section 2.6.1. For the complex hypergraphs used in Section 4.4.4, we use the two approaches of Section 3.6.2. With this two techniques we gain two types of graphs: non-inner/simple and inner/complex graphs.

As has being said, cardinalities and selectivities are generated in a second step. For this, we follow the approach of [24], which is based on a proposal by Steinbrunn et al. [30]. Our method is described in [12]. According to the kind of join, we can distinguish between foreign-key key joins (or FFK-joins for short) and other joins, which we call non-foreign-key key joins (or non-FFK-joins for short). Based on this, we generate FFK-join queries and non-FFK-join queries. For non-FFK-join queries, cardinalities and domain sizes are generated according to the scheme in Fig. 4.5. If — as proposed in [30] — selectivities are computed by choosing two random attributes and using $\frac{1}{max(dom(A_1), dom(A_2))}$, this often leads to intermediate cardinalities less than 1, which then are successively increased to become huge again. As this does not seem to be realistic, we propose and use foreign-key join queries. For relation and domain sizes, the same scheme as before is used. Then, with a probability of 10%, the selectivity of a join edge is computed as described above for non-FFK-join queries, and with a probability of 90% the selectivity is computed such that the cardinality of the result is equal to the cardinality of the relation with the foreign key.

As DeHaan and Tompa pointed out, pruning techniques are quite unsuccessful with star queries [5]. This makes them perfect for analyzing the overhead of a branch-and-bound pruning strategy. To use them for this purpose, we decrease the chances for pruning down to zero by setting the join selectivity of an edge to the reciprocal of the dimension's cardinality.

Abbreviated Name	Partitioning Strategy	Pruning Type
TDMcL	MINCUTLAZY	none
TDMcL$_{PCB}$	MINCUTLAZY	TDPG$_{PCB}$
TDMcL$_{APCB}$	MINCUTLAZY	TDPG$_{APCB}$
TDMcL$_{APCBI}$	MINCUTLAZY	TDPG$_{APCBI}$
TDMcL$_{APCBI\_Opt}$	MINCUTLAZY	TDPG$_{APCBI\_Opt}$
TDMcC	MINCUTCONSERVATIVE	none
TDMcC$_{PCB}$	MINCUTCONSERVATIVE	TDPG$_{PCB}$
TDMcC$_{APCB}$	MINCUTCONSERVATIVE	TDPG$_{APCB}$
TDMcC$_{APCBI}$	MINCUTCONSERVATIVE	TDPG$_{APCBI}$
TDMcC$_{APCBI\_Opt}$	MINCUTCONSERVATIVE	TDPG$_{APCBI\_Opt}$
TDMcB	MINCUTBRANCH	none
TDMcB$_{PCB}$	MINCUTBRANCH	TDPG$_{PCB}$
TDMcB$_{APCB}$	MINCUTBRANCH	TDPG$_{APCB}$
TDMcB$_{APCBI}$	MINCUTBRANCH	TDPG$_{APCBI}$
TDMcB$_{APCBI\_Opt}$	MINCUTBRANCH	TDPG$_{APCBI\_Opt}$

Table 4.2.: Abbreviated names of different partitioning algorithms and pruning strategies.

For a description of how the query graphs for the TPC-H [34], TPC-DS [33] and SQLite yes suite [29] queries have been computed, we refer to Section 3.6.2.

4.4.3. Performance Evaluation with Simple Query Graphs

We start with an organizational overview. After that, we evaluate the pruning performance of acyclic query graphs and follow with cyclic queries later. At the end, we investigate our different pruning advancements.

Organizational Overview

In our empirical analysis for simple graphs, we compare the accumulated-predicted cost bounding algorithm named TDPG$_{APCB}$, which was given by DeHaan and Tompa (Section 4.2.4) [5], to our novel branch-and-bound pruning algorithm called TDPG$_{APCBI}$. We instantiate both algorithms with three different partitioning strategies for simple graphs to calculate the ccps: MINCUTLAZY [5] (Appendix A), MINCUTCONSERVATIVE [12] (Section 2.4) and MINCUTBRANCH [8] (Section 2.5). We use the abbreviated names, as shown in Table 4.2. By TDPG$_{APCBI\_Opt}$, we indicate the APCBI pruning strategy with pre-calculated optimal (tight) upper bounds. We derive those by extracting the costs of the optimal subjoin trees of each plan class after a run of DPCCP [22] and make them available with a lookup to $uB[S]$ (Line 11 of TDPG$_{APCBI}$). Since APCBI_OPT is of no practical use, it is only shown here to indicate the theoretical lower bound of ACB. Therefore, we do not include the pre-computation time of the optimal upper bound's runtime results for TDPG$_{APCBI\_Opt}$.

In order to put all top-down join enumeration algorithms into perspective, we include the results of Moerkotte and Neumann's DPCCP [22] as a very efficient bottom-up join enumeration algorithm via dynamic programming. We present our results in terms of the quotient of the algorithm's execution time and the execution time of DPCCP. We refer to this quotient as the *normed time*. Tables 4.3, 4.4 and 4.5 show the average, minimum, and maximum normed time over the whole workload for a particular graph type. Since the normed time for DPCCP is always 1, we rather give its elapsed time in seconds.

Table 4.6 shows the details of the pruning behavior. With max_s or avg_s, we refer to the maximum or average of the following quotient. We divide the number of times a join tree was requested and successfully returned by the number of built join trees by DPCCP. Note that the divisor corresponds to the number of plan classes, which equals the number of connected subgraphs. As a consequence, the subscript s indicates that we are talking about the normed number of plan classes for which a plan was *successfully* built. Analogously, max_f (avg_f) denotes the maximum (average) of the quotient where we divide the number of times a join tree was requested but not built by the number of join trees built by DPCCP. The latter quotient gives us the ratio of *failed* builds compared to the total number of DPCCP's optimal join tree builds.

In order not to overload the evaluation charts, we decided to include only a subset of the possible combinations between algorithms and pruning strategies we investigated. We present TDMcL and TDMcC to show the performance difference to DPCCP. According to [5], this deficiency can be overcome by pruning (TDMcL$_{APCB}$). We also present TDMcC$_{APCB}$, TDMcB$_{APCB}$ and TDMcB$_{APCBI}$ to allow for a comparison of the two pruning strategies. Finally, the results for TDMcC$_{APCBI}$ are presented because it dominates all the other combinations. The workload consists of more than 20000 query graphs. Our experiments were conducted on an Intel Pentium D with 3.4 GHz, 2 Mbyte second level cache and 3 Gbyte of RAM running openSUSE 12.1. We used the Intel C++ compiler with the compiler option O3.

Acyclic Query Graphs

The minimum, maximum, and average normed runtimes over the whole acyclic workload for chain, star, and random acyclic queries are given in Tables 4.3 and 4.4.

We see that, except for star queries (Table 4.3, Figure 4.7), pruning (TDPG$_{PCB}$, APCPI) decreases the optimization time for acyclic graphs. However this is not true for TDPG$_{APCB}$, which performs worse when either star or random acyclic queries are considered. TDPG$_{APCB}$ exhibits extremely high average normed runtimes for random acyclic queries. In fact, accumulated-cost-bounding without our improvements does not pay off, as the much lower average normed runtimes of TDPG$_{PCB}$ show.

In contrast, DeHaan and Tompa [5] reported performance gains by combining the methods ACB and TDPG$_{PCB}$ into TDPG$_{APCB}$. The main reason for the different findings lies in the different workload settings. In particular, it mainly depends on how the cardinalities and selectivities are computed. Our workload predominantly consists of key foreign-key join scenarios, which are not that advantageous for accumulated-cost bounding.

We also see that for TDPG$_{APCB}$ the maximum normed runtimes sometimes deviate substantially from the average. TDPG$_{APCBI}$ does not show this behavior. Hence, TDPG$_{APCBI}$ exhibits a much better worst case behavior than TDPG$_{APCB}$.

Table 4.6 gives us the explanation for TDPG$_{APCB}$'s worst case behavior by looking at the values of max_f. Through the *improved lower bounds*, our *rising budget* and the

Algorithm	min	max	avg	min	max	avg
	Chain			Star		
DPCCP	0.0001 s	0.0082 s	0.0032 s	0.0001 s	15.490 s	2.1200 s
TDMCL	0.9468 ×	2.2641 ×	1.3133 ×	0.9613 ×	2.2923 ×	1.3712 ×
TDMCL$_{PCB}$	0.3291 ×	2.5645 ×	0.8881 ×	1.0090 ×	2.5045 ×	1.3920 ×
TDMCL$_{APCB}$	0.3544 ×	3.3335 ×	0.9926 ×	1.2113 ×	3.2712 ×	1.7285 ×
TDMCL$_{APCBI}$	0.1091 ×	2.9416 ×	0.5742 ×	0.8470 ×	3.6037 ×	1.4289 ×
TDMCL$_{APCBI\_Opt}$	0.0584 ×	2.8568 ×	0.3974 ×	0.8627 ×	2.0956 ×	1.3285 ×
TDMCC	0.6399 ×	1.8050 ×	1.0381 ×	0.6923 ×	1.5193 ×	1.0386 ×
TDMCC$_{PCB}$	0.1593 ×	1.6809 ×	0.5570 ×	0.7458 ×	1.7192 ×	1.0804 ×
TDMCC$_{APCB}$	0.1481 ×	2.4412 ×	0.5572 ×	0.9938 ×	2.1116 ×	1.3987 ×
TDMCC$_{APCBI}$	0.0488 ×	1.6809 ×	0.2959 ×	0.6648 ×	2.0689 ×	1.1306 ×
TDMCC$_{APCBI\_Opt}$	0.0426 ×	0.9265 ×	0.2500 ×	0.6845 ×	2.7019 ×	1.0724 ×
TDMCB	0.5000 ×	1.7394 ×	1.0119 ×	0.7306 ×	1.6003 ×	1.0324 ×
TDMCB$_{PCB}$	0.2000 ×	1.1538 ×	0.5449 ×	0.7402 ×	1.7192 ×	1.0522 ×
TDMCB$_{APCB}$	0.1579 ×	2.5000 ×	0.6001 ×	0.9847 ×	2.0950 ×	1.3738 ×
TDMCB$_{APCBI}$	0.0610 ×	1.1333 ×	0.3369 ×	0.6387 ×	1.8019 ×	1.0866 ×
TDMCB$_{APCBI\_Opt}$	0.0380 ×	0.9091 ×	0.2390 ×	0.6431 ×	1.5999 ×	1.0282 ×

Table 4.3.: Minimum, maximum and average of the normed runtimes for chain and star queries.

Algorithm	min	max	avg	min	max	avg
	random Acyclic			random Cyclic		
DPCCP	0.0002 s	2.5436 s	0.0990 s	0.0002 s	55.394 s	4.9052 s
TDMCL	0.8333 ×	2.3437 ×	1.2584 ×	1.0000 ×	2.5975 ×	1.6741 ×
TDMCL$_{PCB}$	0.0786 ×	2.6177 ×	0.7999 ×	0.0383 ×	1.7500 ×	0.3036 ×
TDMCL$_{APCB}$	0.0263 ×	613.08 ×	13.591 ×	0.0256 ×	25.366 ×	0.3909 ×
TDMCL$_{APCBI}$	0.0049 ×	2.7344 ×	0.4924 ×	0.0100 ×	1.3125 ×	0.1291 ×
TDMCL$_{APCBI\_Opt}$	0.0025 ×	1.8861 ×	0.4178 ×	0.0085 ×	1.0000 ×	0.1238 ×
TDMCC	0.6467 ×	1.7032 ×	1.0482 ×	0.6635 ×	3.6544 ×	1.0391 ×
TDMCC$_{PCB}$	0.0440 ×	1.5627 ×	0.6136 ×	0.0081 ×	1.1450 ×	0.1051 ×
TDMCC$_{APCB}$	0.0132 ×	193.45 ×	3.1745 ×	0.0082 ×	15.866 ×	0.3971 ×
TDMCC$_{APCBI}$	0.0027 ×	1.9800 ×	0.2863 ×	0.0030 ×	0.6250 ×	0.0397 ×
TDMCC$_{APCBI\_Opt}$	0.0017 ×	1.4849 ×	0.2772 ×	0.0030 ×	0.6112 ×	0.0387 ×
TDMCB	0.6250 ×	1.6279 ×	1.0201 ×	0.6535 ×	1.5474 ×	1.0485 ×
TDMCB$_{PCB}$	0.0721 ×	1.5939 ×	0.5708 ×	0.0078 ×	0.9589 ×	0.1022 ×
TDMCB$_{APCB}$	0.0150 ×	325.28 ×	7.6074 ×	0.0058 ×	11.231 ×	0.1394 ×
TDMCB$_{APCBI}$	0.0023 ×	1.4554 ×	0.3130 ×	0.0034 ×	0.5471 ×	0.0444 ×
TDMCB$_{APCBI\_Opt}$	0.0030 ×	1.4854 ×	0.2671 ×	0.0030 ×	0.5624 ×	0.0393 ×

Table 4.4.: Minimum, maximum and average of the normed runtimes for random acyclic and random cyclic queries.

initialized lower bounds, TDPG$_{APCBI}$ can prevent the negative effect (described in Section 4.3) as the corresponding values of max_f verify.

Algorithm	min	max	avg	min	max	avg
	Cycle			Clique		
DPCCP	$0.0001\ s$	$0.0224\ s$	$0.0080\ s$	$0.0003\ s$	$21.640\ s$	$1.7672\ s$
TDMcL	$0.9576 \times$	$2.0411 \times$	$1.2546 \times$	$1.4167 \times$	$2.0689 \times$	$1.7085 \times$
TDMcL$_{PCB}$	$0.2857 \times$	$1.5464 \times$	$0.6312 \times$	$0.0605 \times$	$1.3684 \times$	$0.4030 \times$
TDMcL$_{APCB}$	$0.2267 \times$	$6.8493 \times$	$0.6792 \times$	$0.0440 \times$	$9.5792 \times$	$0.5870 \times$
TDMcL$_{APCBI}$	$0.0859 \times$	$1.2343 \times$	$0.3236 \times$	$0.0178 \times$	$0.8420 \times$	$0.1768 \times$
TDMcL$_{APCBI\_Opt}$	$0.0567 \times$	$0.9336 \times$	$0.2162 \times$	$0.0178 \times$	$0.5833 \times$	$0.1653 \times$
TDMcC	$0.6626 \times$	$1.2886 \times$	$1.0312 \times$	$0.8333 \times$	$1.1183 \times$	$1.0294 \times$
TDMcC$_{PCB}$	$0.1636 \times$	$1.2243 \times$	$0.4036 \times$	$0.0132 \times$	$0.8421 \times$	$0.1340 \times$
TDMcC$_{APCB}$	$0.1200 \times$	$3.5790 \times$	$0.3801 \times$	$0.0166 \times$	$9.7472 \times$	$0.8473 \times$
TDMcC$_{APCBI}$	$0.0521 \times$	$0.7510 \times$	$0.1833 \times$	$0.0045 \times$	$0.3449 \times$	$0.0508 \times$
TDMcC$_{APCBI\_Opt}$	$0.0412 \times$	$0.6058 \times$	$0.1382 \times$	$0.0044 \times$	$0.2158 \times$	$0.0458 \times$
TDMcB	$0.5001 \times$	$1.6596 \times$	$1.0168 \times$	$0.8333 \times$	$1.3000 \times$	$1.0422 \times$
TDMcB$_{PCB}$	$0.1888 \times$	$0.8908 \times$	$0.4106 \times$	$0.0114 \times$	$0.6947 \times$	$0.1324 \times$
TDMcB$_{APCB}$	$0.1100 \times$	$6.9825 \times$	$0.4009 \times$	$0.0102 \times$	$5.7806 \times$	$0.2438 \times$
TDMcB$_{APCBI}$	$0.0533 \times$	$0.8164 \times$	$0.1934 \times$	$0.0051 \times$	$0.2828 \times$	$0.0541 \times$
TDMcB$_{APCBI\_Opt}$	$0.0412 \times$	$0.5425 \times$	$0.1334 \times$	$0.0046 \times$	$0.2106 \times$	$0.0474 \times$

Table 4.5.: Minimum, maximum and average of the normed runtimes for cycle and clique queries.

Also TDPG$_{APCB}$ is much less robust (Section 4.1) than TDPG$_{APCBI}$, as the deviation of the avg_s and avg_f values between the corresponding three different TDMcX$_{APCB}$ results compared to TDMcX$_{APCBI}$ prove.

When comparing the performance of TDMcL$_{APCB}$ and TDMcC$_{APCBI}$ for random acyclic graphs, we can determine an improvement factor of about 47 made through our contributions.

For chain queries using TDPG$_{APCBI}$ instead of TDPG$_{APCB}$ improves the average normed runtime of all three enumerators by a factor of $1.7 - 1.9$. For random acyclic queries the average normed runtimes difference are much higher with a factor of $11 - 28$. Figure 4.6 confirms that all pruning methods speed-up the planing process when chain queries are considered. Figure 4.8 shows how for random acyclic queries with an increasing number of vertices the performance of TDPG$_{APCB}$ diminishes while on the other hand the performance of TDPG$_{PCB}$ and TDPG$_{APCBI}$ improves. Note that in both Figures the relative order of the algorithms is independent of the number of relations.

Figure 4.9 depicts the density plot of the normed runtimes for random acyclic graphs. Again we can see that in the majority of cases TDPG$_{APCB}$ performs worse than DPCCP regardless of the partitioning algorithm (MINCUTLAZY or MINCUT-BRANCH). TDPG$_{APCBI}$ clearly shows the highest improvement factor of the normed runtimes for a large part of the queries. Thereby TDMcC$_{APCBI}$ is slightly better then TDMcB$_{APCBI}$. There are only some minor exceptions where TDMcC$_{APCBI}$ and TDMcB$_{APCBI}$ performs worse than DPCCP. Thus our novel pruning strategy, proves to be risk free, again with the exception of star queries.

Algorithm	avg_s	max_s	avg_f	max_f	avg_s	max_s	avg_f	max_f
	Chain				Star			
TDMCL_{PCB}	0.87	1.00	0.00	0.00	1.00	1.00	0.00	0.00
TDMCL_{APCB}	0.63	1.00	0.47	4.01	1.00	1.00	0.00	0.00
TDMCL_{APCBI}	0.41	0.87	0.19	0.76	1.00	1.00	0.00	0.00
TDMCL_{APCBI_Opt}	0.33	0.90	0.16	0.62	1.00	1.00	0.00	0.00
TDMCC_{PCB}	0.78	1.00	0.00	0.00	1.00	1.00	0.00	0.00
TDMCC_{APCB}	0.56	1.00	0.36	7.45	1.00	1.00	0.00	0.00
TDMCC_{APCBI}	0.33	0.80	0.17	0.67	1.00	1.00	0.00	0.00
TDMCC_{APCBI_Opt}	0.32	0.71	0.18	0.60	1.00	1.00	0.00	0.00
TDMCB_{PCB}	0.84	1.00	0.00	0.00	1.00	1.00	0.00	0.00
TDMCB_{APCB}	0.59	1.00	0.52	7.30	1.00	1.00	0.00	0.00
TDMCB_{APCBI}	0.41	0.87	0.19	0.76	1.00	1.00	0.00	0.00
TDMCB_{APCBI_Opt}	0.32	0.90	0.16	0.62	1.00	1.00	0.00	0.00
	random Acyclic				random Cyclic			
TDMCL_{PCB}	0.84	1.00	0.00	0.00	0.26	1.00	0.00	0.00
TDMCL_{APCB}	0.38	1.00	36.6	1674	0.07	0.80	1.15	344
TDMCL_{APCBI}	0.36	1.00	0.30	1.43	0.03	0.72	0.03	0.72
TDMCL_{APCBI_Opt}	0.34	1.00	0.27	0.96	0.03	0.65	0.03	0.65
TDMCC_{PCB}	0.82	1.00	0.00	0.00	0.23	1.00	0.00	0.00
TDMCC_{APCB}	0.42	1.00	12.5	1295	0.06	0.77	24.05	1122
TDMCC_{APCBI}	0.31	0.96	0.30	1.40	0.03	0.64	0.03	0.74
TDMCC_{APCBI_Opt}	0.32	0.96	0.30	0.99	0.03	0.65	0.03	0.60
TDMCB_{PCB}	0.84	1.00	0.00	0.00	0.23	1.00	0.00	0.00
TDMCB_{APCB}	0.38	1.00	37.9	2450	0.06	0.73	3.17	405
TDMCB_{APCBI}	0.37	1.00	0.30	1.44	0.04	0.73	0.03	0.77
TDMCB_{APCBI_Opt}	0.34	1.00	0.28	0.98	0.03	0.65	0.03	0.69
	Cycle				Clique			
TDMCL_{PCB}	0.74	0.96	0.00	0.00	0.35	0.84	0.00	0.00
TDMCL_{APCB}	0.44	0.78	0.68	24.7	0.11	0.51	3.47	124
TDMCL_{APCBI}	0.27	0.53	0.12	0.54	0.04	0.26	0.04	0.18
TDMCL_{APCBI_Opt}	0.19	0.61	0.11	0.42	0.04	0.23	0.04	0.18
TDMCC_{PCB}	0.66	0.99	0.00	0.00	0.33	0.95	0.00	0.00
TDMCC_{APCB}	0.43	0.78	0.44	20.7	0.10	0.56	47.81	665
TDMCC_{APCBI}	0.24	0.61	0.12	0.46	0.04	0.32	0.04	0.18
TDMCC_{APCBI_Opt}	0.19	0.61	0.11	0.42	0.04	0.25	0.04	0.19
TDMCB_{PCB}	0.74	0.98	0.00	0.00	0.31	0.95	0.00	0.00
TDMCB_{APCB}	0.42	0.88	0.68	45.9	0.10	0.53	9.51	474
TDMCB_{APCBI}	0.27	0.61	0.12	0.47	0.04	0.23	0.04	0.20
TDMCB_{APCBI_Opt}	0.19	0.63	0.11	0.41	0.04	0.21	0.04	0.19

Table 4.6.: Average and maximum: Number of optimal join trees built ($_s$) and number of failed join tree requests ($_f$) normed with the number of all possible join trees.

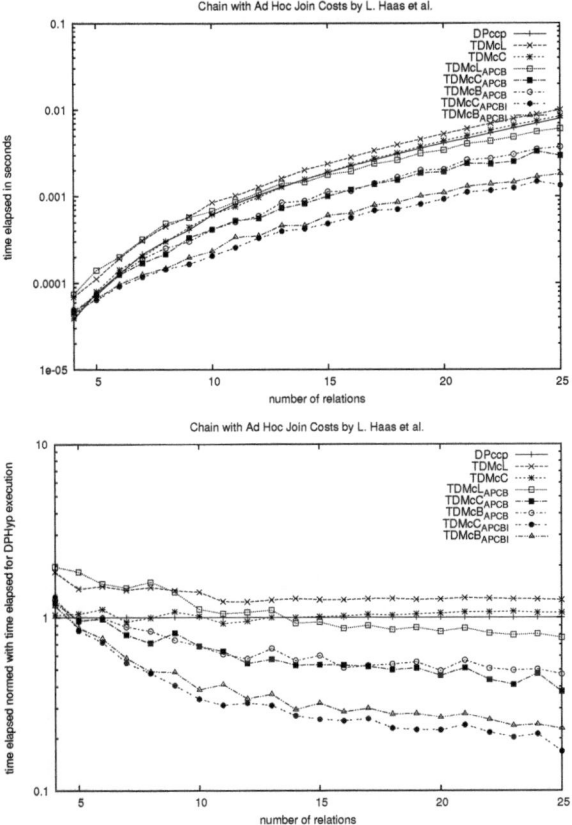

Figure 4.6.: Performance results for chain queries.

In general the star queries in our workload are not beneficial for pruning. We generated the selectivities for star queries in a way that disabled pruning (Section 4.4.2). This is confirmed by $avg_s = 1$. Consequently, the normed runtime for star queries gives us an idea of the overhead of the pruning techniques. The overhead is largest for TDMCL_{APCB} and TDMCL_{APCBI}, as indicated by the average normed runtimes of 1.73 and 1.43 compared to 1.37 (TDMCL).

The novel algorithm TDPG_{APCBI} not only decreases the optimization time, but also requires less space for its memotable, as the avg_s values in Table 4.6 indicate. For random acyclic graphs, TDMCC_{APCB} had to build 42% of DPCCP built join trees, whereas TDMCC_{APCBI} could drop this to a value of 31%.

Cyclic Query Graphs

The minimum, maximum, and average normed runtimes over the whole cyclic workload for cycle, clique, and random cyclic queries are given in Tables 4.4 and 4.5.

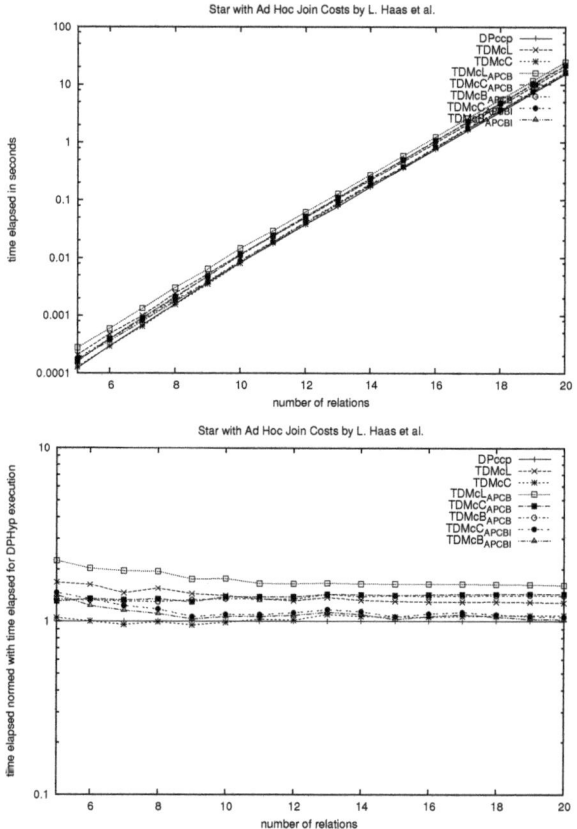

Figure 4.7.: Performance results for star queries.

We see, for example, for random cyclic queries that using TDPG_{APCBI} instead of TDPG_{APCB} improves the average normed runtime of all three enumerators by an average factor of $3-10$. We also see that for TDPG_{APCB} the maximum normed runtimes sometimes strongly deviate from the average. On the other hand, TDPG_{APCBI} does not show such a worst case behavior. Our results indicate that TDPG_{APCB}'s maximum normed runtime is by a factor of 25 higher than maximum normed runtime of TDPG_{APCBI}.

As already outlined for acyclic graphs, TDPG_{APCBI} compared to TDPG_{APCB} proves to be much more robust. Again, we determine this from the deviation among the avg_s and avg_f values, which verify that the enumeration order has much less impact on the pruning behavior of TDPG_{APCBI} than on the pruning behavior of TDPG_{APCB}. Also, comparing the average normed runtime of TDMCC_{APCB} and TDMCB_{APCB} indicates an average deviation of 2.8. Furthermore the charts for clique queries (Fig-

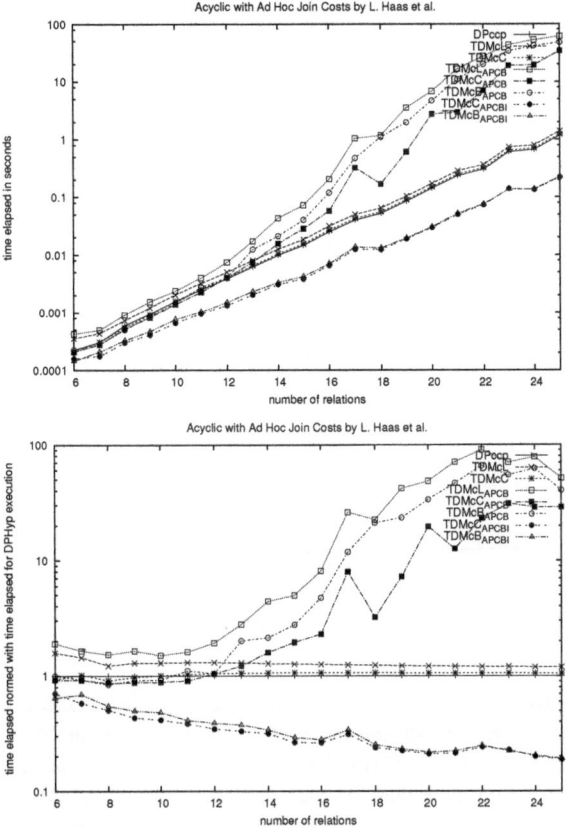

Figure 4.8.: Performance results for random acyclic queries that are neither chain nor star queries.

ure 4.11) and random cyclic queries with 15 vertices (Figure 4.13) show the same evidence: The performance of TDMCC$_{APCB}$ and TDMCB$_{APCB}$ deviate strongly.

As already mentioned cycle and clique queries belong to the same group of cyclic graphs, but in terms of the number of *ccp*s, they are on two opposite sides of the spectrum. Cycles have the lowest number of edges that is possible for cyclic graphs, removing one edge would result in a chain query. Cliques have the maximal number of edges possible. Therefore, the potential for performance improvements through pruning is much higher for the latter, as the results in Table 4.5 show. The average normed time for TDMCC$_{APCBI}$ and TDMCB$_{APCBI}$ decreases by a factor of 3.6 between the two graphs. This is also true for the space requirements of the memotable, as can be seen from the different avg_s values (Table 4.6). Whereas TDMCC$_{APCBI}$ still requires 24% of DPCCP's size of the memotable, the space requirement drops down to 4% when clique queries are optimized.

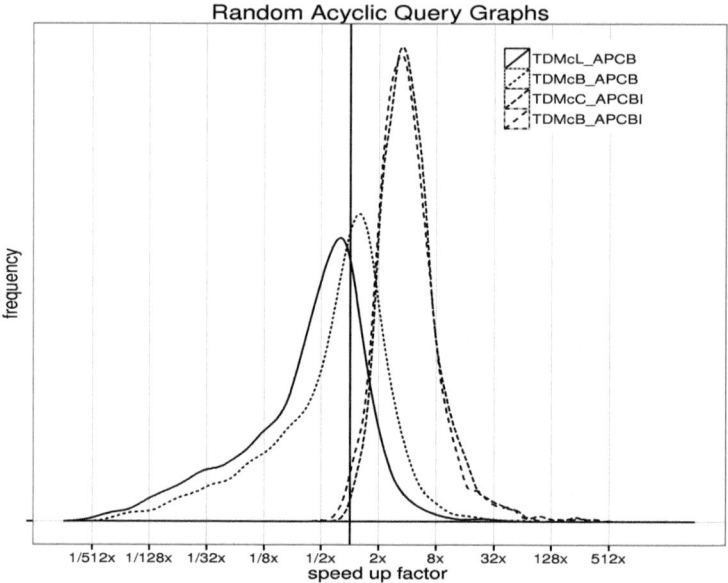

Figure 4.9.: Density plot of random acyclic queries.

Comparing the average normed runtime of TDMcL$_{APCB}$ and TDMcC$_{APCBI}$ for random cyclic graphs, we see an improvement factor of 9.8. Figure 4.12 and Figure 4.13 support our claim that TDMcC$_{APCBI}$ and TDMcB$_{APCBI}$ are the best performing join enumeration algorithm for cyclic graphs. Thereby TDMcC$_{APCBI}$ is slightly faster. The average speedup between TDMcC$_{APCBI}$ and DPccp is a factor of 25. This factor increases significantly with the number of relations in the query.

Figure 4.14 shows the corresponding density plot. As can be seen, TDMcC$_{APCBI}$ and TDMcB$_{APCBI}$ are much farther to the right than the other competitors. This means that for a much higher fraction of queries it achieves a far lower runtime.

Impact of Technical Advances

This section investigates how the seven new pruning advancements (Section 4.3) improve the efficiency of TDPG$_{APCB}$. Figure 4.15 presents the averaged relative runtime ratios. By relative runtime ratio we refer to the runtime result of the investigated pruning method divided by the runtime of TDPG$_{APCB}$ for the same query graph. For our investigation we used MINCUTBRANCH (Section 2.5) as partitioning algorithm. Thus we took the runtime of TDMcB$_{APCB}$ as divisor for the relative runtime ratio computation. We measured the runtime of every single pruning advancement on top of TDMcB$_{APCB}$. This was done with the exception of *remapping the query graph* (Advancement no. 6) and the *join heuristic* (Advancement no. 2), which we measured as a whole, since remapping depends on a heuristic. As already mentioned, the join heuristic we implemented is GOO [7].

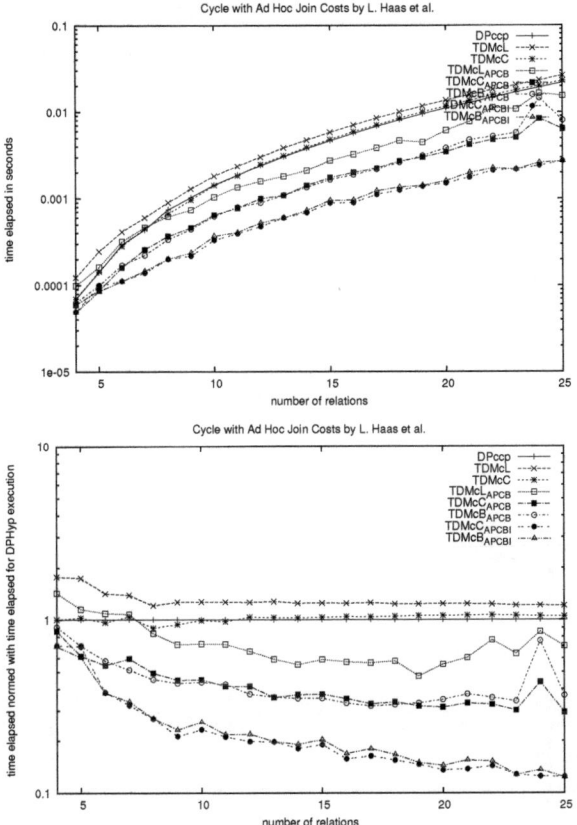

Figure 4.10.: Performance results for cycle queries.

Looking at the results (Figure 4.15) for the acyclic queries, we can see that all advancements have a relative runtime ratio significantly below 1, with the exception of GOO and remapping the graph, which itself appears to be counter-productive. That is why we also measured all advancements at once, except for the latter. This combination is displayed as the third last bar. When we compare it to TDPG_{APCBI}, we can see that only in combination with the other advancements it further improves runtime. For acyclic graphs the initial lower bounds (Advancement no. 7) are the most significant improvement.

Considering cyclic queries, all advancements have a relative runtime ratio below 0.79. Again, the initial lower bounds exhibit the highest performance gains. Note that the performance improvements of all advancements become more significant for workloads with a larger number of vertices.

The last bar shows TDPG_{APCBI} with the upper bounds for all different connected plan classes set to the cost of the corresponding optimal plan. But compared to the

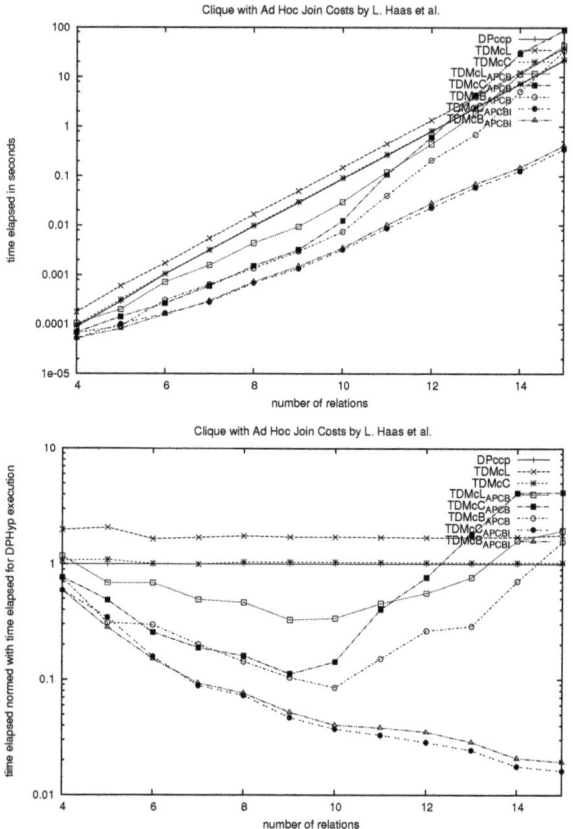

Figure 4.11.: Performance results for clique queries.

relative runtime ratio of TDPG$_{APCBI}$, it brings an improvement of 12% at the most. Hence, let us emphasize that there is not much potential for improving accumulated cost bounding strategies in the future, since this number is only of theoretical nature and can never be achieved in practice.

4.4.4. Performance Evaluation with Complex Query Graphs

This section compares the performance of our novel branch-and-bound pruning algorithm TDPG$_{APCBI}$ instantiated with our generic partitioning framework (Section 3.5), with the performance of DPHYP. Thereby, we instantiate PARTITION$_X$ with the best performing partitioning strategies MINCUTCONSERVATIVE (Section 2.4) and MINCUTBRANCH (Section 2.5). Furthermore, we include the results of TDPG$_{APCBI}$ instantiated with MINCUTCONSERVATIVEHYP (Section 3.4). Table 4.7 gives an overview of the algorithms investigated here.

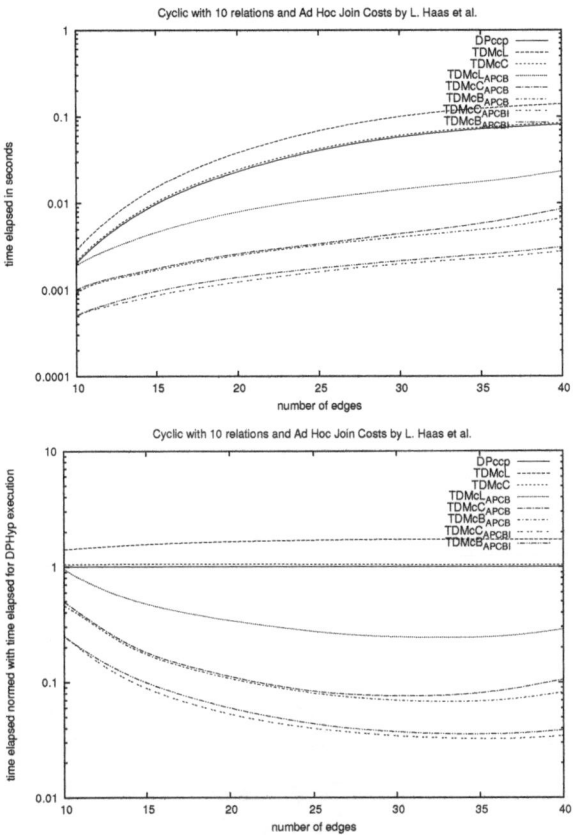

Figure 4.12.: Performance results for random cyclic queries with 10 vertices.

Abbreviated Name	Partitioning Strategy	Pruning Type
TDMcCHyp	MinCutConservativeHyp	none
TDMcCHyp$_{APCBI}$	MinCutConservativeHyp	TDPG$_{APCBI}$
TDMcBHyp	Partition$_X$+MinCutBranch	none
TDMcBHyp$_{APCBI}$	Partition$_X$+MinCutBranch	TDPG$_{APCBI}$
TDMcCFwHyp	Partition$_X$+MinCutConservative	none
TDMcCFwHyp$_{APCBI}$	Partition$_X$+MinCutConservative	TDPG$_{APCBI}$

Table 4.7.: Abbreviated names of different partitioning algorithms and pruning strategies.

As workload, we use the same query graphs as already used in Section 3.6.2. We differentiate between non-inner/simple and inner/complex query graphs.

Let us start with the pruning performance of acyclic queries. Figures 4.16 and 4.17 show the results for acyclic/inner/complex and acyclic/non-inner/simple queries. We

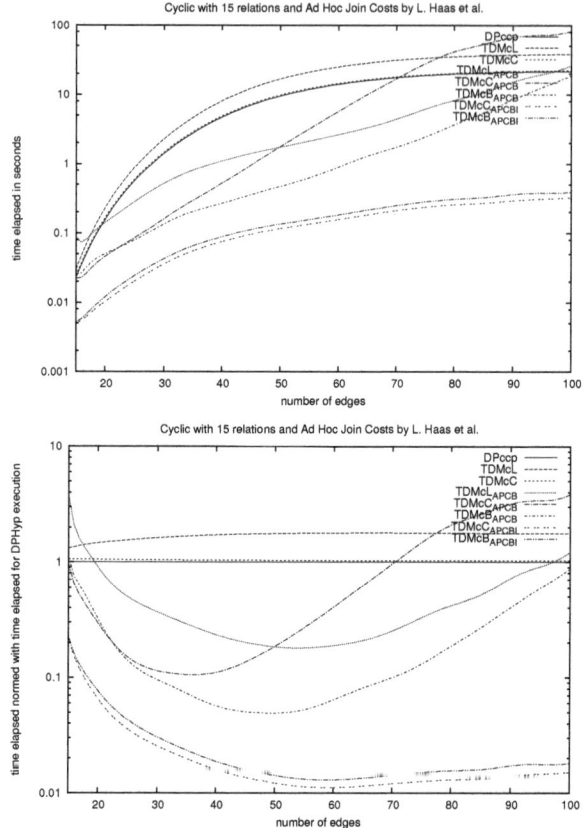

Figure 4.13.: Performance results for random cyclic queries with 15 vertices.

can observe that TDMCBHYP$_{APCBI}$ dominates TDMCCFwHYP$_{APCBI}$, although the differences are not that high. We can make the same observations when looking at the average normed runtimes on the left side of Table 4.8. Further, we can see that the average normed runtimes for acyclic/inner/complex are lower than the values for acyclic/non-inner/simple queries. This is because for an average acyclic/inner/complex query, more *ccp*s exist when compared with an average acyclic/non-inner/simple query, which makes the acyclic/inner/complex query harder to compile. Since more *ccp*s exist, TDMCBHYP$_{APCBI}$ and TDMCCFwHYP$_{APCBI}$ can benefit more from their pruning capabilities. Independent of the acyclic scenario, DPHYP is clearly dominated by TDMCBHYP$_{APCBI}$ either by an average factor of $\frac{1}{0.89} = 1.12$ or by a factor of $\frac{1}{0.49} = 2.04$.

The advantages of branch-and-bound pruning become more distinctive when random cyclic queries are considered. The results for cyclic/inner/complex and cyclic/non-inner/simple queries are given in Figures 4.18, 4.19 and 4.20, 4.21.

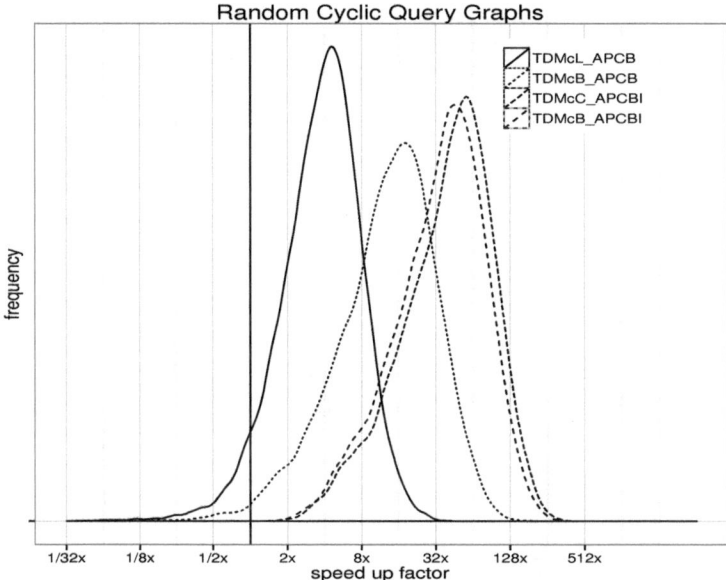

Figure 4.14.: Density plot of random cyclic queries.

Again the pruning performance is better for the inner/complex queries than for the cyclic/non-inner/simple queries of our workload. We can find the same rationale: the number of *ccp*s is higher for cyclic/inner/complex queries than for cyclic/non-inner/simple queries. Again, TDMcCFwHYP$_{APCBI}$ is slightly slower than TDMcBHYP$_{APCBI}$. Comparing the average normed runtimes on the right side of Table 4.8, we can see that TDMcBHYP$_{APCBI}$ outperforms DPHYP with an average factor of up to 0.064.

Looking at all four scenarios ANS (acyclic/non-inner/simple), AIC (acyclic/inner/-complex), CNS (cyclic/non-inner/simple) and CIC (cyclic/inner/complex), we can conclude: Different queries together with different cardinalities and selectivities embed different inherent pruning potentials.

We thus decided to illustrate this potential using density plots, as shown in Figures 4.22 and 4.23. The x-axis gives the speed-up factor achieved by pruning. The y-axis shows its frequency, i.e., how often a certain speed-up factor was observed during our experiments with random cyclic and acyclic queries. Thereby, Figure 4.22 gives the density plot for the speed-up factor of TDMcBHYP$_{APCBI}$ when compared with TDMcBHYP. The speed-up factor in comparison to DPHYP is given in Figure 4.23. Both figures support our claim: The pruning behavior for our four cases is rather different. First, in the worst case (ANS), we have a steep peak around 1. This means that the pruning potential is poor. It becomes larger in case of AIC, but still for cyclic queries in the cases CNS and CIC, we observe a much higher optimization potential.

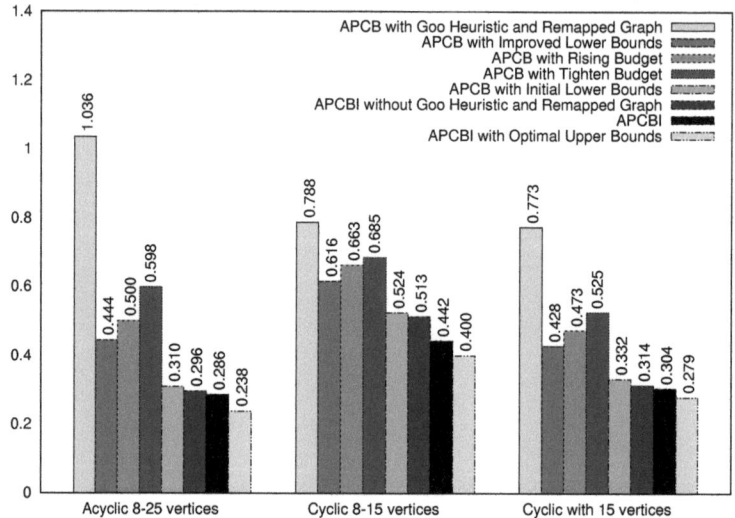

Figure 4.15.: Performance of different Pruning Advancements.

Algorithm	min	max	avg	min	max	avg
	acyclic/non-inner/simple			cyclic/non-inner/simple		
DPHYP	$0.000\ s$	$0.059\ s$	$0.001\ s$	$0.000\ s$	$1.235\ s$	$0.008\ s$
TDMCCHYP	$0.189 \times$	$4.011 \times$	$1.218 \times$	$0.119 \times$	$3.568 \times$	$1.153 \times$
TDMCBHYP	$0.105 \times$	$2.639 \times$	$0.975 \times$	$0.093 \times$	$2.142 \times$	$0.876 \times$
TDMCCFwHYP	$0.105 \times$	$2.500 \times$	$1.002 \times$	$0.096 \times$	$2.064 \times$	$0.892 \times$
TDMCCHYP$_{APCBI}$	$0.070 \times$	$3.409 \times$	$1.041 \times$	$0.040 \times$	$2.920 \times$	$0.574 \times$
TDMCBHYP$_{APCBI}$	$0.065 \times$	$2.640 \times$	$0.893 \times$	$0.018 \times$	$2.034 \times$	$0.450 \times$
TDMCCFwHYP$_{APCBI}$	$0.065 \times$	$3.689 \times$	$1.066 \times$	$0.022 \times$	$2.547 \times$	$0.539 \times$
Algorithm	min	max	avg	min	max	avg
	acyclic/inner/complex			cyclic/inner/complex		
DPHYP	$0.000\ s$	$0.438\ s$	$0.010\ s$	$0.000\ s$	$44.306\ s$	$2.176\ s$
TDMCCHYP	$0.655 \times$	$3.234 \times$	$1.380 \times$	$0.829 \times$	$2.026 \times$	$1.351 \times$
TDMCBHYP	$0.436 \times$	$2.433 \times$	$1.016 \times$	$0.757 \times$	$1.573 \times$	$1.027 \times$
TDMCCFwHYP	$0.473 \times$	$1.879 \times$	$1.049 \times$	$0.760 \times$	$1.607 \times$	$1.036 \times$
TDMCCHYP$_{APCBI}$	$0.030 \times$	$3.797 \times$	$0.712 \times$	$0.004 \times$	$1.391 \times$	$0.096 \times$
TDMCBHYP$_{APCBI}$	$0.027 \times$	$2.206 \times$	$0.486 \times$	$0.003 \times$	$1.084 \times$	$0.065 \times$
TDMCCFwHYP$_{APCBI}$	$0.027 \times$	$2.559 \times$	$0.583 \times$	$0.003 \times$	$1.217 \times$	$0.073 \times$

Table 4.8.: Performance results for random queries

4.4.5. Performance Evaluation with Different Benchmarks

Whereas in Section 4.4.4 we have investigated the pruning potential for random query graphs, we now want to analyze the pruning potential for standard benchmark queries.

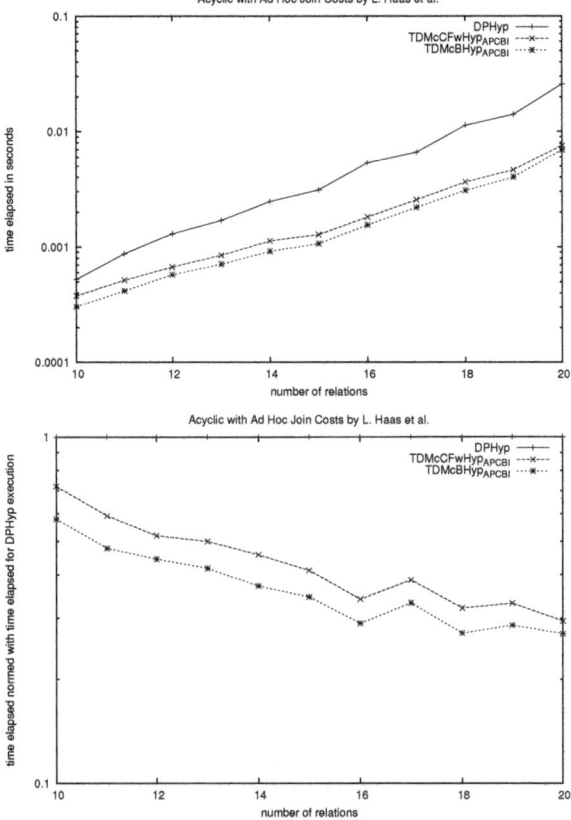

Figure 4.16.: Acyclic/inner/complex

Therefore, we consider the queries of the TPC-H [34] and TPC-DS [33] benchmarks as well as the queries obtained from the SQLite test suite [29]. We refer to Section 3.6.2 for a description of how the query graphs have been computed.

Again, we instantiate TDPG_{APCBI} with PARTITION$_X$ and employ MINCUT-CONSERVATIVE and MINCUTBRANCH as graph-partitioning strategies. We use the performance results of DPHYP to put our results for TDMCBHYP_{APCBI} and $\text{TDMCCFWHYP}_{APCBI}$ (Table 4.7) into perspective.

Tables 4.10, 4.11 and 4.12 give the summarized results for the three benchmarks. Thereby, the first column gives the overall runtime for processing the workload with a given plan generator. We refer to that value as H/DS/SQLite total time. In the second column the overall normed runtime is given. Thus, the H/DS/SQLite total time for a given algorithm is divided by DPHYP's H/DS/SQLite total time. We refer to that value as overall normed runtime. For the value in the third column, we take the normed runtime for every query and compute the average of all normed runtimes of the whole workload. To be more precise, for that value we compute the sum of all

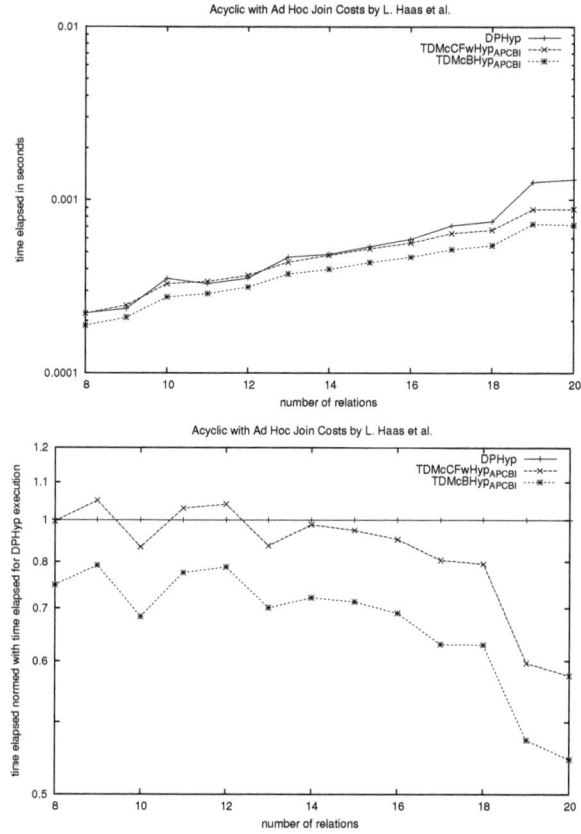

Figure 4.17.: Acyclic/non-inner/simple

Algorithm	Q2	Q5	Q7	Q8	Q9	Q20	Q21
TDMcCFwHyp$_{APCBI}$	0.70 ×	0.40 ×	0.40 ×	0.59 ×	0.54 ×	0.61 ×	1.05 ×
TDMcBHyp$_{APCBI}$	0.65 ×	0.36 ×	0.36 ×	0.43 ×	0.49 ×	0.63 ×	0.84 ×

Table 4.9.: Normed runtimes for TPC-H Queries with more than 4 tables referenced

query-specific normed runtimes and divide the sum by the number of query graphs the workload consists of. We call this value averaged normed runtime.

TPC-H

We considered all TPC-H [34] queries except for those that did not contain any join (Q1 and Q6). For Q14 and Q17 we gained the same query graph. Hence, we consider only the graph for Q14.

For those queries referencing more than 4 tables, we give the normed runtime results in Table 4.9. For the 19 TPC-H queries we investigated, we give the summarized

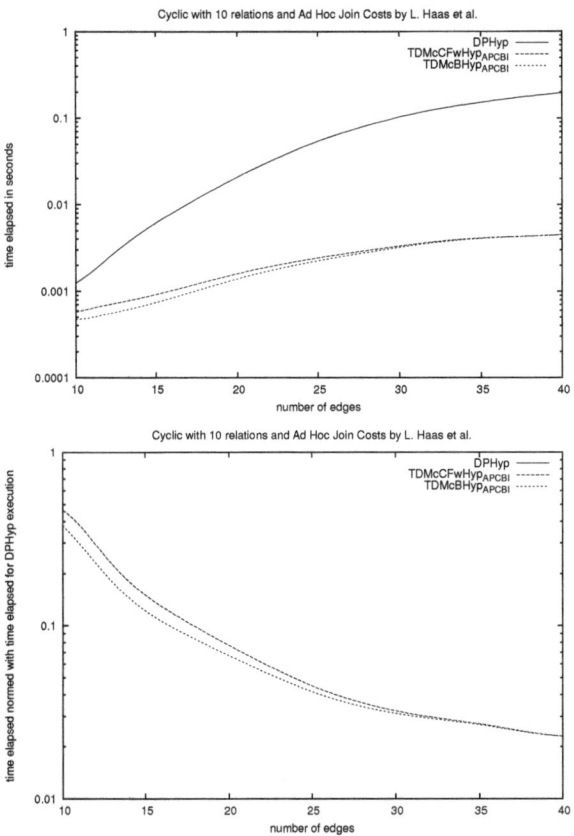

Figure 4.18.: Cyclic/inner/complex with 10 relations

Algorithm	$\sum$	overall normed	average normed
DPHYP	0.00069 s	1.0000 $\times$	1.0000 $\times$
TDMCCFWHYP$_{APCBI}$	0.00044 s	0.6350 $\times$	1.1955 $\times$
TDMCBHYP$_{APCBI}$	0.00038 s	0.5504 $\times$	1.0917 $\times$

Table 4.10.: Overall sum of elapsed time, overall normed runtime and average normed runtime for TPC-H Queries

results in Table 4.10. Since the TPC-H queries reference 8 relations at the most, the H-total time is very low. Thus, the number of *ccp*s is low as well. This leads to a lower pruning potential, as the overall normed time for TDMCBHYP$_{APCBI}$ with a value of 0.55 shows. TDMCCFWHYP$_{APCBI}$ is even 15% slower then TDMCBHYP$_{APCBI}$. Nevertheless, DPHYP is clearly outperformed by both algorithms when the whole TPC-H workload is considered.

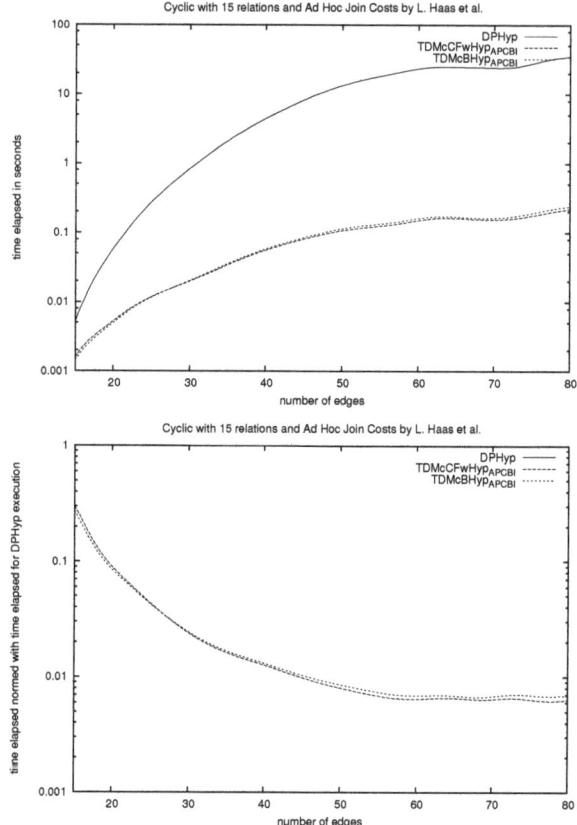

Figure 4.19.: Cyclic/inner/complex with 15 relations

TPC-DS

In Table 4.11 we give the summarized results for the TPC-DS benchmark [33]. Since on average more relations are referenced than in a TPC-H query, the pruning potential should be higher. This is confirmed by an overall normed runtime of 0.23 for TDMCBHYP$_{APCBI}$. With an overall normed runtime of 0.58, TDMCCFWHYP$_{APCBI}$ is by a factor of 2.43 slower than TDMCBHYP$_{APCBI}$, but still distinctly faster than DPHYP. The speed-up factor of TDMCBHYP$_{APCBI}$ in comparison to DPHYP is $\frac{1}{0.23} = 4.35$.

SQLite Test Suite

The summarized results for the SQLite Test Suite [29] are given in Table 3.9. From the SQLite-total time, we can see that the queries take on average much longer to compile than the TPC-H and TPC-DS queries. In fact, the queries considered here reference up to 32 relations. Hence, we might expect a larger pruning potential. But taking a look

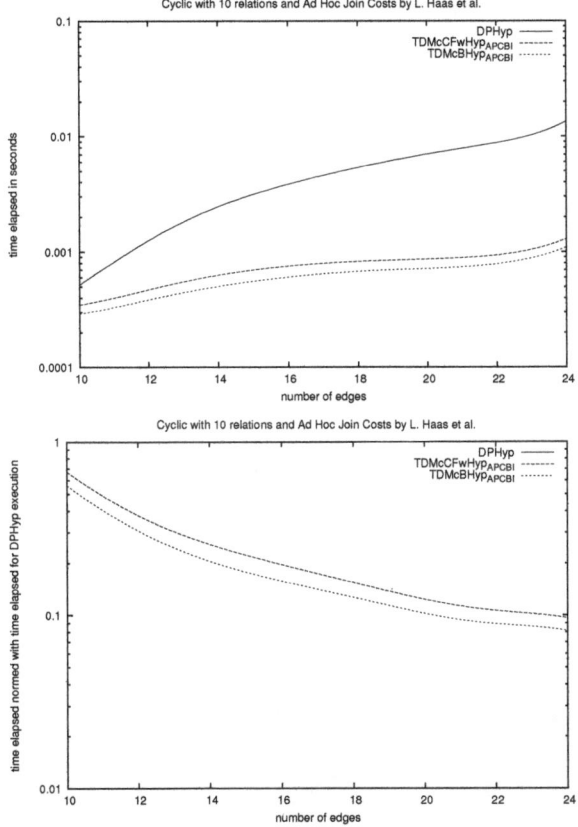

Figure 4.20.: Cyclic/non-inner/simple with 10 relations

Algorithm	$\sum$	overall normed	average normed
DPHYP	0.40295 s	1.0000 ×	1.0000 ×
TDMCCFWHYP$_{APCBI}$	0.23423 s	0.5813 ×	0.9825 ×
TDMCBHYP$_{APCBI}$	0.09636 s	0.2391 ×	0.9716 ×

Table 4.11.: Overall sum of elapsed time, overall normed runtime and average normed runtime for TPC-DS Queries

at the selectivities and cardinalities of the query graphs tells us something different. There is only one cardinality for all relations, which is 10 tuples. The selectivities of the join edges are either 0.04 or 1. Those values lead to many equivalent (sub)plans of equal costs, which in turn minimize the pruning potential. Nevertheless, the overall normed runtime of 0.52 for TDMCBHYP$_{APCBI}$ and 0.59 for TDMCCFWHYP$_{APCBI}$ shows that DPHYP is outperformed distinctively. Under the given circumstances, this is still a very good result.

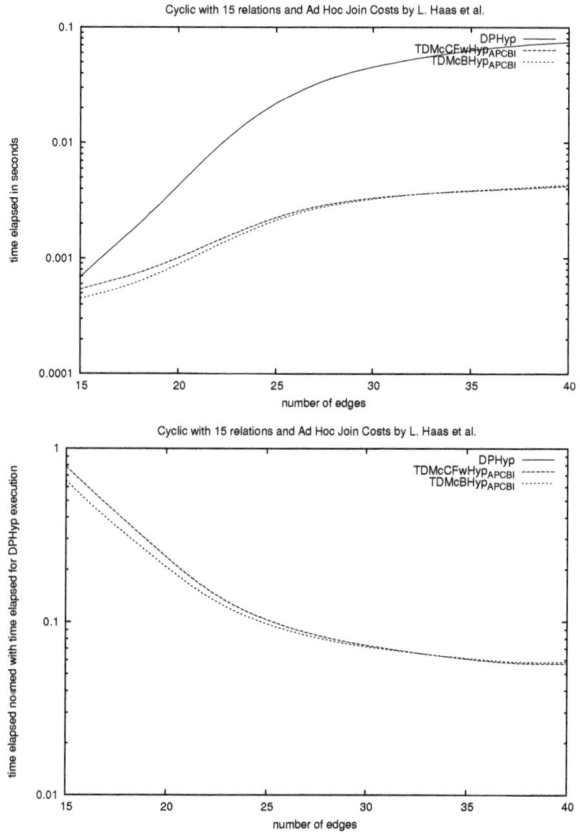

Figure 4.21.: Cyclic/non-inner/simple with 15 relations

Algorithm	$\sum$	overall normed	average normed
DPHYP	981.00958 s	1.0000 $\times$	1.0000 $\times$
TDMCCFWHYP$_{APCBI}$	576.05450 s	0.5872 $\times$	0.7324 $\times$
TDMCBHYP$_{APCBI}$	510.90008 s	0.5208 $\times$	0.6690 $\times$

Table 4.12.: Overall sum of elapsed time, overall normed runtime and average normed runtime for 337 queries of the SQLite test suite

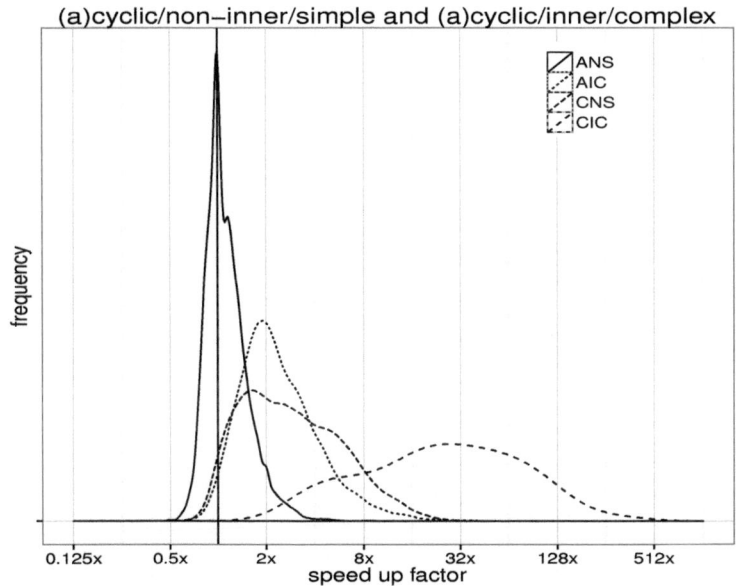

Figure 4.22.: Density plots for TDMCBHYP$_{APCBI}$ with TDMCBHYP as norm

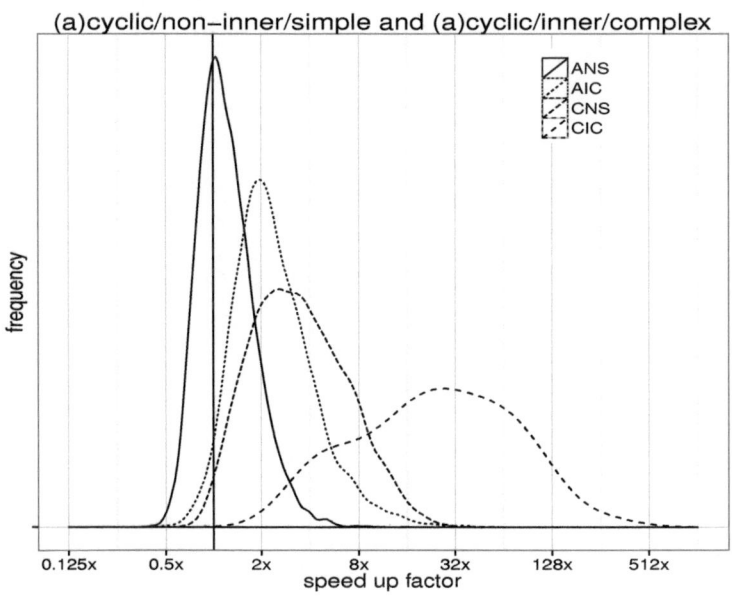

Figure 4.23.: Density plots for TDMCBHYP$_{APCBI}$ with DPHYP as norm

5. Conclusion

Dynamic programming-based join enumeration is a common and well-accepted approach for plan generation. However, this approach is not suitable for every type of query, i.e., if the query is to complex because it references too many relations or it consists of too many join predicates. For those type of queries, plan generation often relies on computationally less intensive greedy join heuristics or modifies the query graph, as proposed in [24]. As a consequence, the produced plans are often not optimal, and, thus, the compiled query takes longer to execute. The first who analyzed the search space for dynamic programming-based/memoization-based plan generation were Ono and Lohman [26].

This work motivated Moerkotte and Neumann [22] to analyze different dynamic programming-based plan generation algorithms. As it turned out, depending on the shape of the query, all dynamic programming plan generation variants known to the literature were far from optimal when compared with the lower bounds given by Ono and Lohman [26]. As a consequence, Moerkotte and Neumann proposed DPCCP [22] as the first dynamic programming-based plan generator meeting those bounds.

For top-down join enumeration, no equivalent efficient solution was known. On the other hand, due to its demand-driven processing nature, top-down join enumeration is amenable to branch-and-bound pruning techniques. The beauty of branch-and-bound pruning is that it can speed up plan generation by several orders of magnitude while guaranteeing the optimality of the produced plan.

This gave rise to a rivalry between bottom-up plan generation via dynamic programming and top-down plan generation via memoization. DeHaan and Tompa followed with a memoization-based plan generator called TDMINCUTLAZY. Although distinctly more efficient than the naive generate-and-test based memoization algorithm, TDMINCUTLAZY is still outperformed by DPCCP when not relying on its branch-and-bound pruning capabilities.

Both DPCCP and TDMINCUTLAZY could only handle graphs and thus only a subset of real-world queries. Therefore, Moerkotte and Neumann [21] developed DPHYP, which was the first efficient plan generator that could deal with hypergraphs. Thus, top-down join enumeration had a couple of disadvantages:

- There was a distinctive performance gap towards bottom-up plan generation.

- Only a subset of queries could be compiled, i.e., those that contained inner joins and simple join predicates only.

- The proposed branch-and-bound pruning techniques were not safe. In particular, there are scenarios with a worst-case runtime behavior that is by several orders of magnitude higher than if no branch-and-bound pruning is applied.

By making a series of contributions, this book dealt with these disadvantages. We summarize the contributions in the following.

5.1. Graph-Aware Join Enumeration Algorithms

We motivated our work with a complexity analysis of TDBASIC. The analysis showed that the naive generate-and-test partitioning strategy used by TDBASIC has a complexity in $O(2^{|V|})$ per emitted *ccp* where $|V|$ is the number of vertices in the query graph. In Appendix A, we analyzed MINCUTLAZY and showed that it has a worst case complexity in $O(|V|^2)$ per emitted *ccp*. Further, we improved upon TDMIN-CUTLAZY and presented TDMINCUTLAZYIMP. Most importantly, we proposed three new graph-partitioning algorithms: MINCUTAGAT [9], MINCUTCONSERVATIVE [12] and MINCUTBRANCH [8]. We showed that the complexity of MINCUT-BRANCH is in $O(1)$ for standard and acyclic graphs per emitted *ccp*. We presented two efficient implementations in C++ for MINCUTCONSERVATIVE (Appendix B.1) and MINCUTBRANCH (Appendix B.2). In our evaluation, MINCUTCONSERVATIVE and MINCUTBRANCH proved to be competitive with DPCCP. For random acyclic queries they outperformed DPCCP, for random cyclic queries they were dominated by DPCCP. But altogether, the performance differences were marginal. In summary, we closed the performance gap between top-down versus bottom-up plan generation by presenting MINCUTCONSERVATIVE and MINCUTBRANCH.

5.2. Hypergraph-Aware Join Enumeration Algorithms

Previous work emphasized that a plan generator has to deal with hypergraphs [2, 21, 27, 20, 35], otherwise it can compile only a subset of real-world queries. Therefore, we presented MINCUTCONSERVATIVEHYP [11] as an extension of MINCUT-CONSERVATIVE as the first efficient partitioning algorithm for hypergraphs. Furthermore, we proposed a generic graph partitioning framework that enables any graph-aware partitioning algorithm to handle hypergraphs [10]. The beauty of this approach is that we could reuse our efficient and competitive graph-partitioning algorithms MIN-CUTCONSERVATIVE and MINCUTBRANCH.

In our performance evaluation, we compared TDMCBHYP as our generic top-down join enumeration algorithm instantiated with our generic graph-partitioning framework and MINCUTBRANCH as partitioning algorithm with DPHYP. As our results proved, TDMCBHYP is indeed competitive with DPHYP, even without exploiting its branch-and-bound pruning capabilities. We were able to support this claim by the performance results of the TPC-H, TPC-DS and the SQLite test suite benchmarks.

5.3. Branch and Bound Pruning

The main advantage of top-down join enumeration over bottom-up join enumeration is that it allows for branch-and-bound pruning. Two branch-and-bound pruning methods are known to the literature: accumulated cost bounding and predicted cost bounding. It has been shown how both methods can be combined. Through seven advancements we achieved an improvement to the combined pruning method (a) in terms of effectiveness, (b) in terms of robustness and (c), most importantly, by avoiding the worst-case behavior otherwise observed. For the workload considered in our evaluation, we improved the average pruning performance by a factor of 10 and decreased the worst-case behavior by a factor of 25 − 225. By considering the TPC-H, TPC-DS and SQLite queries, we have shown that our improvements speed up plan generation by 100% when compared with DPHYP as the state-of-the-art in bottom-up plan generation.

5.4. Graceful Degradation

As has been mentioned, for complex queries, i.e., queries that reference many relations or queries that consist of many join predicates, plan generation relies often on computationally less intensive greedy join heuristics. With the contributions of this book, we showed how compile time can be decreased by orders of magnitude while still preserving plan optimality. Thus, in order to produce an optimal plan, we are able to consider much more complex queries than before.

This leads to an important question: When should plan generation rely on dynamic programming/memoization and when should it use a greedy join heuristic? The problem with dynamic programming is that it does not exhibit graceful degradation. This means that a complete query execution plan is produced very late in the plan generation process. One solution to this is to limit the query by a certain number of relations/join edges or a combination of both. Queries with a higher number of relations/join edges are not considered for dynamic programming. Another solution gives the dynamic programming-based search process a time constraint. If the search takes longer, it is aborted and a greedy join heuristic is used. A more elegant solution modifies the query graph beforehand such that the search space for dynamic programming is decreased [24].

For top-down join enumeration, the latter solution can still be applied, but the whole problem is less immanent. For our improved accumulated predicted cost bounding method, we produce an initial plan by utilizing a greedy join heuristic. Thus, the search process can be stopped at any time, and we already have a usually relatively good plan. Moreover, top-down processing produces a complete plan, i.e. a plan that contains all relations of the query, much faster. Thus, it exhibits graceful degradation. Due to the demand-driven nature of top-down join enumeration, we have the means of prioritizing the optimization of certain (sub)plans. In such a way, we can consider the (sub)plans of the initial plan at a faster rate. This is achieved by the sixth advancement of our pruning method. Hence, if the search process needs to be stopped, we do have a plan that has the same or even and most likely smaller cost than our initial plan.

5.5. Summary

With TDMCBHYP$_{APCBI}$ and TDMCCFWHYP$_{APCBI}$, we presented two top-down join enumeration algorithms that are based on our generic partitioning framework and use the improved accumulated predicted cost-bounding method. Whereas TDMCBHYP$_{APCBI}$ relies on MINCUTBRANCH as graph-partitioning method, TDMCCFWHYP$_{APCBI}$ utilizes MINCUTCONSERVATIVE.

Our experiments with the TPC-H, TPC-DS and SQLite queries showed that both TDMCBHYP$_{APCBI}$ and TDMCCFWHYP$_{APCBI}$ dominate DPHYP, which is the state-of-the-art in bottom-up processing. Thereby, TDMCBHYP$_{APCBI}$ performs best. In fact, TDMCBHYP$_{APCBI}$ is on average by a factor of two faster than DPHYP.

Moreover, for our generated workloads we have shown that TDMCBHYP$_{APCBI}$ and TDMCCFWHYP$_{APCBI}$ have a better worst-case performance than DPHYP.

Because of the distinctive performance advantage, a better worst-case behavior and graceful degradation, we can conclude: When building a query optimizer, top-down processing, and, in particular, TDMCBHYP$_{APCBI}$ should be the alternative of choice.

A. TDMinCutLazy

A.1. Important Notions

Lazy minimal cut partitioning makes use of a data structure called *biconnection tree* [8]. We give its definition:

Definition A.1.1. Let $G = (V, E)$ be a connected undirected graph and $BCC = \{G_1^{BCC}(V_1, E_1), ..., G_k^{BCC}(V_k, E_k)\}$ the set of biconnected components of which G consists such that $V = \bigcup_{1 \leq i \leq k} V_i$ holds. For an arbitrary vertex $t \in V$, a set of vertex nodes V_{vn} and a set of set nodes V_{sn} where $V_{tree} = V_{vn} \cup V_{sn}$ and $V_{vn} \cap V_{sn} = \emptyset$ holds, we call $\mathcal{T} = (V_{tree}, E_{tree}, t)$ a biconnection tree if

- $V_{vn} = V$,

- $V_{sn} = \{s_{V_i} \mid s \text{ representing a set of vertices } V_i \text{ of a biconnected component } G_i^{BCC}(V_i, E_i)\}$, and

- the set of tree edges $E_{tree} = \{(s_{V_i}, v) \mid s_{V_i} \in V_{sn} \land v \in V_i\}$.

The vertex t is called root of $\mathcal{T}$.

Within a biconnection tree $\mathcal{T}$, the *descendants* $\mathcal{D}_\mathcal{T}$ and the *ancestors* $\mathcal{A}_\mathcal{T}$ of an arbitrary vertex $v \in V$ can be defined as follows.

$$\mathcal{D}_\mathcal{T}(v) = \{u \in V \mid u \text{ occurs in a subtree of } \mathcal{T} \text{ rooted at } v\},$$

$$\mathcal{A}_\mathcal{T}(v) = \{u \in V \mid u \text{ is a vertex node on path } t \xrightarrow{*} v\}.$$

A.2. Lazy Minimal Cut Partitioning

DeHaan and Tompa [5] proposed a partitioning algorithm named MINCUTLAZY that generates the *ccp*s for a set. We give its pseudocode in Figure A.1. MINCUTLAZY can be embedded into a top-down memoization algorithm like TDPLANGEN, as given in Section 2.2.1. We refer to the top-down join enumeration algorithm instantiated with DeHaan's and Tompa's MINCUTLAZY as TDMINCUTLAZY or TDMCL for short.

DeHaan's and Tompa's partitioning algorithm starts with one-element sets of the relations C and expands them recursively by the descendants $\mathcal{D}_\mathcal{T}(v)$ of a neighbor $v \in \mathcal{N}(C)$, but does not cause the complement $S \setminus C$ to become disconnected. Duplicates are avoided through a restricted set X that is enhanced by the ancestors $\mathcal{A}_\mathcal{T}(v)$ of a C's neighbor $v \in \mathcal{N}(C)$ after every recursive call. The calculation of descendants and ancestors is based on a biconnection tree structure $\mathcal{T}$ that is computed by a call to BUILDBCT (Section A.3). We analyze the complexity to build a biconnection tree in Section A.3.2. It is $O(|S|^2)$. To avoid the unnecessary recomputation of the biconnection tree at every invocation of MINCUTLAZY, the reusability test ISUSABLE [5] is proposed. Since the test returns false negatives, the partitioning algorithm in the worst case constructs a biconnection tree for every emitted partition. But in the best case, that is, for all acyclic graphs, only one biconnection tree is constructed.

PARTITION$_{MinCutLazy}(G_{|S})$
    ▷ **Input:** a connected (sub)graph $G_{|S}$
    ▷ **Output:** $P_{ccp}^{sym}(S)$
1    $t \leftarrow$ arbitrary vertex of S
2   MINCUTLAZY$(G_{|S}, \emptyset, \emptyset, \{t\}, \text{NULL}, t)$

MINCUTLAZY$(G_{|S}, C, C_{diff}, X, \mathcal{T}', t)$
    ▷ **Input:** connected set S, $C \cap X = \emptyset$, $C_{diff} \subseteq C$
    ▷ **Output:** *ccps* for S
1   **if** $C \neq \emptyset$
2   emit $(C, S \setminus C)$
3   **if** $\mathcal{N}(C) \subseteq X$
4   **return**
5   **if** ISUSABLE$(\mathcal{T}', C_{diff})$
6        $\mathcal{T} \leftarrow \mathcal{T}'$
7   **else** $\mathcal{T} \leftarrow$ BUILDBCT$(G_{S \setminus C}, t)$
8    $P \leftarrow \{v \in \mathcal{N}(C) | v \in (S \setminus X) \land (\mathcal{D}_\mathcal{T}(v) \cap \mathcal{N}(C)) = \{v\}\}$
9    $X' \leftarrow X$
10   **for all** $v \in P$
11   **do** MINCUTLAZY$(G_{|S}, C \cup \mathcal{D}_\mathcal{T}(v), \mathcal{D}_\mathcal{T}(v), X', \mathcal{T}, t)$
12       $X' \leftarrow X' \cup \mathcal{A}_\mathcal{T}(v)$
    ▷ $\mathcal{N}(\emptyset) = S \setminus \{t\}$

Figure A.1.: Pseudocode for MINCUTLAZY

A.3. Biconnection Tree Building

Unfortunately, DeHaan and Tompa omitted some important implementation details about how to build a biconnection tree efficiently. This section fills some gaps. First the biconnection tree construction (Section A.3.1) is explained, and then implementation alternatives for precomputing the ancestors and descendants (Section A.3.2) are discussed through a complexity analysis.

A.3.1. Biconnection Tree Construction

The pseudocode for constructing a biconnection tree is given in Figures A.2 and A.3 as a modification of [6] [1]. The variables are initialized in BUILDBCT, and the recursive search and building procedure is implemented within BUILDBCTSUB. We presume that the details of depth-first search and pre-order numbering are known and omit any further explanation [4].

The stack of graph edges E_{stack} is used to distinguish between the tree edges and back edges that are not captured. Tree edges are those that lead to all the accessed vertices during the discovery of vertices. Back edges are the rest of the graph edges that would close the cycles to already visited vertices. We denote the set of tree edges with E_t and the set of back edges with E_b. It holds that $E = E_t \cup E_b$ with $E_b \cap E_t = \emptyset$. For the recognition of cycles, we need an additional field low. For its values, it holds:

$$low[v] = Min(\{df[v]\} \cup \{df[w] \mid w \in D(v)\}),$$

where df is the pre-order number and $D(v)$ is defined as:

$$D(v) = \{w \mid \exists x(x,w) \in E_b, w \xrightarrow{*} v \xrightarrow{*} x\}.$$

In other words, the set $D(v)$ includes all vertices w with a back edge $(x,w) \in E_b$, and v is a descendant of w and x a descendant of v in the directed spanning tree $S(V, E_t)$. Note that the vertex v is a descendant of w if $df[w] < df[v]$ holds. Hence, x is also a descendant of w, and it holds that $df[w] < df[v] < df[x]$. The calculation of $low[v]$ can be embedded into the depth-first search procedure if the formula is rewritten in terms of values of $low[s]$ at the direct children $s \in C(v)$ of v in $S(V, E_t)$ and of the preorder numbers of the vertices connected to v via back edges.

$$low[v] = Min(\{df[v]\} \cup \{low[s] \mid s \in C(v)\} \cup \{df[w] \mid w \in D(v)\})$$

The set $C(v)$ is defined as:

$$C(v) = \{s \mid s \in \mathcal{N}(v) \wedge df[v] < df[s]\}$$

Due to the recursive iteration, the final value of $low[v]$ is not known before the list of vertices adjacent to v is fully processed. If a vertex v is an articulation vertex and the entry point of the biconnection $G^{BCC} = (V_i, E_i)$ where $v, s \in V_i$ holds, it is recognized by $low[s] \geq df[v]$. This is also true for a root that is not an articulation vertex because it has just one set node as a child.

In Line 4 of BUILDBCTSUB, the value of $low[v]$ is initialized. Since during processing $low[v] \leq df[v]$ holds, its preorder number is chosen. As the first part of the previous rewritten formula, the value of $low[v]$ is adjusted to the minimum value between $low[w]$ from the son w of v and itself in Line 21. The second part of the definition is implemented in Line 24. The check of Line 22 ensures that $(v,w) \in E_b$ is really a back edge and not just a tree edge.

Knowing the value $low[w]$ of v's descendant w in $S(V, E_t)$, it could be determined whether v is an articulation vertex and as a vertex node, implicitly, the father of a set node $s_{\{v,w,...\}}$ (Line 11). If so, that set node $s_{\{v,w,...\}}$ has to be constructed and added to the set of set nodes V_{sn} (Line 16). Taking all edges from E_{stack} (Line 13) until the edge (v,w) from which w was accessed (Line 15) corresponds to enumerating the recognized biconnected component. To complete the set node, all its child vertex nodes have to be attached by adding an edge to the edge set E_{tree} of the biconnection tree (Line 19). They can be taken from the stack of vertex nodes v_{stack} (Line 18).

If v is an articulation vertex, then all its set nodes are attached in Line 28. The set nodes which belong to v and all contain v have to be on top of s_{stack}. In case that v is not an articulation vertex, there will be no items on top of s_{stack} containing v. This follows from the observation that the set node corresponding to the biconnection is not constructed until the recursive call (Line 9) returns to its articulation vertex or root t in $S(V, E_t)$.

```
BUILDBCT(G, t)
        ▷ Input: connected query graph G = (V, E), t ∈ V
        ▷ Output: biconnection tree T for G rooted at t
1       for each vertex v ∈ V
2           color[v] ← WHITE
3           df[v] ← |V| + 1
4           low[v] ← |V| + 1
5           π[v] ← NIL
6       count ← 0
7       declare stack of edges E_stack
8       declare stack of vertex nodes v_stack
9       declare stack of set nodes s_stack
10      BUILDBCTSUB(t)
11      return (V_sn ∪ V, E_tree, t)
```

Figure A.2.: Pseudocode for BUILDBCT

A.3.2. Complexity of Biconnection Tree Construction

Now we pay attention to the complexity of constructing a biconnection tree. Recognizing the biconnected components of a graph has a complexity of $O(|E|)$ [1]. But BUILDBCT contains three more loops, which we have to examine additionally.

The loop in Line 13 iterates over the edges that are part of a biconnection, not including their back edges $b_i \in E_b$. Since a tree edge $e_i \in E_t$ is never pushed twice on E_{stack} within all invocations of BUILDBCTSUB, this loop increases complexity by $|E_t|$, where $E_t = E - E_b$. Note that $|E_t| = |V| - 1$ holds.

The second loop (17) iterates over vertices in v_{stack} and attaches each vertex to its corresponding set node. That adds $|V| - 1$ to the complexity. Note that the -1 comes from the root t, which does not have to be attached to a set node.

The third loop (26) runs over all set nodes that need to be linked to their corresponding articulation vertex or root t, respectively. If A is the set of all articulation vertices, then in all calls to BUILDBCTSUB there will be $|A|$ set nodes added to s_{stack} if $t \in A$, or $|A| + 1$ set nodes otherwise. This increases complexity by at least $|A|$.

A.3.3. Computation of Ancestors and Descendants

DeHaan and Tompa suggest [5] to incorporate the computation of $\mathcal{D}_\mathcal{T}(v)$ and $\mathcal{A}_\mathcal{T}(v)$ for all $v \in V$ into the biconnection tree building without increasing its complexity, but do not explain how this can be done.

The children as direct descendants can be part of more than one biconnected component bcc. Therefore, in addition to bcc (12) in BUILDBCTSUB, the field *descendants* is introduced preferably before Line 5. After a new bcc is constructed (16), the *descendants* should be updated with the descendants of those vertices which have been calculated in previous recursions. This means adding $O(|bcc| - 1)$ for each bcc and in total $O(|V| - 1)$.

BUILDBCTSUB(v)
  ▷ **Input:** vertex $v \in V$
1 $color[v] \leftarrow$ GRAY
2 $count \leftarrow count + 1$
3 $df[v] \leftarrow count$
4 $low[v] \leftarrow df[v]$
5 **for all** $w \in \mathcal{N}(v)$
6   **if** $color[w] =$ WHITE
7   PUSH$(E_{stack}, (v, w))$
8      $\pi[w] \leftarrow v$
9   BUILDBCTSUB(w)
10   PUSH(v_{stack}, v)
11   **if** $low[w] \geq df[v]$
12       $bcc \leftarrow \emptyset$
13   **repeat** $(e_1, e_2) \leftarrow$ POP(E_{stack})
14         $bcc \leftarrow bcc \cup \{e_1\} \cup \{e_2\}$
15   **until** $(e_1, e_2) = (v, w)$
16       $V_{sn} \leftarrow V_{sn} \cup \{s_{bcc}\}$
17   **while** TOP$(v_{stack}) \in bcc$
18         $c \leftarrow$ POP(v_{stack})
19         $E_{tree} \leftarrow E_{tree} \cup \{(s_{bcc}, c)\}$
20   PUSH(s_{stack}, s_{bcc})
21     $low[v] \leftarrow$ MIN$(low[v], low[w])$
22   **else if** $w \neq \pi[v]$
23   PUSH$(E_{stack}, (v, w))$
24     $low[v] \leftarrow$ MIN$(low[v], df[w])$
25 $color[v] \leftarrow$ BLACK
26 **while** $v \in$ TOP(s_{stack})
27   $s_{bcc} \leftarrow$ POP(s_{stack})
28   $E_{tree} \leftarrow E_{tree} \cup \{(s_{bcc}, v)\}$

Figure A.3.: Pseudocode for BUILDBCTSUB

At the same time, to all those vertices in the biconnected component the direct ancestor v can be assigned. Since the other ancestors, which are all articulation vertices on the path to the root t, are not known at this point, only the parent can be linked.

To calculate $\mathcal{A}_\mathcal{T}(v)$, the indirections of the parent articulation vertices and their ancestors need to be followed until the root t is reached. In the worst case scenario, i.e., a chain query where one end is the root and the other end has $|V| - 1$ ancestors, this means that $|V| - 2$ indirections have to be followed for one computation of $\mathcal{A}_\mathcal{T}(v)$.

The other alternative is to update not only the direct descendants but the whole set. That means in the worst case with a chain query $|V| - 1$ update operations for the opposite end of t and $(|V| - 1)!$ updates in total. It is cheaper not to follow DeHaan's and Tompa's suggestion and to postpone the calculation of the ancestors to the end of the tree construction. Knowing all direct descendants, the computation can be done top-down in $O(|V| - 1)$ by revisiting the root and all the articulation vertices. Going down this path enables us to postpone the update operation of the current descendants with the descendants of the children in BUILDBCTSUB, which saves us $O(|V|-1)$ compared to incorporating it in the biconnection tree building.

A.3.4. An Alternative to Tree Construction

Looking at MINCUTLAZY raises the question whether the overhead of the biconnection tree building is necessary, since just the ancestors and descendants of a vertex v need to be computed. The only method which depends on a biconnection tree structure is ISUSABLE. For this reason, we suggest to reformulate the usability test and to use just the information of the vertex set V_i of a $G_i^{Bcc}(V_i, E_i)$ to which a vertex v belongs. If a vertex is an articulation vertex, i.e., an inner vertex node of the biconnection tree, it must be part of more than one set node or biconnected component, respectively (Definition 2.1.17). Therefore, we map only V_i to a vertex v in case that v is not the parent vertex node p of the set node s_{V_i} in a biconnection tree. To optimize the usability test, we suggest for the mapping of v to V_i that the vertex set V_i is reduced by $\{p\}$.

Following this suggestion, we do not need the stacks s_{stack} and v_{stack} and the loop in Line 17 of BUILDBCTSUB any more, which saves us $O(|V|-1)$.

We can conclude that in spite of our suggested improvements, the additional demands on the algorithm of [1] increase the complexity by $2*|V|-2+|A|$ to an overall complexity of $|E|+2*|V|-2+|A|$.

A.4. Complexity of Lazy Minimal Cut Partitioning

We analyze the complexity of DeHaan's and Tompa's MINCUTLAZY for fixed shape query graphs, which are chain, star, cycle and clique queries. We base our calculations on the proposed improvements of Section A.3.4 [9]. Thus the complexity for building a biconnection tree is $|E|+2|S|-2+|A|$, where A is the set of articulation vertices (Definition 2.1.17) of a $G=(S,E)$. Furthermore, our analysis presumes a simplification of Line 8, which saves unnecessary iterations during the calculation of the pivot set. Now the revised computation in Line 8 is: $P \leftarrow \{v \in \mathcal{N}(C) \setminus X \mid (\mathcal{D}_\mathcal{T}(v) \cap \mathcal{N}(C)) = \{v\}\}$. For one call to PARTITION$_{MinCutLazy}$, we compute the algorithm's complexity in the form of $O(\frac{O_t+O_u+O_p+O_i}{|P^{sym}ccp(S)|})$, where O_t is the complexity of all biconnection tree buildings, O_u the complexity of all usability tests, O_p the complexity for computing all pivot sets P, and O_i the complexity of all iterations of the loop in Line 10.

First, we consider chain queries. We know that $|A|=|S|-2$ holds and only one biconnection tree has to be built. Hence, $O_t = |S|-1+2|S|-2+|S|-2 = 4|S|-5$ holds. The number of usability tests will be $|S|-3$ times at minimum and $|S|-2$ times at maximum at $O(1)$ cost each, because at every step $|\mathcal{D}_\mathcal{T}(v)|=1$ holds. The condition of Line 8 $(\mathcal{D}_\mathcal{T}(v) \cap \mathcal{N}(C)) = \{v\}$ for computing the pivot set P is evaluated $2|S|-4$ times at least and $2|S|-3$ times at most at $O(1)$ cost each. MINCUTLAZY is invoked $|S|-1$ times in Line 11, which we account with $O(1)$ cost each. In total, the complexity is $4|S|-5+|S|-2+2|S|-3+|S| = 8|S|-11$, and there are $|S|-1$ ccps emitted, whereas symmetric ccps are counted only once. Therefore, the complexity of MINCUTLAZY to emit a ccp corresponds to $O(1)$.

Next, star queries are to be considered. Again, there will be only one biconnection tree building with a complexity of $|S| - 1 + 2|S| - 2 + 1 = 3|S| - 2$, because $|A| = 1$ holds. Depending on whether the hub of the star is chosen as the root vertex t of the biconnection tree, there is no usability test required and otherwise, one usability test at $O(1)$ cost. The condition of Line 8, $(\mathcal{D}_T(v) \cap \mathcal{N}(C)) = \{v\}$, is computed $|S| - 1$ times at least and $|S|$ times at most at $O(1)$ cost each. There are $|S| - 1$ times that MINCUTLAZY is invoking itself in Line 11, which we account with $O(1)$ cost each. In total, the complexity is $3|S| - 2 + 1 + |S| + |S| = 5|S| - 2$, and since there are $|S| - 1$ ccps emitted, the complexity of MINCUTLAZY to emit a ccp is in $O(1)$.

Let us now consider cycle queries. First of all, we know that $|E| = |S|$ holds. There are $|S|$ many connected subgraphs of size k, with $k < |S|$ and $(|S|-1)|S| = |S|^2 - |S|$ in total. When we count symmetric ccps only once, the number of ccps is $\frac{1}{2}|S|^2 - \frac{1}{2}|S|$. Lazy minimal cut partitioning needs one initial biconnection tree building for S and at the most $|S| - 2$ buildings for the complements of size $|S| - 1$ that are chain graphs, because the cycle is broken off. This yields a worst case complexity of $|S|-2|S|-2+1+(|S|-1)(|S|-2+2(|S|-1)-2+|S|-3) = 4|S|^2 - 18|S| + 17$ for all tree buildings. MINCUTLAZY invokes itself $\frac{1}{2}|S|^2 - \frac{1}{2}|S|$ times. The same holds for the number of times that the condition of Line 8, $(\mathcal{D}_T(v) \cap \mathcal{N}(C)) = \{v\}$, is computed, again at $O(1)$ cost each. The number of tree usability tests evaluated is at least $|S| - 1$ lower than MINCUTLAZY invokes itself, because of the early exit in Line 1. Therefore, there are $\frac{1}{2}|S|^2 - \frac{3}{2}|S| + 1$ usability tests with $O(1)$ cost each. In total, the worst case complexity is $4|S|^2 - 18|S| + 17 + \frac{1}{2}|S|^2 - \frac{3}{2}|S| + 1 + 2(\frac{1}{2}|S|^2 - \frac{1}{2}|S|) = \frac{11}{2}|S|^2 - \frac{41}{2}|S| + 18$. Therefore, the complexity of MINCUTLAZY to emit a ccp is in $O(1)$.

Finally, we analyze the algorithm's complexity for clique queries. For every clique, it holds that $|E| = \frac{|S|(|S|-1)}{2}$. Since a powerset of a set with n elements has $2^n - 1$ nonempty subsets, for a clique $|P^{sym}ccp(S)| = 2^{|S|-1} - 1$ holds. When determining the complexity of the biconnection tree buildings for clique queries, it is important how often the tree building algorithm is called for a subgraph $G_{S \setminus C}$. Since the vertex t, arbitrarily chosen during the invocation of PARTITION$_{MinCutLazy}$, must always be part of a complement $S \setminus C$, there are $\binom{|S|-1}{k-1}$ possible complements of size k. Because of the early exit in Line 1 of MINCUTLAZY, there are no biconnection trees built for complements of size $k = 1$ or if $S \setminus C = X$ holds. This means that there are only $\binom{|S|-2}{k-2}$ biconnection tree buildings of size k. In total, there are $\sum_{K=1}^{|S|} \binom{|S|-2}{k-2} = 2^{|S|-2}$ biconnection tree buildings with a complexity of $\sum_{K=1}^{|S|}(\binom{|S|-2}{k-2}\frac{k^2+3k-4}{2}) = \frac{1}{32}2^{|S|}(|S|^2 + 11|S| - 2)$. There are as many tree usability tests as biconnection tree buildings, each at $O(1)$ costs, since $\forall v \in S : |\mathcal{D}_T(v)| = 1$ holds. This results in a complexity of $2^{|S|-2}$ for all tests. MINCUTLAZY is called $2^{|S|-1}$ times, which we count with a complexity of $2^{|S|-1}$. The condition $(\mathcal{D}_T(v) \cap \mathcal{N}(C)) = \{v\}$ is calculated $2^{|S|-1}$ times at cost of $O(1)$ each. The total complexity is $\frac{1}{32}2^{|S|}(|S|^2 + 11|S| - 2) + 2^{|S|-2} + 2 * 2^{|S|-1} = \frac{1}{32}2^{|S|}(|S|^2 + 11|S| + 38)$. When we assume that the number of ccps is $|P^{sym}ccp(S)| = 2^{|S|-1}$ instead of $2^{|S|-1} - 1$, we have a complexity of $\frac{1}{16}|S|^2 + \frac{11}{16}|S| + \frac{19}{8}$ per emitted ccp, which corresponds to $O(|S|^2)$.

A.5. Improved Version

In this subsection, we present an improvement of TDMINCUTLAZY. We call the improvement TDMINCUTLAZY$_{Imp}$ or TDMCL$_{Imp}$ for short. First, we explain the idea of our improvement and then, we analyze the number of tree buildings for both versions.

A.5.1. Global Reuse of the Biconnection Tree

In [5], the reusability of the biconnection tree within a call to the minimal cut partitioning algorithm is discussed. We propose a global reuse of the biconnection tree. We observe that once MINCUTLAZY emits a ccp $(C, S \setminus C)$ for a set S, the top-down memoization algorithm recursively invokes himself, one time with the C and the other time with $(S \setminus C)$ as the next S. Hence, the minimal cut partitioning algorithm is called again with connected subsets of the old S. Our idea is to share the biconnection tree with the memoization algorithm TDPLANGEN and reuse it for the subsequent call to the partitioning algorithm with $S \setminus C$ as the next S. Therefore, the recursion of MINCUTLAZY must be transformed into an iterative stack implementation such that the emitted ccps for a set are available before the call of the partitioning algorithm returns to TDPLANGEN. This way, one instance of the biconnection tree can be shared at a time. Note that the existing tree cannot be reused for the top-down descent with C, since the root t of the biconnection tree is not an element of C, which is necessary, as pointed out in [5].

A.5.2. Analyzing the Number of Tree Buildings

We have analyzed the potential of our improvement. Therefore, we derived formulas for the number of biconnection tree buildings in the best and the worst case that TDMINCUTLAZY needs for enumerating chain, star and clique query graphs. The formulas hold if one of two strategies for choosing the root vertex for a new biconnection tree (or tree for short) is consistently applied: we either determine the root by appointing the vertex with the lowest index or the vertex with the highest index of the set.

Chain Queries

In case of TDMINCUTLAZY, there are as many tree buildings as there are calls to PARTITION$_{MinCutLazy}$ and as there are connected subsets S, $|S| > 1$ of V from the query graph $G = (V, E)$. We define k as the cardinality of a connected subset of V. Because we only account for subsets with more than one vertex, $2 \leq k \leq |V|$ holds. Since there are $|V| - k + 1$ different connected subsets of size k, the total number of subsets with more than one vertex is $\#t^{chain}(|V|) = \sum_{k=2}^{|V|}(|V| - k + 1) = \frac{|V|^2}{2} - \frac{|V|}{2}$.

We observe that only the tree for the whole set V can be reused. This is because in every possible case, only one vertex is added to C so that $|\mathcal{D}_\mathcal{T}(v)| = 1$ holds. Furthermore, the number of times the top-level tree for all vertices in V is reused depends on the choice of the root t. If the root is chosen from one end, we have the worst case, since there are only $|V| - 2$ different connected and proper subsets of V containing t. The best case we have if t is chosen as the middle vertex of the chain query. Then if $|V|$ is even, we have $2 * \sum_{i=2}^{\frac{1}{2}*|V|} i = \frac{|V|^2}{4} + \frac{|V|}{2} - 2$, and if $|V|$ is odd, we have $2 * \sum_{i=2}^{\frac{|V|-1}{2}} i = \frac{|V|^2}{4} + \frac{|V|}{2} - \frac{7}{4} = \lceil \frac{|V|^2}{4} + \frac{|V|}{2} - 2 \rceil$ connected and proper subsets of V containing t. By subtracting our results for the number of times the tree can be reused from the number of connected subsets with more than one vertex, we get the final result. For the best case, we then have $\#t_{imp}^{chain}(|V|) = \lfloor \frac{(|V|-2)^2}{4} \rfloor + 1$, and for the worst case $\#t_{imp}^{chain}(|V|) = \frac{|V|^2 - 3*|V|}{2} + 2$ tree buildings.

Star Queries

For TDMINCUTLAZY, we have $\binom{|V|-1}{k-1}$ different connected subsets of size k and in total $\#t^{star}(|V|) = \sum_{k=2}^{|V|} \binom{|V|-1}{k-1} = 2^{|V|-1} - 1$ different connected subsets with more than one vertex. In the best case, the root t of the tree is chosen from the hub vertex of the star. Then we have $\#t_{imp}^{star}(|V|) = 1$. The worst case happens when the hub vertex has an index that would be the last or second last choice for the root of the trees among all other indices. We observe that we need one tree construction less if the hub's index is the third last choice for being the root, and $i - 2$ tree constructions less if it is the ith last choice. Therefore, for the worst case we have $\#t_{imp}^{star}(|V|) = \sum_{i=3}^{|V|}(i - 2) + 1 = \frac{|V|^2 - 3*|V|}{2} + 2$ tree buildings.

Clique Queries

There are $\binom{|V|}{k}$ connected subgraphs with k vertices. For TDMINCUTLAZY, we need 2^{k-2} tree buildings per call to PARTITION$_{MinCutLazy}$. Since we need a tree only for graphs with more than one vertex, we have for the non-improved version $\#t^{clique}(|V|) = \sum_{k=2}^{|V|} \binom{|V|}{k} * 2^{k-1} = \frac{1}{4} * 3^{|V|} - \frac{|V|}{2} - \frac{1}{4}$. We observe for $|V| > 2$ that for the improved version we reuse $2^{|V|} - |V|$ biconnection trees more than in the case of a clique query of $|V| - 1$ vertices. We give the number of reuses by $\sum_{k=1}^{|V|-2}(2^k - k) = 2^{|V|-1} - \frac{|V|^2}{2} + \frac{3*|V|}{2} - 3$. The total number of tree buildings for TDMINCUTLAZY$_{Imp}$ then is the difference between the number of tree buildings of TDMINCUTLAZY and the number of reuses. We give it with $\#t_o^{clique}(|V|) = \frac{1}{4} * 3^{|V|} - 2^{|V|-1} + \frac{|V|^2}{2} - 2 * |V| + \frac{11}{4}$.

In Table A.1, we give the number of tree buildings for TDMINCUTLAZY with $\#t$ and for TDMINCUTLAZY$_{Imp}$ with $\#t_{imp}$.

	Chain			Star			Clique	
$|V|$	$\#t$	$min(\#t_{imp})$	$max(\#t_{imp})$	$\#t$	$min(\#t_{imp})$	$max(\#t_{imp})$	$\#t$	$\#t_{imp}$
3	3	1	2	3	1	2	5	4
4	6	2	4	7	1	4	18	15
5	10	3	7	15	1	7	58	50
10	45	17	37	511	1	37	14757	14283
15	105	43	92	16383	1	92	3587219	3570928
20	190	82	172	524287	1	172	871696090	871171975

Table A.1.: Number of biconnection tree buildings for TDMINCUTLAZY and TDMINCUTLAZY$_{Imp}$.

B. Iterator Implementations

B.1. Conservative Partitioning

In the following we present the C++ Code for an iterator implementation of MINCUT-CONSERVATIVE (Section 2.4). The Code compiles with the Intel C++ compiler only, since Intel Intrinsics are used. The iterator is initialized by invoking the constructor MINCUTCONSERVATIVE. Here, s will be the bitvector representation of the vertex (sub)set S and $neighborhood$ will hold a pointer to the precomputed neighborhood array. We loop over P_{ccp}^{sum} (Line 1 of Figure 2.2) by utilizing a while loop. For the stop condition, we use the iterator's HASNEXT method. A result of TRUE indicates if there is another ccp. Otherwise, all ccps for S have already been enumerated (FALSE). NEXT then stores a ccp $(left, right)$ into $left$ and $right$ and computes the next ccp.

Conservative partitioning is a recursive algorithm, but we transformed the recursion by using a loop and making use of a stack (struct $stack\_entry$) to store the values of the local variables. Therefore, we differentiate between different cases (= $\_state$): Case 1 handles the emission of ccps (Line 4 of Figure 2.10) by assigning C to $left$ and $S \setminus C$ to $right$. Case 2 computes the next v (Line 6 of Figure 2.10). Case 3 invokes GETCONNECTEDCOMPONENTS. In case $|O| = 1$ holds, Case 3 also covers the recursive descent. Case 4 handles the scenarios where $|O| > 1$ holds. Finally, Case 5 is important for determining if there exists another ccp that has not been emitted yet, i.e. if the next call of HASNEXT has to return TRUE or FALSE. Our approach is simple: We know that there must exists at least one ccp. Hence, the first invocation of HASNEXT always returns TRUE. We compute the first ccp during the subsequent and first invocation of NEXT. But in order to have an answer ready for the next call to HASNEXT, we continue computing until we have found the second ccp. Then the second ccp is stored and $\_hasNext$ is set to TRUE. In case the computation terminates without finding another ccp we assign $\_hasNext$ with FALSE. Thus, we use Case 5 to differentiate between the first invocation of NEXT, where we essentially compute two ccps, and all other subsequent invocations. Moreover, Case 5 emulates the return of the recursive sub invocation by popping the stack. If the stack is empty, we know that there is no other ccp for S. In that case, we terminate the computation by setting $\_hasNext$ to FALSE and return the call.

```
#ifndef MINCUTCONSERVATIVE_HH_
#define MINCUTCONSERVATIVE_HH_

class MinCutConservative {

public:
    MinCutConservative(const uint32_t s, uint32_t const* neighborhood);

    virtual ~MinCutConservative();
    void next(uint32_t& left, uint32_t& right);
```

```cpp
    bool hasNext() { return _hasNext; }
  private:
    int getConnectedComponents(const uint32_t& s, const uint32_t& c_new,
        const uint32_t& neigh_it_no_c, const uint32_t& neigh);

    inline uint32_t getNeighbourhood(const uint32_t c) const {
      uint32_t result = 0;
      uint32_t c_prim = c;
      while(c_prim != 0) {
        unsigned int index = leastSignificantSetBit(c_prim);
        result = setunion(result, _neighborhood[index]);
        c_prim = reset(c_prim, index);
      }
      return difference(result, c);
    }

    inline uint32_t difference(uint32_t x, uint32_t y) const {
      x &= (~y); return x; }
    inline uint32_t intersect(uint32_t x, uint32_t y) const {
      x &= y; return x; }
    inline uint32_t setunion(uint32_t x, uint32_t y) const {
      x |= y; return x; }
    inline uint32_t reset(uint32_t x, unsigned int i) const {
      x &= ~(((uint32_t) 1) << i); return x; }
    inline uint32_t lowest_bit(uint32_t x) const {
      return (x & (-x)); }
    inline unsigned int leastSignificantSetBit(uint32_t x) const {
      return _bit_scan_forward(x); }
    inline unsigned int cardinality(uint32_t x) const {
      return _popcnt64(x); }
    inline bool disjoint(uint32_t x, uint32_t y) const {
      return (0 == (x & y)); }

  private:
    uint32_t _s;
    uint32_t const* _neighborhood;

    int _s_card;
    int _state;
    bool _hasNext;

    struct stack_entry {
      uint32_t c;
      uint32_t c_new;
      uint32_t x;
      uint32_t neigh;
      uint32_t neigh_new;
      uint32_t iter;
      int num_bccs;
      int num_bccs_found;
    };
    stack_entry* _stack;
    stack_entry* _stackPointer;
    int _stackIndex;

    uint32_t* _bccStack;
    int _bccIndex;
```

```cpp
};

MinCutConservative :: MinCutConservative (const uint32_t s,
    uint32_t const* neighborhood )
        : _s(s), _neighborhood(neighborhood), _stackIndex(0) {
  _state = 2;
  _hasNext = true;
  _s_card = cardinality(s);

  _stack = new stack_entry[_s_card];
  _stackPointer = &_stack[0];
  _stackPointer->c = 0;
  _stackPointer->neigh = lowest_bit(_s);
  _stackPointer->x = 0;
  _stackPointer->iter = _stackPointer->neigh;
  _stackIndex = 0;

  _bccStack = new uint32_t[(_s_card * (_s_card - 1)) / 2];
  _bccIndex = 0;
}

MinCutConservative ::~MinCutConservative () {
  delete[](_stack);
  delete[](_bccStack);
}

void MinCutConservative :: next(uint32_t& left, uint32_t& right) {
  bool did_emit = false;

  while(true) {
    switch(_state) {
    case 1:
      {
        left = _stackPointer->c;
        right = difference(_s, left);
        did_emit = true;
      }
    case 2:
      {
        _stackPointer->iter = difference(_stackPointer->neigh,
            _stackPointer->x);
      }
    case 3:
      if(_stackPointer->iter != 0) {
        uint32_t current = lowest_bit(_stackPointer->iter);
        uint32_t c_new = setunion(_stackPointer->c, current);

        uint32_t neigh_iter = intersect(difference(_neighborhood[
            leastSignificantSetBit(current)], c_new), _s);
        _stackPointer->neigh_new = difference(setunion(
            _stackPointer->neigh, neigh_iter), current);

        if(_stackPointer->neigh_new == 0) {
          _state = 5;
          break;
        }
```

```
        _stackPointer ->c_new = c_new;
        _stackPointer ->num_bccs_found = getConnectedComponents(
            _s, c_new, neigh_iter, _stackPointer ->neigh_new);
        _stackPointer ->num_bccs = _stackPointer ->num_bccs_found;

        if(_stackPointer ->num_bccs_found == 0) {
          _stackIndex++;          // descend recursively
          _stack[_stackIndex].num_bccs = 0;
          _stack[_stackIndex].c = c_new;
          _stack[_stackIndex].x = _stackPointer ->x;
          _stack[_stackIndex].neigh = _stackPointer ->neigh_new;

          _stackPointer ->x = setunion(_stackPointer ->x, current);
          _stackPointer = &_stack[_stackIndex];
          _state = 1;
          if(did_emit)
            return;
          else
            break;
        }
      } else {
        _state = 5;
        break;
      }
    case 4:
      if(_stackPointer ->num_bccs > 0) {
        _stackPointer ->num_bccs--;
        uint32_t c_jump = _bccStack[_bccIndex -
            _stackPointer ->num_bccs];
        uint32_t c_jump_no_c = difference(c_jump, _stackPointer ->c);
        uint32_t neigh_jump = setunion(intersect(getNeighbourhood(
            c_jump_no_c), _s), _stackPointer ->neigh_new);
        neigh_jump = difference(neigh_jump, c_jump);

        if(disjoint(c_jump, _stackPointer ->x) && c_jump < _s) {
          ++_stackIndex;         // descend recursively
          _stack[_stackIndex].num_bccs = 0;
          _stack[_stackIndex].c = c_jump;
          _stack[_stackIndex].x = _stackPointer ->x;
          _stack[_stackIndex].neigh = neigh_jump;

          _stackPointer = &_stack[_stackIndex];
          _state = 1;
          if(did_emit)
            return;
          else
            break;
        } else {
          _state = 4;
          break;
        }
      } else {
        uint32_t current = lowest_bit(_stackPointer ->iter);
        _stackPointer ->x = setunion(_stackPointer ->x, current);
        _bccIndex -= _stackPointer ->num_bccs_found;
        _stackPointer ->iter = difference(_stackPointer ->iter, current);
        _state = 3;
```

```cpp
          break;
        }
      case 5:
        --_stackIndex;
        _stackPointer = &_stack[_stackIndex];
        if(_stackIndex < 0) {
          _hasNext = false;
          return;
        }
        if(_stackPointer->num_bccs_found == 0) {
          _stackPointer->iter = difference(_stackPointer->iter,
              lowest_bit(_stackPointer->iter));
          _state = 3;
        } else {
          _state = 4;
        }
        break;
    }
  }
}

int MinCutConservative::getConnectedComponents(const uint32_t& s,
    const uint32_t& c_new, const uint32_t& neigh_it_no_c,
    const uint32_t& neigh) {

  uint32_t check_points = neigh_it_no_c;

  if(cardinality(check_points) <= 1) {
    return 0;
  }
  uint32_t con_points(neigh);

  uint32_t to_discover = lowest_bit(check_points);
  check_points = difference(check_points, to_discover);

  uint32_t checked = c_new;
  uint32_t previous_checked = c_new;
  int numBcc = 0;
  bool do_con_test = true;
  while(con_points != 0) {

    while(to_discover != 0) {
      uint32_t next = lowest_bit(to_discover);
      checked = setunion(checked, next);

      to_discover = difference(to_discover, next);
      uint32_t reached = _neighbourhood[leastSignificantSetBit(next)];

      reached = intersect(difference(reached, checked), s);

      if(do_con_test) {
        check_points = difference(check_points, reached);
        if(check_points == 0) {
          return 0;
        }
      }
      to_discover = setunion(to_discover, reached);
```

```
        }
        // not connected at this point
        do_con_test = false;
        _bccIndex++;
        numBcc++;
        _bccStack[_bccIndex] = setunion(difference(s, checked),
                    previous_checked);

        previous_checked = checked;
        con_points = difference(con_points, checked);
        to_discover = lowest_bit(con_points);
    }
    return numBcc;
}
#endif /* MINCUTCONSERVATIVE_HH_ */
```

B.2. Branch Partitioning

In this section, we give the C++ Code for the iterator implementation of MINCUT-BRANCH (Section 2.5). Since we make use of the Intel Intrinsics the Code needs to be compiled with the Intel C++ compiler. The iterator interface is the same as described in Section B.1. Branch partitioning is a recursive algorithm like the previously described conservative partitioning algorithm. We remove the recursion by applying the same transformation through using a loop and making use of a stack (struct $stack\_entry$) to store the values of the local variables.

Here we differentiate between five different cases ($= \_state$): Case 1 handles the emission of ccps (Line 27 of Figure 2.13) by assigning R_{tmp} to $left$ and $S \setminus R_{tmp}$ to $right$. Case 2 models the handling of the three different cases as described in Section 2.5.2, which covers Lines 7 to 19 of Figure 2.13. Note that in the iterator implementation, the handling of the first and second case of Section 2.5.2 is merged into one. The computation of $\mathcal{N}(C)$ is also optimized by merging the result of $\mathcal{N}(L)$ with the result of the previous $\mathcal{N}(C)$. Case 3 covers Lines 20 to 26. Case 4 is important for determining if there exists an other ccp that has not been emitted yet. Thereby, we follow the same idea as discussed in Section B.1. Finally, Case 5 emulates the return of the recursive sub invocation by popping the stack. If the stack is empty, we know that there is no other ccp for S. In that case, we terminate the computation by setting $\_hasNext$ to FALSE and return the call.

```
#ifndef MINCUTBRANCH_HH_
#define MINCUTBRANCH_HH_

class MinCutBranch {
public:
    MinCutBranch(const uint32_t s, uint32_t const* neighborhood);
    ~MinCutBranch();

    void next(uint32_t& left, uint32_t& right);
    bool hasNext() { return _hasNext; }

private:
    void reachable(const uint32_t& c, const uint32_t& current,
                    uint32_t& s_no_c) const;
```

```cpp
    inline uint32_t getNeighbourhood(const uint32_t c) const {
      uint32_t result = 0;
      uint32_t c_prim = c;
      while(c_prim != 0) {
        unsigned int index = leastSignificantSetBit(c_prim);
        result = setunion(result, _neighborhood[index]);
        c_prim = reset(c_prim, index);
      }
      return difference(result, c);
    }

    inline uint32_t difference(uint32_t x, uint32_t y) const {
      x &= (~y); return x; }
    inline uint32_t intersect(uint32_t x, uint32_t y) const {
      x &= y; return x; }
    inline uint32_t setunion(uint32_t x, uint32_t y) const {
      x |= y; return x; }
    inline uint32_t reset(uint32_t x, unsigned int i) const {
      x &= ~(((uint32_t) 1) << i); return x; }
    inline uint32_t lowest_bit(uint32_t x) const {
      return (x & (-x)); }
    inline unsigned int leastSignificantSetBit(uint32_t x) const {
      return _bit_scan_forward(x); }
    inline unsigned int cardinality(uint32_t x) const {
      return _popcnt32(x); }
    inline bool disjoint(uint32_t x, uint32_t y) const {
      return (0 == (x & y)); }

private:
    uint32_t const* _neighborhood;
    int _state;
    bool _hasNext;
    uint32_t _s;
    uint32_t _r_tmp;
    uint32_t _s_no_r_tmp;

    struct stack_entry {
      uint32_t c;
      uint32_t x;
      uint32_t x_prim;
      uint32_t neigh;
      uint32_t n_x;
      uint32_t n_l;
      uint32_t n_b;
      uint32_t next_neigh;
      uint32_t r;

      int next_state;
    };

    stack_entry* _stack;
    stack_entry* _stackPointer;
    int _stackIndex;
};

MinCutBranch::MinCutBranch(const uint32_t s,
```

```cpp
        uint32_t const* neighborhood)
        : _s(s), _neighborhood(neighborhood), _stackIndex(0) {
  _state = 2;
  _hasNext = true;
  _stack = new stack_entry[cardinality(_s)];
  _stackPointer = &_stack[0];
  _stackPointer->c = 0;
  _stackPointer->next_neigh = 0;
  _stackPointer->x = 0;
  uint32_t neigh = lowest_bit(_s);
  _stackPointer->neigh = neigh;
  _stackPointer->n_1 = neigh;
  _stackPointer->n_x = 0;
  _r_tmp = 0;
  _stackPointer->r = 0;
  _stackPointer->x_prim = 0;
  _stackPointer->n_b = 0;
  _stackPointer->next_state = 0;
}

MinCutBranch::~MinCutBranch() {
  delete[](_stack);
}

void MinCutBranch::next(uint32_t& left, uint32_t& right) {
  bool did_emit = false;

  while(true) {
    switch(_state) {
    case 1:
      {
        left = _r_tmp;
        right = _s_no_r_tmp;

        did_emit = true;
        _state = 2;
      }
    case 2:
      {
        if(_stackPointer->n_1 != 0) {
          uint32_t l_prim = lowest_bit(intersect(
              _stackPointer->n_1, _r_tmp));
          int next_state = 2;
          if(l_prim == 0) {
            next_state = 3;
            l_prim = lowest_bit(_stackPointer->n_1);
            _stackPointer->x_prim = _stackPointer->x;
          }

          _stackPointer->n_1 = difference(_stackPointer->n_1, l_prim);
          uint32_t c_prim = setunion(_stackPointer->c, l_prim);

          if(c_prim < _s) {
            uint32_t neigh(_neighborhood[
                leastSignificantSetBit(l_prim)]);
            neigh = difference(intersect(neigh, _s), c_prim);
            if(neigh == 0) {
```

```
        _r_tmp = l_prim;
        _state = 3;
        break;
      }

      const uint32_t x = _stackPointer ->x_prim;
      _stackPointer ->next_state = next_state;
      _stackPointer ->x_prim = setunion(
          _stackPointer ->x_prim, l_prim );
      _stackIndex++;
      _stack[_stackIndex].next_neigh = _stackPointer ->next_neigh;
      _stackPointer = &_stack[_stackIndex];
      _stackPointer ->next_neigh = difference(setunion(
          _stackPointer ->next_neigh, neigh), c_prim);
      _stackPointer ->n_b = difference(difference(
          _stackPointer ->next_neigh, neigh), x);
      _stackPointer ->n_l = difference(neigh, x);
      _stackPointer ->n_x = intersect(neigh, x);
      _stackPointer ->c = c_prim;
      _stackPointer ->x = x;
      _r_tmp = 0;
      _stackPointer ->r = l_prim;
      _stackPointer ->n_l = difference(_stackPointer ->n_l, x);

      _state = 2;
      break;
    }
    _r_tmp = l_prim;
    _state = next_state;
  } else {
    _stackPointer ->n_x = difference(_stackPointer ->n_x,
        _stackPointer ->r);
    if(_stackPointer ->n_x != 0) {
      uint32_t l_prim = lowest_bit(_stackPointer ->n_x);
      _stackPointer ->x_prim = _stackPointer ->x;

      uint32_t c_prim = setunion(_stackPointer ->c, l_prim);
      if(c_prim < _s) {
        reachable(c_prim, l_prim, _r_tmp);
      } else {
        _r_tmp = l_prim;
      }

      if(!disjoint(_r_tmp, _stackPointer ->x_prim))
        _stackPointer ->n_b = intersect(
            _stackPointer ->n_b, _r_tmp);

      _s_no_r_tmp = difference(_s, _r_tmp);
      if(!disjoint(_s_no_r_tmp, _stackPointer ->x)) {
        _stackPointer ->n_b = difference(
            _stackPointer ->n_b, _r_tmp);
      }

      _stackPointer ->x_prim = setunion(_stackPointer ->x_prim,
          l_prim);
      _state = 4;
      break;
```

```
          } else {
            _state = 5;
            break;
          }
        }
      }
    case 3:
      {
        if(!disjoint(_r_tmp, _stackPointer->x)) {
          _stackPointer->n_x = difference(setunion(
              _stackPointer->n_x, _stackPointer->n_l), _r_tmp);
          _stackPointer->n_l = intersect(_stackPointer->n_l, _r_tmp);
          _stackPointer->n_b = intersect(_stackPointer->n_b, _r_tmp);
        }

        _s_no_r_tmp = difference(_s, _r_tmp);
        if(!disjoint(_s_no_r_tmp, _stackPointer->x)) {
          _stackPointer->n_l = difference(_stackPointer->n_l, _r_tmp);
          _stackPointer->n_b = difference(_stackPointer->n_b, _r_tmp);
        }
      }
    case 4:
      {
        _stackPointer->n_l = setunion(_stackPointer->n_l,
            intersect(_stackPointer->n_b, _r_tmp));
        _stackPointer->r = setunion(_stackPointer->r, _r_tmp);

        if(disjoint(_s_no_r_tmp, _stackPointer->x_prim) &&
            _r_tmp < _s) {
          if(did_emit) {
            _hasNext = true;
            _state = 1,
            return;
          } else {
            _state = 1;
            break;
          }
        } else {
          _state = 2;
          break;
        }
      }
    case 5:
      {
        _stackIndex --;
        if(_stackIndex >= 0) {
          _r_tmp = _stackPointer->r;
          _stackPointer = &_stack[_stackIndex];
          _state = _stackPointer->next_state;
          break;
        }
        _hasNext = false;
        return;
      }
    }
  }
}
```

```cpp
void MinCutBranch::reachable(const uint32_t& c, const uint32_t& l,
        uint32_t& s_no_c) const {
    s_no_c = 1;
    uint32_t neigh = _neighborhood[leastSignificantSetBit(l)];
    neigh = intersect(difference(neigh, c), _s);
    while(neigh != 0) {
        s_no_c = setunion(s_no_c, neigh);
        neigh = getNeighbourhood(neigh);
        neigh = intersect(difference(difference(neigh, c), s_no_c), _s);
    }
}
#endif /* MINCUTBRANCH_HH_ */
```

Bibliography

[1] Alfred V. Aho, John E. Hopcroft, and Jeffrey D. Ullman. *The Design and Analysis of Computer Algorithms*. Addison-Wesley, 1974.

[2] Gautam Bhargava, Piyush Goel, and Bala Iyer. Hypergraph based reorderings of outer join queries with complex predicates. In *Proceedings of the 1995 ACM SIGMOD International Conference on Management of Data*, pages 304–315, 1995.

[3] Sophie Cluet and Guido Moerkotte. On the complexity of generating optimal left-deep processing trees with cross products. In *Proceedings of the 5th International Conference on Database Theory*, pages 54–67, 1995.

[4] Thomas H. Corman, Charles E. Leiserson, Ronald L. Rivest, and Clifford Stein. *Introduction to Algorithms*. MIT Press, 2001.

[5] David DeHaan and Frank Wm. Tompa. Optimal top-down join enumeration. In *Proceedings of the 2007 ACM SIGMOD International Conference on Management of Data*, pages 1098–1109, 2007.

[6] David DeHaan and Frank Wm. Tompa. Optimal top-down join enumeration (extended version). Technical report, University of Waterloo, 2007.

[7] Leonidas Fegaras. A new heuristic for optimizing large queries. In *Proceedings of the 9th International Conference on Database and Expert Systems Applications*, DEXA, pages 726–735, 1998.

[8] Pit Fender and Guido Moerkotte. A new, highly efficient, and easy to implement top-down join enumeration algorithm. In *Proceedings of the 27th International Conference on Data Engineering*, pages 864–875, 2011.

[9] Pit Fender and Guido Moerkotte. Reassessing top-down join enumeration. *IEEE Transactions on Knowledge and Data Engineering*, 24(10):1803–1818, 2012.

[10] Pit Fender and Guido Moerkotte. Counter strike: Generic top-down join enumeration for hypergraphs. *Proceedings of the VLDB Endowment*, 6(14):1822–1833, September 2013.

[11] Pit Fender and Guido Moerkotte. Top-down plan generation: From theory to practice. In *Proceedings of the 29th International Conference on Data Engineering*, pages 1105–1116, 2013.

[12] Pit Fender, Guido Moerkotte, Thomas Neumann, and Viktor Leis. Effective and robust pruning for top-down join enumeration algorithms. In *Proceedings of the 28th International Conference on Data Engineering*, pages 414–425, 2012.

[13] César A. Galindo-Legaria, Arjan J. Pellenkoft, and Martin L. Kersten. Cost distribution of search spaces in query optimization. In *Proceedings of the 5th International Conference on Database Theory*, pages 280–293, 1995.

[14] César A. Galindo-Legaria and Arnon Rosenthal. Outerjoin simplification and reordering for query optimization. *ACM Transactions on Database Systems (TODS)*, 22(1):43–73, March 1997.

[15] Goetz Graefe. The cascades framework for query optimization. *IEEE Data Engineering Bulletin*, 18(3):19–29, 1995.

[16] Goetz Graefe and William J. McKenna. The volcano optimizer generator: Extensibility and efficient search. In *Proceedings of the Ninth International Conference on Data Engineering*, pages 209–218. IEEE Computer Society, 1993.

[17] Laura M. Haas, Michael J. Carey, Miron Livny, and Amit Shukla. Seeking the truth about ad hoc join costs. *VLDB Journal*, 6(3):241–256, 1997.

[18] International Business Machines Corporation. IBM DB2 LUW database software. http://www-01.ibm.com/software/data/db2/.

[19] Rosana S. G. Lanzelotte, Patrick Valduriez, and Mohamed Zaït. On the effectiveness of optimization search strategies for parallel execution spaces. In *Proceedings of the 19th International Conference on Very Large Data Bases*, pages 493–504, 1993.

[20] Guido Moerkotte, Pit Fender, and Marius Eich. On the correct and complete enumeration of the core search space. In *Proceedings of the 2013 ACM SIGMOD International Conference on Management of Data*, pages 493–504, 2013.

[21] Guido Moerkotte and T. Neumann. Dynamic programming strikes back. In *Proceedings of the 2008 ACM SIGMOD International Conference on Management of Data*, pages 539–552, 2008.

[22] Guido Moerkotte and Thomas Neumann. Analysis of two existing and one new dynamic programming algorithm for the generation of optimal bushy join trees without cross products. In *Proceedings of the 32nd International Conference on Very Large Data Bases*, pages 930–941, 2006.

[23] T. Neumann and Guido Moerkotte. A combined framework for grouping and order optimization. In *Proceedings of the 13th International Conference on Very Large Data Bases*, pages 960–971, 2004.

[24] Thomas Neumann. Query simplification: graceful degradation for join-order optimization. In *Proceedings of the 2009 ACM SIGMOD International Conference on Management of Data*, pages 403–414, 2009.

[25] Thomas Neumann and Guido Moerkotte. An efficient framework for order optimization. In *In Proceedings of the 20th International Conference on Data Engineering*, pages 461–472, 2004.

[26] Kiyoshi Ono and Guy M. Lohman. Measuring the complexity of join enumeration in query optimization. In *Proceedings of the 16th International Conference on Very Large Data Bases*, pages 314–325, 1990.

[27] Jun Rao, Bruce Lindsay, Guy M. Lohman, Hamid Pirahesh, and David E. Simmen. Using EELs: A practical approach to outerjoin and antijoin reordering. In *Proceedings of the 17th International Conference on Data Engineering*, pages 585–594, 2001.

[28] Leonard D. Shapiro, David Maier, Paul Benninghoff, Keith Billings, Yubo Fan, Kavita Hatwal, Quan Wang, Yu Zhang, Hsiao min Wu, and Bennet Vance. Exploiting upper and lower bounds in top-down query optimization. In *Proceedings of the International Database Engineering & Applications Symposium*, pages 20–33, 2001.

[29] SQLite Consortium. SQLite Test Suite. http://www.sqlite.org/testing.html.

[30] Michael Steinbrunn, Guido Moerkotte, and Alfons Kemper. Heuristic and randomized optimization for the join ordering problem. *The VLDB Journal*, 6:191–208, August 1997.

[31] Kian-Lee Tan and Hongjun Lu. A note on the strategy space of multiway join query optimization problem in parallel systems. *SIGMOD Record*, 20(4):81–82, December 1991.

[32] Technische Universität München. Hyper – a hybrid oltp&olap high performance dbms. http://hyper-db.de.

[33] Transaction Processing Performance Council. TPC-DS Benchmark. http://www.tpc.org/tpcds/.

[34] Transaction Processing Performance Council. TPC-H Benchmark. http://www.tpc.org/tpch/.

[35] Jeffrey D. Ullman. *Database and Knowledge Base Systems*, volume 2. Computer Science Press, 1989.

[36] Bennet Vance and David Maier. Rapid bushy join-order optimization with cartesian products. In *Proceedings of the 1996 ACM SIGMOD International Conference on Management of Data*, pages 35–46, 1996.